Whispers

ACROSS THE
ATLANTICK

General William Howe and the
American Revolution

DAVID SMITH

OSPREY
PUBLISHING

Osprey Publishing
c/o Bloomsbury Publishing Plc
PO Box 883, Oxford, OX1 9PL, UK
Or
c/o Bloomsbury Publishing Plc
1385 Broadway, 5th Floor, New York, NY 10018, USA
E-mail: info@ospreypublishing.com

www.ospreypublishing.com

OSPREY is a trademark of Osprey Publishing, a division of Bloomsbury Publishing Plc.

First published in Great Britain in 2017

A CIP catalog record for this book is available from the British Library.

David Smith has asserted his right under the Copyright, Designs and
Patents Act, 1988, to be identified as the Author of this Work.

ISBN: HB: 978-1-4728-2795-1
ePub: 978-1-4728-2796-8
ePDF: 978-1-4728-2797-5
XML: 978-1-4728-2798-2

17 18 19 20 21 10 9 8 7 6 5 4 3 2 1

Index by Kate Inskip
Typeset in Bell MT Std by Deanta Global Publishing Services, Chennai, India
Printed in Great Britain by CPI Group (UK) Ltd, Croydon CR0 4YY

Osprey Publishing supports the Woodland Trust, the UK's leading woodland
conservation charity. Between 2014 and 2018 our donations are being
spent on their Centenary Woods project in the UK.

Front Cover: *Battle of Bunker Hill* by Percy Moran, 1909. (Photo by: Universal History
Archive/UIG via Getty Images)
Back Cover: Color mezzotint of William Howe by Richard Purcell, 1777. (Anne S. K. Brown
Military Collection, Brown University)

To find out more about our authors and books visit www.ospreypublishing.com.
Here you will find extracts, author interviews, details of forthcoming events
and the option to sign up for our newsletter.

*This book is dedicated to my wife Shirley and
my boys Harry and Joshua.*

ACKNOWLEDGMENTS

The staff at libraries and museums in Britain and America have proved extremely helpful during the research needed both for this book and the Ph.D. it is based upon. Most notably, Clayton Lewis, Brian Leigh Dunnigan, Cheney Schopieray, Barbara DeWolfe, Meg Hixon, Diana Sykes, Valerie Proehl, Terese Austin, and the rest of the staff of the William L. Clements Library at the University of Michigan were welcoming, encouraging, and helpful during my study visits, which were the undoubted highlights of my research. Richard Dabb at the National Army Museum, Ben Cunliffe at the Staffordshire Record Office, Sandra Blake at the Northumberland Estates, and the staff at The National Archives at Kew also offered valuable help and support. My thanks also go to Peter Harrington at the Anne S. K. Brown Military Collection, for permission to reproduce many of the excellent artworks in their collection.

Dr. Keith A. J. McLay and Professor Peter Gaunt were patient and supportive during four years of Ph.D. research. Their advice, experience, and knowledge greatly strengthened my thesis and, therefore, this book. In addition, Professor John W. Shy at the University of Michigan, Professor Gregory J. W. Urwin at Temple, and Professor Jeremy Black at the University of Exeter were generous with their time when discussing my research.

Finally, I owe thanks to Jenny Clark at Bloomsbury and Lucy Doncaster and Mandy Woods for their work in the production of this book.

CONTENTS

PREFACE

William Howe does not hold a place among the list of revered 18th-century British generals. Following John Churchill and James Wolfe there is a long gap before Arthur Wellesley nips in just before the close of the century, a gap in which Howe resides alongside Henry Clinton, John Burgoyne, and John Carleton. If not entirely forgotten, he has at least been dismissed as a mediocrity; he commanded an army for just two campaigns and is generally considered to have been outgeneraled by George Washington, the American commander-in-chief who was learning his job as he went along. Yet how could he be a mediocrity when he won every battle in which he commanded, never tasting defeat and usually winning with some ease? Such questions make Howe an intriguing figure, but a lack of primary source material has made it difficult to gain a better understanding of this enigmatic general (the Howe family papers are believed to have been destroyed in a fire).

For the bulk of his life, Howe remained in the background. He would sometimes make a fleeting appearance in a letter or report, but rarely took center stage. Like a figure caught in the glare of a flashbulb, Howe can be seen at critical points through his career, but seldom as a moving image. The snapshots are often striking—he sits at a desk, broken by grief over the death of his oldest brother, he scales a cliff-side path to glory, he demonstrates light infantry tactics to the King—but he only becomes a living, breathing, complex man during his period in command in North America and immediately afterward, when a relative abundance of source material is available.

This book is an attempt to understand Howe better. It takes an unapologetically narrow view of the first two campaigns of the War of Independence, mostly considering events through Howe's eyes. Where the opinions, perspectives, and comments of others are included, they are generally done so to add to our understanding of Howe's decisions or to demonstrate how he so often left everyone around him guessing as to what he was really up to. Howe, an enigma to historians today, was no less so to his contemporaries, friend and foe alike.

A conversation with Professor Shy in 2011 ran along the lines of "what does the historian do when the evidence runs out?" Perhaps the easiest thing to do is to admit defeat, to own up when no firm and supported conclusions can be drawn. There is little alternative when you're writing a Ph.D., where all statements need to be firmly underpinned with evidence, but my research was helped when it turned out the evidence had not yet quite run out. A draft of Howe's famous "narrative" to the House of Commons, delivered during a parliamentary inquiry into his conduct while commander-in-chief, was sold at auction while I was still working on my Ph.D. and suddenly delivered 85 pages of precious new primary source material. The draft offered telling insights into some of Howe's biggest decisions and added subtle detail to the picture of the man. In any case, a book such as this offers a little more leeway than a Ph.D. thesis, and if I have managed to make Howe more of a human being, with all the complexities that come with that, then I will be happy.

PROLOGUE

April 22, 1779

The man standing in the House of Commons was tall and dark, and
had retained the athletic build of his youth. If he seemed nervous,
that was understandable. Nothing less than his professional
reputation was on the line as he prepared to deliver a speech to
the House. In his hands was a thick sheaf of papers and although
the majority of the men ready to hear him speak already knew
which side they would be on during the coming days, there was
still a sense of anticipation. That sheaf of papers might contain
answers, and the career of Lieutenant General Sir William Howe
had generated plenty of questions.

Howe's situation, if not unique, was certainly remarkable.
It was more than a year since he had resigned his position as
commander-in-chief of the British army in North America and
18 months since he had last led troops in battle against the
rebellious colonists. Howe had returned to Britain after winning
every major engagement he had fought, after his troops had
beaten the rebels at Bunker Hill, Long Island, White Plains, Fort
Washington, and the Brandywine. He had returned at his own
request and, if not to a hero's welcome, at least to a civil one,
from the King and the administration of Lord North. He had been
rewarded for his efforts with the red ribbon of the Order of the
Knights of the Bath.

Yet he now stood before a committee made up of the entire
House of Commons, at an inquiry he himself had demanded in
an effort to silence the growing whispers from critics who had
dogged him almost since he had taken command in America four
years previously. For although Howe had won his battles, he had
not won his war, and the Americans now seemed close to achieving

what at one time had seemed an unthinkable independence from their mother state.

Had Howe been blessed with an awareness of his own limitations he might have entertained doubts over how his speech would be received, because the arena in which he was now engaged was unfamiliar and unsuited to his skills. Physically imposing and a natural leader of men on the battlefield, he was politically naive and a poor speaker off it. There is no evidence that Howe had ever possessed such self-awareness and he was unlikely to suddenly acquire it at the age of 49. How else could he have stood patiently waiting for the House to fall quiet, with only that sheaf of papers to offer them? His speech, the lengthy opening statement in the case to clear his name, was grossly unfit for purpose and some of the sharpest minds (and sharpest tongues) of the day were waiting to hear it. Pathetically ill-equipped to defend his conduct, Sir William nevertheless acted as he had always done and stepped bravely out onto what was to be his last battlefield. He started to speak...

ONE

The Narrative

"If the peculiarities of my situation be considered, I shall not be thought presumptuous in desiring the indulgence of the committee during the trespass I must this day commit upon their patience. The repugnance of his Majesty's ministers (in this house at least) to declare any opinion concerning the transactions of the American war during my command, although possessed of all the necessary, and only, documents, upon which a judgement could have been formed, impelled me to move, that my correspondence with the Secretary of State for the American Department, might be laid before you. The most material parts of my conduct, the reasons upon which I acted, the plans which I suggested and executed, appear in that correspondence; and therefore to those who may have connected the whole in a regular series of dates and events, the detail into which I propose to enter may seem unnecessary. But I cannot flatter myself that the papers have been considered with such minute attention, nor can I presume to suppose, that all the circumstances of the American war have been invested with the partial view of clearing the conduct of the man who commanded the army."

Howe's narrative, April 22, 1779

*I*T WAS AN UNCERTAIN *start, but one that held the promise of better things to come. Howe claimed to be about to answer all the questions—what he had done in America and why—and although some in the House may have already trawled through the lengthy* *correspondence between Howe and Lord George Germain, the American Secretary, many undoubtedly had not. Howe's speech plowed on through its cumbersome opening, as he laid out what he intended to present to the House. He spoke of censures passed upon him and of conclusions too hastily drawn. He was not concerned, he insisted, with the justice of the war itself, or with the policies adopted by the government, only with explaining his own conduct. Those listening, perhaps still patiently, perhaps already starting to fidget in their seats, might have raised an eyebrow as Howe set a generously low bar for himself to clear, setting out the four facts that he hoped to establish: that he had kept Germain informed of his plans; that he had given his opinion on what could be achieved with the forces available; that he had carried out his plans with as little deviation as possible; that he had never deceived the American Secretary with hopes of ending the war in a single campaign. It was Howe's inquiry and he could set his own agenda, but this was already sounding less like an attempt to clear a reputation and more like a damage-limitation exercise.*

Still, the preliminaries appeared to be nearly over and Howe seemed ready to get to the meat of his speech. The promise of drama and adventure remained and all might yet end well for him, if he could only get over a tendency to plod. But then the same could so easily have been said of his period in command in America.

Howe was not meant to be a plodder; he had never been one before he took command of the army. Like his older brothers, George Augustus and Richard, William had bypassed university and gone straight into the military after a period at Eton. Whether any of the three had been fit for higher education is not possible to say, but they each quickly proved that they were suited to life in the armed forces. George became one of the foremost exponents of light infantry warfare, while Richard embarked on an illustrious career as a naval officer. The young William was walking in very big footprints when he joined the 15th Light Dragoons, as a 17-year-old cornet, in 1746.

The details of his life before this time are uncertain. His father, Emanuel Scrope Howe, died while governor of Barbados when William was just six years old. Having previously been Member of Parliament for Nottingham, Emanuel had run into severe financial problems and the governorship of Barbados had offered a solution that proved, like Emanuel himself, to be short-lived. William's years at Eton would have been spent translating and reciting Greek and Latin, and it is difficult to imagine the young Howe enjoying it. Not that it was a particularly grueling curriculum (a 17-hour working week left plenty of time for other activities), but he was not considered to be a great intellect. Failure to complete a year's work satisfactorily would lead, shamefully, to being "kept back," and although there is no evidence that this ever happened to Howe, several of his contemporaries would later comment on his lack of education.

Howe would have been on more solid ground when it came to physical activities, but he went to school at a time when exercise for the young was viewed with suspicion. The boys were not encouraged to exert themselves, especially during the summer months, and this mistrust of exertion was demonstrated by the changes made to a peculiar and barbarous tradition known as the "ram hunt." A horde of Eton schoolboys chasing a terrified ram through the streets of Windsor and Eton would have made an arresting sight, but many would no doubt have turned away when the "hunt" reached its conclusion, with the boys battering the ram to death with cudgels. Howe would undoubtedly have taken part in this macabre spectacle, but by the time he attended Eton it had been modified. Out of a fear that that the boys might over-exert themselves, the ram was hamstrung before the chase commenced. Still concerned over the dangers of physical endeavor (and perhaps feeling that the health and safety brigade had already taken all the fun out the affair), the ram hunt was abandoned completely the year after Howe left Eton.

Advancement through the army in the 18th century was often as much to do with wealth and patronage as it was to do with talent. The Howes had little in the way of the former attributes, but plenty of the latter. Although related to the King (their grandmother was an illegitimate half-sister to George I), the Howes were poor and they had to progress by the less sure means of aptitude and luck. Luck would prove fickle for William, but he enjoyed two major strokes of good fortune early in his career. The first saw him serving alongside, and forging a friendship with, James Wolfe in the 20th Regiment. When Wolfe later commanded an army in North America, during the French and Indian War of 1754–1763 (the North American counterpoint to the Seven Years War), he was generous in his praise of Howe, referring to him as "our old comrade" and claiming that he headed the best-trained battalion in all of America.

The fates smiled upon Howe a second time with the creation of a new form of soldiering that fit him like a bespoke suit. The idea of light troops was not new and European armies had a long history of employing them in various capacities, from screening the main army as it advanced, to scouting for enemy formations and pursuing a defeated opponent. These men were usually, however, irregular troops, often hired from the local population and thus able to bring their own knowledge and experience to bear in their duties. They could be ill-disciplined, difficult to recall once unleashed, and, at their worst, prone to committing atrocities indiscriminately. They excelled in the *petit guerre*, the "little war" that was waged between the main enemy lines. In North America, the British realized this sort of fighting was so important it should not be left solely to the enthusiastic part-timer; the professionals needed to be trained in irregular tactics as well.

Conventional wisdom has it that the European armies of the 18th century were unwieldy and hampered by their need to retain rigid, parade-ground formations. It is true that tightly packed ranks and metronomic maneuvers (known as "evolutions") helped retain discipline and order on the battlefields of Europe, as massive armies slogged their way through brutal attritional battles, and it is equally true that such tactics were ill-suited to the forests of Canada and the American colonies. But the tradition of using Hussars, Cossacks, and Pandours proved that European military minds were not as hidebound as is often thought, and British officers were prepared for the irregular warfare waged by Native American tribes and French Canadians during the French and Indian War. The British Army received one of the harshest lessons in its entire history on July 9, 1755, when Major General Edward Braddock's command was annihilated by a smaller enemy force at the Monongahela River, but the lesson is often misunderstood. The defeat has been characterized as a clear-cut case of stiff-backed redcoats standing in their ranks as opportunistic enemies took potshots at them from behind trees. In fact, Braddock's command, with troops flanking the main column to guard against partisan attacks, had been progressing nicely on its march to take the French-held Fort Duquesne. The redcoats had been in the wilderness for a month with no serious problems, employing Indian and colonial scouts and posting around a third of the army in flanking parties. It appears that a lapse in this careful progress, as the army neared its target, coincided disastrously with a surprise meeting with a smaller enemy force. In the confused fighting that followed, panic set in; Braddock lost his life, as did close to a thousand of his men, while his French, Canadian, and Indian opponents lost around 30. The image of red-coated automatons employing inflexible formations was seared into the British imagination and has proved difficult to shake, but the lesson was not so much that European tactics were out of place in North America, but rather that any lapse in concentration could prove fatal when facing an alert and opportunistic opponent. Local men, with their knowledge of an area and adeptness at fighting within it, would remain valued, but the British also wanted their own redcoats to learn the job of the irregular soldier, adding an extra element of discipline to the role. Such a man would combine the best elements of the professional soldier and the specialized hireling, an irregular regular. He would be a light infantryman.

Recruited from the ablest, nimblest men of the regiments, light infantrymen were selected on the basis of their intelligence, resourcefulness, and physical fitness. Pure size was not important. Unlike the grenadiers, the existing elite of the regiments who were picked based on height and strength, the light infantryman was often a short, scrappy character, able to live off the land and willing to engage in a particularly savage form of warfare, frequently removed from the battlefield itself. He screened the main army, engaged his opponents from behind trees or any other cover that offered itself, retreated when his enemy advanced, pursued when his enemy fled, harried, hounded, and generally made a thorough nuisance of himself. Discipline remained important, but this was a different form of discipline. It wasn't an automated, ingrained response to orders, it was based on a deep understanding of the responsibilities a man bore for the safety of his fellow light infantrymen, as well as pride in his own skill. The men fought in pairs (one usually keeping watch while the other reloaded his weapon after firing), developing an instinctive understanding of their roles in any situation. There was little place for formality when living rough in hostile territory, but equally there was no place for dissent when the enemy showed itself. The light infantry units therefore formed bonds stronger than those of their regular counterparts and became experts at their peculiar form of warfare.

Howe loved it. With his athletic build he was an obvious candidate for light infantry duty, but there was more to it than this. He also had a dislike of formality and deference. Sharing the discomforts of his men, sleeping rough, and existing on his wits were far more to his taste. This rugged form of soldiering so suited Howe, in fact, that he came to believe that light infantry was the future of the British Army and he envisioned a time when they would undertake all the active duties required. Howe was also following in the illustrious footsteps of his oldest brother George, a recognized expert in light infantry warfare. The brothers might have carved out a glorious future in tandem had George not been killed while fighting near Fort Ticonderoga in 1758, which provides our first clear snapshot of Howe. In one of the most personally illuminating letters the younger Howe wrote, he poured out his anguish to his surviving brother, Richard: "What a loss we have sustained!" he wrote on November 23, 1758. "If it is a weakness I acknowledge to you the stroke was such a one I had not firmness to bear."

The first clear view we have of Howe, then, is that of a devastated 29-year-old, far from home (he was in Halifax, Nova Scotia, when writing the letter), reaching out to a surviving sibling for comfort. "Live," he entreated Richard, "and be a comfort to us all."

A single moment on the battlefield can make or break a career. Two such moments, in 1759, irrevocably changed the careers of two British officers. One set himself on the road to future advancement and, eventually, command of an army; the other inexplicably snuffed his military future out. Six weeks and 3,000 miles (4,800 kilometers) separated the two moments.

There had been plenty of glory up for grabs during that remarkable year, the *annus mirabilis* of British military fortunes, but not everyone was able to secure their share. Most notable among those who missed out was Lord George Sackville, who was commander-in-chief of British forces in Germany at the Battle of Minden on August 1, 1759. Sackville did more than just miss out—his part in the battle saw him court-martialed and disgraced. Sackville had failed to advance with the British cavalry when ordered to do so by the allied commander, Prince Ferdinand of Brunswick-Lüneburg, and he revealed a stubborn streak in insisting upon a court martial in an attempt to clear his name. Despite the complexities of the events on the battlefield, there was little appetite among the British establishment to hear excuses, and Sackville's arrogance during the trial could not have helped his case; he was found guilty of disobeying an order and, infamously, condemned as "unfit to serve his Majesty in any military capacity whatever." The only consolation for Sackville, who would never shake off this disgrace, was that "his Majesty" was George II. Sackville had long aligned himself with the King's grandson, the future George III, so there was hope for rehabilitation when the young man ascended the throne.

Six weeks later, during Wolfe's campaign to capture Quebec from the French, Howe stepped into the spotlight for a dazzling cameo. At the head of the light infantry, his job was to seize control of a narrow road leading up to a French defensive position near the Plains of Abraham, overlooking the city of Quebec. On the night of September 12–13, however, the boats carrying Howe's men were swept further downriver than anticipated and he found himself some distance from the road. It was to prove one of the most important moments of his life. Thinking quickly in the murky pre-dawn light, Howe sent some of his men back along the coast to find the road, but also led a small force up a cliff-side path. Reaching the top of the cliffs behind the French defensive works, Howe was able to secure the route for the bulk of Wolfe's army. It was as neat an encapsulation of the value of light infantry as could be hoped for. Howe had encountered an unexpected problem in tremendously difficult circumstances and had responded with initiative, boldness, and bravery. His star was rising.

Almost as quickly as fortune had smiled on Howe, however, it turned away. Wolfe was killed during the battle that followed on the Plains of Abraham; Britain had lost a great general and Howe had lost a powerful friend. Even so, his part in the triumph was clear and he made an eye-catching appearance in the 1770 depiction of the death of Wolfe by Benjamin West, leaning in to draw the dying general's attention to the victory unfolding in the background. Howe's dress in the painting contrasts sharply with the red-coated officers around him and has more in common with the contemplative Native American warrior sitting beside him. In leggings, moccasins, and a green coat more suited to service in woodland, this depiction of Howe goes a long way toward explaining why his relatives referred to him (it is to be hoped affectionately) as "the savage." As Britain's *annus mirabilis* drew to a close, it would have been difficult to find two men with more contrasting career trajectories than Howe and Sackville, but those trajectories would bring them together 16 years later, at the head of an unprecedented war effort.

With the loss of Wolfe, Howe's military education continued under the more cautious Earl of Albemarle in the 1762 Havana campaign. Following a rousing opening scene (Howe leading the waves of flat-bottomed boats that brought the army to shore on Cuba), the campaign had degenerated into a drawn-out siege punctuated initially by heat and thirst and later by sickness and death. Fewer than 600 men lost their lives in action during the campaign. Almost 5,000 died of disease. The situation at one stage was so bleak it was feared the siege might be abandoned, and only the arrival of fresh troops from the colonies salvaged the situation and allowed Havana to be captured. Having been taken at exorbitant cost, it was handed back to the Spanish in peace negotiations the following year.

Howe had distinguished himself still further—not in so gaudy a manner as he had done in leading the light troops up the cliff-side path at Quebec, but still with a dash of bravado. He had been given the critical job of securing the water supply for the army as it endured its grueling siege (not a job for a soldier who did not have the complete trust of his commanding officer), and had also performed admirably on the night of June 8, when he had led a small party of men to scout out Spanish positions at La Cabaña, unnerving them so completely that they had actually fled from their defensive works.

However, bold action was only possible in wartime, and the Seven Years War was coming to its conclusion. As always, peace was accompanied by a vast culling of the regiments that had been raised during the conflict. The British Army, 92,000 strong at the end of the war, was quickly pared back to around 45,000. The French had effectively been kicked out of North America under the terms of the 1763 Treaty of Paris, but despite the acquisition of vast new territories, Britain remained suspicious of large standing armies. Four years after the end of the war, there were just 15 regiments of redcoats in North America, with the largest concentration being a mere nine companies at Nova Scotia.

Among the disbanded troops were the specialist light infantry companies that had performed such distinguished service in

North America. Howe's particular brand of soldiering no longer officially existed, although few doubted that it would one day be called upon once more. In a book charting the progress of an expedition against the Ohio Indians in 1764, William Smith noted the essential qualities of the light infantryman, or "hunters," declaring that they should be lightly armed and equipped and dressed in modified, cut-down uniforms. Recruited at the age of 15 and taught to do just about everything, they would eventually become "tolerable good carpenters, joiners, wheelwrights, coopers, armourers, smiths, masons, brickmakers, saddlers, tailors, butchers, bakers, shoemakers, curriers, etc." Such soldiers would be able to pursue an enemy like a pack of terriers, fire and reload with great rapidity, swim across rivers (pushing clothing and weapons ahead of themselves on improvised rafts), and perform complex maneuvers on the run. It is easy to see why Howe came to believe that, given enough men like this, no other type of soldier would be needed.

Three years later, Captain Bennett Cuthbertson also extolled the virtues of the light infantryman, pointing out that he could not simply be conjured up in time of war; the intensive training necessary to master the role required time and Cuthbertson pressed for new companies to be raised and drilled in peacetime. For most, the light infantrymen were something of an afterthought. Even Cuthbertson did not get around to them until the very last chapter of his book, after he had dealt with marriage, bookkeeping, and (perhaps naively) the "suppression of all sorts of immoralities." The establishment also had no plans to make them central to the army, and as the light infantrymen departed the scene, so too did Howe, whose career now threatened to stagnate.

A soldier in peacetime was something of an embarrassment in 18th-century Britain. His existence was graciously tolerated while spilling his blood for glory and empire, but such tolerance was quickly withdrawn if he survived and came home. For many, there was little alternative but to wait for another war, but after peace arrived in 1763, uninvited by the career soldiers of the British Army and most definitely unwelcome, the next war proved to be slow in arriving. There was growing unrest in the North American colonies, at least in part because of the removal of the French threat, but this was never going to turn into a war. There was a certain level of paranoia in Britain that the colonists might one day become an independent nation, as well as recognition of the powerful force they might quickly become, but surely nothing more than a tightening of the mother country's grip on the colonial reins was necessary to restore harmony. The trouble, as quickly became apparent, was that Britain had not so much loosened its grip on the reins as dropped them altogether.

North America had been a relatively insignificant part of the British Empire at the start of the century. With a population estimated at around a quarter of a million, it contributed just six percent to the British economy. The War of the Spanish Succession, which ended in 1713 (for Britain at least), added some important new territories, including Nova Scotia, Hudson's Bay, and the island of St. Kitt's, but the boundaries of empire were often sketchy, inviting trouble with neighboring French and Native American territories. One solution, beefing up the colonial population by encouraging mass immigration of non-British Europeans, had unforeseen consequences. By 1750 the colonial population had increased by 500 percent, but their essential "Englishness" had been diluted. An estimated 100,000 Germans and 250,000 Scots-Irish had been part of the influx.

Edmund Burke referred to the "wise and salutary neglect" that had characterized British colonial policy, but it quickly appeared neither wise nor salutary when attempts were made to reassert control. Immediately after the French and Indian War came to a close, Britain was faced with defending a larger empire and it was reasonably expected that the colonists themselves would contribute to the expense. Even a modest army of 7,500 in North America was expected to cost something like £200,000 per year (it turned out to be twice as much), so a series of acts was passed to raise revenue, including the notorious Stamp Act of 1765. Requiring any legal documents to be printed on stamped paper, the act pushed lawyers and printers into the opposition camp, which was always going to have unpleasant consequences. At the same time as the colonists began to chafe under the unwanted return of parental guidance, they were beginning to develop their own identity. This included an emerging colonial elite, a savvy and experienced political class, and a distinctive culture. Disturbingly (both in terms of their quality and for the implication that the colonists were starting to think of themselves as different), the first American plays and novels started to appear in the 1760s. Perhaps most dangerously, there was an uncomfortable feeling in the colonies that they were looked down upon by the more cultured and cosmopolitan gentlemen in London.

By the early 1770s it seemed that matters in the colonies had calmed, but in an uncharacteristic moment of prescience the British Army reinstated the light companies in 1771. Perhaps startled by its own boldness, the Army then ignored the fact that the new light infantrymen had no idea what they were doing. The warnings about the amount of time needed to train such men had proved to be prophetic; with the last major battles fought by the British Army now more than a decade in the past, the hard lessons learned in North America had been forgotten. Something needed to happen, but there was apparently no rush, for nothing was actually done for three years.

Howe had loved his service in North America and had developed strong feelings of affection for the colonists, who had paid for a memorial to his fallen brother after the war. He had served alongside provincial troops both on the North American continent and in Cuba, where the Connecticut Brigade had shared the miseries of the prolonged siege. Peacetime was not so absorbing for him. He took over as Member of Parliament for Nottingham on the death of George but, although maintaining another family tradition, this one was less appealing. Life as a politician was never likely to hold his interest; it was a poor substitute for life as a soldier and, in any case, he was not good at it. Bewildered at being put forward as a candidate, he had attempted to persuade his older brother, Richard, to step in instead, but he was not allowed to pass on the honor. His ambitious mother had done his political campaigning for him, since he was still fighting in America when he was elected Member of Parliament for Nottingham.

The House of Commons held no allure for Howe, but he was able to step back into a more agreeable spotlight in the summer of 1774. He had not seen action for 12 years (although he became colonel of the 46th Regiment in 1764 and made major general in 1772) when he devised and supervised a six-week light infantry training camp at Salisbury. Surviving manuals from the camp demonstrate that far from merely recapping what had been learned in the previous war, Howe had been developing new ideas. His final vision was for an entirely new way of waging war, with the light infantryman at the forefront.

The traditional view of light infantry tactics holds that they were best suited for screening the movements of the main army. They could operate in the dangerous area between opposing forces or even behind enemy positions. They could play a role as skirmishers, in an advanced line on the battlefield, but they were expected to melt back into the massed ranks of the heavy infantry before the real battle started. Their opponents would usually be the light infantry or irregular soldiers of the enemy, and although their clashes might be savage, the proper fighting would be done by others.

Howe's vision was different. He believed that, since the light infantry were the best and brightest of the army, they should be capable of fulfilling all roles. With the light infantry companies of each regiment combined into composite battalions, the light infantry could become the cutting edge of the British Army. Far from being a mere nuisance to an enemy force, like a swarm of mosquitoes, they could actually take on and defeat that force. Combining the companies was not a new idea, but the way Howe envisioned using them was, and it was demonstrated on October 3, 1774 in Richmond Park, Surrey, in front of an audience that included King George III.

Following their six weeks of drill, the light companies from the 3rd, 11th, 21st, 29th, 32nd, 36th, and 70th regiments were fluent in their new discipline and they put on quite a show. A range of tactical situations was presented that allowed the men to demonstrate their ability to flow from one formation to another at speed. Staging simultaneous assaults on a house and an "enemy" position on rising ground, the lights advanced in two groups of three companies each, with a single company in extended order (with intervals of 10 feet [3 meters] between each man) maintaining communications between the two sections. Firing was done on the move. The traditional static volleys delivered by the line infantry were replaced by single, aimed shots. The use of cover was encouraged, especially that offered by trees, and "tree" was even used as a verb ("March thro' the wood in extended order, halt at the edge of it, tree and fire by files").

At one stage in the maneuvers, three companies lined up for a frontal assault on a hilltop position (something that would usually be left to the regular infantry or grenadiers), with a further company engaged as skirmishers ahead of them. The advance included simulation of casualties taken from a defensive volley by the enemy troops. Once the enemy had been driven from their cover, the lights pursued them relentlessly: "they fire upon the flying enemy, continuing to pursue from one strong post to another, until at length he surrenders."

This was not merely a complementary part of the army. In Howe's eyes, this *was* the army, or at least it would be in an ideal world. The problem would be finding enough of these super-soldiers to operate in the manner Howe envisioned. For now, he would have to be content with spreading the word about his new infantry tactics. With his maneuvers drawing praise from all who witnessed them, the army ordered that every regiment should spend time practicing them. Veterans of the camp itself became evangelists, passing on their skills to other units. A year after the camp closed, the men of the 9th Regiment were given instruction from the 33rd, which had not itself been at the original camp. Word of Howe's new drill was spreading effectively.

It needed to. The situation in North America had deteriorated and the colonists now seemed, shockingly, to be on the brink of outright rebellion. The administration of Lord North, rather bemused by the turn of events, struggled to find a coherent response. With a strong faction pushing for stern treatment of the ungrateful colonists, and with the King himself in no mood for conciliation, a high-handed attitude was adopted that was never likely to be well received in America. The awful prospect of war with a group of men who, if no longer brothers, could still be looked upon as favored cousins seemed increasingly likely.

Dissatisfaction with the course of events in North America fastened upon the commander-in-chief in the colonies, Sir Thomas Gage. Replace Gage with a more dynamic commander, it was believed, and the problem could be resolved and peaceful relations with the colonists restored. Gage was unfortunate to be dismissed so easily. As a fighting soldier his career had never really taken off. His chance had come (as it had for so many others) in 1759, when he had been ordered to launch an offensive operation against a French position at La Galette during the French and Indian War. His failure to act led the commander-in-chief, Sir Jeffery Amherst, to comment that "he may not have such an opportunity again as long as he lives."

Gage did, however, become respected as an administrator and diplomat, having an easy-going manner that sat well with the colonists. As governor of Massachusetts and commander of British forces in North America, Gage was the symbolic figurehead of what was increasingly being viewed as an oppressive British policy, yet he remained popular with many of the colonists right up until the moment he was recalled. It might not have required much of a general to replace Gage on the battlefield, but it would take a special man to fill his boots as a bridge to the colonists.

As it happened, the British government thought it had just the man.

TWO

The Letter

"In the course of the great variety of business which fell to my lot, during such a wide and extensive command, faults must undoubtedly be perceived, but none I hope which can be suspected to have arisen from want of zeal, or from inactivity. In all military transactions, but more particularly in those of America, where the nature of the war, in all its points, is without example, the happiest commander will be he who escapes with the fewest blots."

Howe's narrative, April 22, 1779

*M*ANY BRITISH OFFICERS HAD *withdrawn themselves from contention for the American command, and many had said they would never serve in America in any capacity, so Howe's comments on the peculiar difficulties of service on that continent may have drawn understanding nods. But he was saying more than that, and he might also have received some quizzical looks as he claimed that the best a commander could hope for was to make as few mistakes as possible. Was it not also possible to find glory and fame? Was it not possible, even if glory had no intention of showing up, to still win a war?*

His comment on "want of zeal" and "inactivity" was also puzzling. They were the two main charges laid against him, the main ingredients in the sniping that had attempted to undermine his credibility even while he had still been serving in America. He would need to prove that what had looked very much like inactivity, especially in his second campaign in America, had been something else, and a glib dismissal of the notion was not going to be enough.

But that wasn't the most notable inference to be drawn from the latest section of his lengthy introduction. "The happiest commander," he had just claimed, "will be he who escapes with the fewest blots." Sir William seemed to be suggesting that he had entertained serious doubts from the start, in which case it might be reasonable to ask why he had wanted the command in the first place; yet want it, he most definitely had.

There was a letter to prove it.

Thomas Gage had been out of favor with the British government long before he sent a column of redcoats to confiscate a colonial arms cache at Concord, near Boston, on April 19, 1775. The column stirred up a hornets' nest of local militia, determined to resist what they saw as an outrageous infringement of civil liberty—the liberty to amass arms and ammunition in preparation for a full-scale rebellion.

Gage's main problem, aside from the small matter of being the man on the spot when the colonies erupted into revolution, was that he had failed to live up to his own hype. In a meeting with George III, while tensions were steadily rising in America in 1773, he had assured the monarch that he would pursue a firm policy against any acts of dissent. The colonists would be lions while the British were lambs, he insisted (and presumably they would become lambs if the British were lions). It was good rhetoric, and enough to please the King, but Gage had failed to follow his own bold words after returning to his post as governor of Massachusetts in Boston. Gage had found himself in an impossible position—the great hope of both sides of the argument. To the colonists, he was the voice of reason and promised a calm resolution to the crisis. To Britain, and the King in particular, he was the hard-hearted enforcer of British supremacy. He could not possibly be both, and he promptly made matters worse by being neither. As the situation deteriorated, he wrote to London asking for instructions. He then, in November 1774, recommended that Britain withdraw all armed forces from the colonies, before building up a bigger army (including German mercenaries) to return and restore order.

Gage's recommendation was viewed with horror in London—as was his passivity in the face of colonial impertinence—and not having the ability to see into the future, he was unable to point out

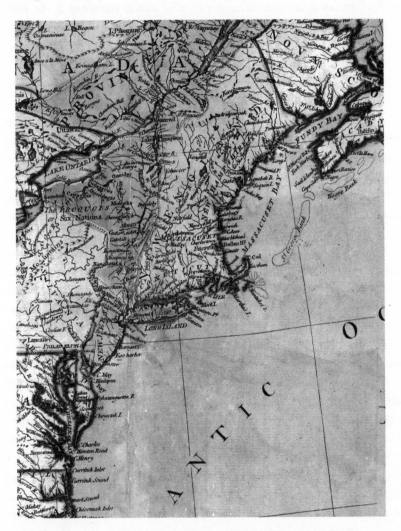

'A New and accurate Map of North America.' Bell, P., Seale, R. W., Bowles, C. & Anville, J. B. B. D. (1771). London, printed for Carington Bowles. (Geography and Map Division, Library of Congress.)

that the British would ultimately do exactly as he had suggested. Patience with him was lost and the process of finding a replacement began. Any doubts that Britain saw Gage as the main problem in America were removed when the British frigate *Cerberus* weighed anchor and headed for Boston in April of 1775; aboard were three major generals. Henry Clinton and John Burgoyne were considered to be aggressive, highly capable commanders, but they were outranked, in terms of seniority, by their companion, and this made William Howe the de facto replacement for Gage. Howe, at the age of 45, was on the verge of becoming commander-in-chief of the British army in America.

It was just six months since he had wowed onlookers, including the King, with his demonstration of light infantry tactics at Richmond Park, yet at one time he had seemed an unlikely candidate to command in America, or even to serve there. During the 1774 election campaign he had assured his constituents that he would never serve against the colonists, but now he offered a simple excuse—he had been asked by his king and could not refuse. Few people could have been seriously affronted in any case; people no more expected election promises to be kept in the 18th century than they do today.

Events in America were already getting out of hand as the *Cerberus* carried its precious cargo toward Boston. Aware that the colonists were building up an arms cache in the region, Gage organized an expedition to seize it. The British commander was acting under a direct order from Lord Dartmouth, Secretary of State for the Colonies (a cabinet position also referred to as "the American Secretary"), but he would draw criticism for the organization of the operation. The disastrous march on Concord (taking in a pleasant detour at Lexington, where British troops fired on and killed several colonial militiamen on the common) provoked far more of a response than Gage had anticipated. He had a network of spies in the region, of course, and he was aware of the depth of feeling in the colony. Moreover, he had taken steps to prepare the ground for his expedition, sending regular patrols out into the countryside around Boston to desensitize the locals to the presence of redcoats. The column that set out on the morning of April 19, however, was clearly more than a patrol. And the colonists had their own spies.

The light and grenadier companies of the Boston garrison were selected for the 32-mile (51-kilometer) round trip to Concord. The 800 men represented the best of the British army in the colonies at the time and ought, Gage believed, to have been able to handle anything that colonial militia could throw at them. Gage was in no doubt that violence was threatening to break out. He had been drilling his men for months in preparation, focusing especially on light infantry tactics, which were considered essential in the local terrain. It has often been claimed that the Boston garrison had become complacent, and was inadequately prepared for the fighting just over the horizon. It may have been largely inexperience—the British Army had fought no major battles since those at Minden and Quebec in 1759, and more than a third of the garrison had been in the ranks for three years or less—but it was as ready as possible for hostilities.

The problem was that drill and target practice were no match for battle exposure and the elite troops of the Boston garrison performed badly when faced with the stresses of combat for the first time. At Lexington they lost their heads completely— "the men were so wild they could hear no orders," according to one officer's report—while at Concord they ran into serious opposition and were forced to retreat back toward Boston. With swarms of militia harassing them, the light infantry and grenadiers retreated grimly to safety, but only a relief column sent from Boston assured the final salvation of the exhausted men. Casualties topped 200, with 68 dead.

Following this shocking outbreak of violence, Gage appeared paralyzed, allowing his army (numbering around 6,000) to be effectively besieged in Boston by an ad hoc rebel army of 20,000 New England militiamen. The poor performance of the light infantry and grenadiers was concerning, but it would soon be someone else's concern. On May 25, the *Cerberus* reached Boston.

The ignominious retreat from Concord gave Gage's enemies all the ammunition they needed to oust him. Among the most committed was Lord George Germain. At the age of 59, Germain was maneuvering himself to take over as American Secretary. The peace-loving Dartmouth had no stomach for a fight with America and Germain saw a glittering opportunity. He had stomach in abundance and had waited a long time for the chance to resurrect his career. A change of name (due to an inheritance clause in a will) had gone some way to giving him a fresh start, while the passage of time had worked its usual magic, but Germain was still painfully aware that to many he was still, and always would be, tainted by the past disgrace 16 years ago when he had stood on the battlefield at Minden as Lord George Sackville. His military career had been extinguished on that day, but he now hoped to serve, under a new king, as the energizing force behind the British response to colonial rebellion.

The first task would be replacing Gage at the earliest opportunity. The retreat from Concord was just such an opportunity and Germain took pains to ensure that blame for the debacle fell on the commander-in-chief. Lord Suffolk (the Secretary of State of the Northern Department and a close political ally of Germain's) wrote that reports on the retreat "don't do much credit to the discipline of our troops." Germain was having none of that: "everybody believes that the men behaved with proper spirit," he replied to his friend, before going on to bury the knife:

"The disposition I fear was originally defective … I must then lament that General Gage, with all his good qualitys, finds himself in a situation of too great importance for his talents. The conduct of such a war requires more than common abilities, the distance from the seat of Government necessarily leaves much to the discretion and the resources of the General, and I doubt whether Mr. Gage will venture to take a single step beyond the letter of his instructions, or whether the troops have that opinion of him as to march with confidence of success under his command."

Germain's letter included a detailed analysis of how the British should have performed during the retreat, if only Gage had thought to train them properly: "… the manner of opposing an army that avoids facing you in the open field is totally different from what young officers learn from the common discipline of the army." Germain then referred to the aftermath of Braddock's defeat at the Monongahela River. "Another discipline was then establish'd and all our light troops in America were taught to separate and secure themselves by trees, walls or hedges, and became so formidable to the Indians and Canadians that they were victorious on all occasions, and ever protected the main body of the army from surprise or insult."

Germain was being unfair to Gage, perhaps forgetting that he had been present at the Battle of the Monongahela and had raised a light infantry regiment afterward. Nobody has ever claimed that Gage was a distinguished soldier or an expert on light infantry service, but he was well aware of its importance and had been training the Boston garrison diligently in its principles. The training had been witnessed by a Scottish doctor, Robert Honyman, who had enjoyed a walking tour of the region earlier in the year and left a detailed diary of his wanderings. (Honyman, who had moved to America in the 1770s, was initially a pacifist but later served as a surgeon with the Continental Army.) As well as detailing how the dispute with the mother country was dominating conversation at the coffee houses and inns of the area, he reported on the extent of training being undertaken by the Boston garrison, noting especially the "young active fellows" of the light infantry companies, whom he described as "extremely expert in their discipline." On multiple days, Honyman enjoyed the spectacle of regiments practicing their marksmanship, using human-shaped boards as targets and often braving bitterly cold weather and even snow. Gage himself was spotted overseeing the drill, belying the notion that he was unprepared for the events that followed.

Still, Germain was certain that Gage had to go, and he was no less certain on the matter of his replacement. "Nobody understands that discipline so well as General Howe," he declared, "who had the command of the light troops [during the French and Indian War], and who will, I am persuaded, teach the present army to be as formidable as that he formerly acted with."

Germain's letter was remarkable for many reasons, not least for showing his towering confidence in a man who had never commanded in battle above regimental level before. Easily overlooked is his reference to "the conduct of such a war." Most people still believed the situation in America would be resolved peacefully, that either the colonists would come to their senses or Britain would make a few minor concessions to take the heat out of the situation. Germain held no such illusions; as far as he was concerned, Britain was already at war with its colonies. And he positively relished the fact.

———

Crossing the Atlantic from Britain to America could take anything from six to nine weeks in the 18th century (travel in the opposite direction was quicker, usually taking between four and six weeks). Nobody would ever describe it as a pleasure cruise, but there were compensating elements, especially for those traveling in the relative comfort offered to senior officers. Icebergs taller than a ship's mast would break up the monotony of the view, often delivering spectacular vistas as they were bathed in sunlight. The three major generals aboard the *Cerberus* enjoyed their crossing. The lengthy voyage gave them plenty of time to get to know each other, and they got on famously. Clinton, a notoriously difficult character, was uncharacteristically positive: "I could not have named two people I should sooner wish to serve with in every respect," he later wrote to a friend at home. "We of course differ often in opinion, but in such a manner as, I am sure, I receive great benefit from." The deteriorating situation in Boston might have dampened their spirits had they been aware of it, but the lengthy voyage passed pleasantly. The ambitious officers were no more able to look into the future than Gage had been. If they had been, they might have petitioned the captain of the *Cerberus* to turn around; the colonies were to put an end to all of their careers.

Upon reaching Boston, on May 25, the reality of the situation came as a shock. The British army was besieged, penned into the miserably inadequate area of the city itself. The rebel army, numbering some 20,000, was numerous enough to deter Gage from any sort of breakout attempt; the two sides sat and watched each other warily. If the British government had hoped that Howe, Clinton, and Burgoyne would inject urgency into the British forces, they were to be disappointed very quickly. The siege of Boston was to last for the best part of a year, with no effort made to drive the Americans away. If it had been humiliating to be chased back from Concord with their tails between their legs, it was doubly so for the entire British army in North America to be trapped in Boston.

Howe was not discouraged, at least not at first. Aware that his brother was in correspondence with Germain, Howe penned the admiral a letter. It spelled out what he would do if he were in command of the British army in North America and its intent was clear—to assure Germain that Howe had a clear vision for ending the rebellion. It started with a diplomatic assertion that the rebel numbers around Boston were too great for anything to be attempted until significant reinforcements had arrived. Gage would have been an easy target, and Germain would have lapped up any barbs thrown in his direction, but Howe perhaps realized it would have been bad form to criticize his commanding officer, especially when his recall was just a matter of time.

Howe also revealed that four regiments of reinforcements on their way to New York were to be intercepted and redirected to join the main army. There was no hope of them performing any worthwhile service in New York and they were badly needed at Boston. The rebel numbers were formidable enough, but they were also well entrenched and had a respectable amount of artillery. There was also the matter of the large numbers of additional men that could arrive quickly to augment the rebel army. Militiamen swarming to the scent of blood was a thought to give a British general nightmares: "… the longer the action may last," Howe predicted ominously, "the greater will be the numbers collected in their support."

Some oblique criticism of Gage did now find its way into the letter. The British were "unprovided in many essential particulars," he complained, going on to cite:

> "No survey of the adjacent country. No proper boats for landing troops. Nor horses sufficient for the artillery or baggage of the regiments. No forage, either hay or corn, of any consequence and without a proper quantity of horse-harness. Salt provisions very short. No fascines or pickets and the military chest at the lowest ebb. Not having more than barely for the subsistence of the troops."

Howe continued with a description of the tactics to be employed by the rebels, notably fighting from behind cover and retreating when pressed. The terrain, Howe remarked, was perfectly suited to such a mode of warfare. What he did not need to mention explicitly was the obvious counter to such a mode of warfare, the light infantry tactics he had so recently demonstrated at Richmond Park. In the short term, Howe proposed seizing the high ground on Dorchester Neck, from where the rebels could threaten the city of Boston, and following up with a similar move to take the heights at Charlestown on the other side of Boston. Giving themselves a little breathing room and securing two potentially dangerous areas of high ground seemed logical to the point of being obvious.

Howe then moved on to thoughts of strategy—the manner in which the rebellion might be crushed. Noting that the northern colonies relied upon their southern brethren to provide them with grain, he mused on the desirability of cutting off communications between New England and the rest of the colonies. The most fractious colonies could in this manner be forced into acquiescence. The colony of New York was critical in this regard. "It is my opinion," wrote Howe, "that an army in that province … would sooner reduce these four provinces [New England] than *any army* could do that was to operate from hence [Boston]."

New York seemed perfect for the job of dividing the colonies because it was so neatly divided itself, by the Hudson River, which ran from New York City up to Canada. Howe continued, spelling out his thoughts on what was to be the first campaign of the war:

> "An army of 12,000 men (rank & file) should be appointed for that province, with artillery in proportion and one *or two* regiments of light dragoons. Another corps of about 3,500 should act in the south parts, upon Connecticut River, and an equal number be provided for the garrison of this town [Boston] & necessary posts to be occupied for its defence."

It was not a highly detailed breakdown of strategy, but that was the point. Howe's vision, as laid out in this letter, was beguilingly simple, and he had little doubt about its chances of success. "With this force of 19,000 rank & file," he wrote, "an end I think might be expected to be put to this rebellion in one campaign. With less—I apprehend, the contest may be spun out by these people until G. Britain is heartily weary of the business."

The plan sketched out by Howe, the so-called Hudson strategy, became the focus of the first two campaigns of the war. Howe's championing of it was not surprising because it was already being talked about by almost all of the men involved with shaping Britain's response to the crisis. Dartmouth had already been in touch with Gage to press upon him the desirability of switching the focus to New York. On April 15 he had alerted Gage to the fact that reinforcements were on their way to New York to start operations there. This corps, presumably strengthened with men from Boston, could, "by a proper disposition of it on Hudson's River, defeat with the assistance of a naval force any attempt to send succor to the New England people from the middle colonies." Howe and Burgoyne, Dartmouth revealed, had both expressed their willingness to command such a corps, which must have been thrilling news for Gage.

Burgoyne was also keen to demonstrate that he had firm ideas for the running of the war. Howe had satisfied himself with writing, by circuitous route, to Germain, the prospective Secretary of State for the Colonies. Burgoyne went straight to the King, outlining how two armies could operate on the Hudson, one pushing up from New York, the other moving southward from the British position in Canada. Burgoyne also thought that one such campaign might finish the job, but noted that foreign troops would probably be needed to provide the requisite numbers. He also talked of the need to "awe" the southern provinces with the use of Indian and black troops, and of the desirability of a "numerous fleet to sweep the whole coast."

The Hudson exerted an irresistible pull on the minds of the British establishment. Perhaps dazzled by the apparent simplicity of cutting the colonies in two, no serious consideration appears to have been given to any other course of action—Lord Barrington, Secretary at War, was one of the few dissenting voices, favoring a naval blockade to force the colonists into negotiating. The Hudson strategy promised results out of all proportion to the scale of effort employed and this was important, because almost nobody believed that a simple conquest of America was possible. "Taking America as it presently stands, it is impossible to conquer it with our British Army," commented Sir Edward Harvey, the Adjutant General. "To attempt to conquer it internally by our land force is as wild an idea as ever controverted common sense."

Howe's letter, therefore, was not remarkable for a demonstration of penetrating insight or original thinking. It was little more than a routine rehashing of the strategy that had already attained dominance in the minds of Britain's military and political elite. Rather than an attempt to stand out from the crowd, it was instead a careful declaration that Howe was a safe pair of hands, a man who understood what needed to be done and had firm ideas on how to do it. But the letter is still remarkable, for having apparently outlined his understanding of the Hudson strategy, and upon being given the command he so clearly desired, he made no effort whatsoever to follow the strategy.

Howe's confidence in his older brother's ability to get the contents of his letter into the right hands was justified. Lord Howe was himself eager to be given the role of peace commissioner to the colonies, seeing a chance of personal glory but also genuinely wishing for a peaceful coexistence with America. Anybody with an ear to the ground knew that Germain was the rising force in British politics, which raised an awkward issue—Lord Howe held views on how the unrest in America should be handled that were almost diametrically opposed to Germain's. Recognizing the fact, however, that he needed to be in a position of power to influence events, he began to carefully craft a new image for himself, that of the able naval commander who was willing to resort to force to bring the deluded colonists back to their senses. The letter from his younger brother could not have arrived at a better time, since it gave him the perfect excuse to get in touch with Germain.

Over the coming months, Lord Howe would use correspondence from his younger brother as a repeated pretext for contacting Germain. It needed to be a careful courtship, because Germain was nowhere near as sure of the admiral as he was of the general. Lord Howe mixed in judicious amounts of flattery and took care to create the impression that he would be willing to act forcefully against the rebels. It was a deliberate misrepresentation of himself, and Germain remained cautious. If he had had a better understanding of the general, he would have been more cautious on that front as well.

THREE

The Hill

"I shall now beg leave to trouble the committee with a narrative of those material operations of the war, which may lead to an impartial judgement upon my general conduct, which may obviate misconceived opinions concerning particular events, and which, with some few remarks upon the several passages of the correspondence as they arise, may elucidate the truth of the facts premised.

"The evacuation of Boston was the first material occurrence, after my appointment to the command of his Majesty's forces in North America."

Howe's narrative, April 22, 1779

*E*YEBROWS MUST HAVE BEEN *raised at this. Howe was accurate in his assertion that the evacuation of Boston was the first important occurrence after he finally took over as commander-in-chief in America, but to skip ahead from his arrival, in May 1775, to the evacuation of the following March dismissed the events of ten months. The vast bulk of that time may have been spent in stultifying boredom as the army sat in its Boston billets, but there was also the small matter of a battle. And not just any battle, but the bloodiest battle the British experienced in the entire war.*

And it took place on a hill that Howe had identified just five days earlier as an essential position to be occupied before the rebels took it over.

Following the excitement at Lexington and Concord, things had settled into a sort of phony war. The men who would shape the British response to the rebellion, Howe and Germain, bided their time while the lame ducks of Gage and Dartmouth continued to correspond on the matter. Howe and Burgoyne had made their views (and their awareness of Gage's impending removal) clear in their letters, but they would not get the chance to act upon their own initiative until Gage was officially recalled. Clinton had been no less busy, but as was often his way, many of his thoughts were laid down in private memoranda. Before sailing to America he had sketched out a plan of operations, in which he had commented on New York's ability to "break the chain of rebellion" by isolating the New England colonies from the rest. Clinton was a man brimming with ideas; his problem would be persuading others of their worth.

One notion that all agreed on was the need to do something about the two areas of high ground, on Dorchester Neck and near Charlestown. Not only would occupying these heights provide them with easily defendable outposts, but allowing them to fall into rebel hands might make the British position untenable, since artillery placed on the heights could reach Boston and the British fleet in the harbor. The heights on Dorchester Neck were considered the most important and plans were drawn up for Clinton to lead a body of men to seize them. With impeccable timing—strongly suggesting that the rebel spy network in Boston was functioning efficiently—the Americans made their move first, on the night of June 16–17.

It should not have been a surprise. Indeed, British sentries heard the colonials at work through the night, but did not think to raise the alarm, much to Howe's disgust. Clinton, who had already been impressed by the spirit of the rebels, believed they had made a serious error, occupying a position that could easily be cut off from its support: "... we had the command of the waters on both sides of the peninsula," he later wrote in his personal account of the war, "and consequently their only communication with it (by the short neck which joins it to the continent) liable to

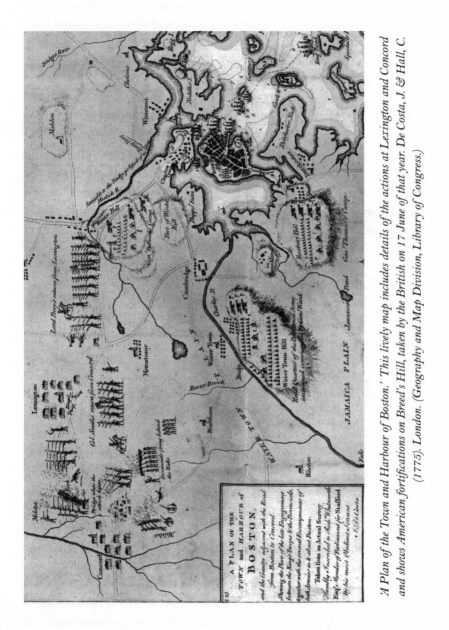

'A Plan of the Town and Harbour of Boston.' This lively map includes details of the actions at Lexington and Concord and shows American fortifications on Breed's Hill, taken by the British on 17 June of that year. De Costa, J. & Hall, C. (1775). London. (Geography and Map Division, Library of Congress.)

be intercepted by the fire from our ships, galleys, gunboats, and other water batteries." Cut off their retreat, Clinton argued, and the British would have secured a respectable bag of prisoners at no cost whatsoever. For the first time, but not the last, Clinton's advice was ignored.

Discounting Clinton's simple scheme, Howe and Gage had their own ideas on how to deal with the rebel position on Breed's Hill. It is uncertain who had the original idea, but Howe, chosen to command the operation, must have been given a deal of leeway in its planning. Perhaps thinking that the position could not be too formidable, having been thrown up in a matter of hours, or perhaps thinking that an encounter with professional soldiers might cause the amateurs in the rebel army to remember pressing matters at home, proposals were drawn up to assault the defensive works. Howe later reported to Gage on the ensuing battle, his detached words giving little indication of the hellish events of the morning of June 17.

"Sir," he reported, rather stiffly, "The troops and artillery ordered by you for the attack of the rebels upon these heights on the 17th instant being landed without opposition, were formed up on the rising ground near the beach in three lines..." There was perhaps just the hint of an apportioning of responsibility, if not exactly blame, in Howe's choice of words; "ordered by you" made it clear that although Howe had led the assault, Gage was still the commander-in-chief. A sense of foreboding had hit Howe the moment he landed and got a closer view of the rebel lines. They were far more substantial than he had expected. Standing on the beach in the early afternoon, he saw a redoubt, cannon, breastworks, and more men than he had anticipated. The rebels' numbers were growing as well, "from the heavy columns of troops which were seen pouring in to their assistance." Clinton, watching from the opposite side of the Charles River, must have felt his stomach tighten at the sight of rebels reinforcing the defensive works on Breed's Hill via the route that would have been cut off had his plan been followed. Howe called for reinforcements, but had no thoughts of canceling the assault.

The best troops available to him, the light and grenadier companies, were formed on the right of the British line, opposing a rebel breastwork that ran down to the beach. This was intended to be the focal point of the battle and Howe's intention was that they should storm the American position with bayonets and then roll up the remainder of the line. "The attack began by a sharp cannonade from our field pieces and howitzers," he recounted, "the lines advancing slowly and frequently halting to give time for the artillery to fire. The light infantry upon the right were directed to keep along the beach and to force the left point of the Rebels' breastwork and then to take their line in flank, the grenadiers being directed to attack it in front, supported by the 5th and 52nd."

Howe's plan was solid and far from the unimaginative frontal assault it has sometimes been portrayed as. The problem was that the unfolding events bore no resemblance to his plan. The lights and grenadiers found their progress impeded by a fence that stretched across the beach. As they struggled to pass it, the first rebel shots began to hit home. The same men who had been harried during their desperate retreat from Concord now found themselves once more under enemy fire, and as the sickening thuds of heavy bullets striking flesh, along with the first screams of the wounded, filled the air, they forgot their orders and began to return fire. The ensuing firefight, one side exposed on a beach and the other nestled behind strong breastworks, was one-sided in the extreme and the British troops broke, streaming back the way they had come. Among the men left behind was Lieutenant Colonel James Abercrombie, commanding the grenadiers, hit by friendly fire in the chaos. He later died.

Howe saw his career flash before his eyes as his men retreated in disorder. His report to Gage gave no hint of the turmoil in his mind at this point, but a second letter, to General Harvey back home, was more revealing. As he watched his best troops milling about in confusion, and then saw his beloved light infantry fall back, he admitted that "there was a moment that I never felt before." This enigmatic statement has been pored over by historians ever since, some suggesting that he felt fear for the first time in his career. It is more likely that his shock stemmed from the failure of his light troops, and the possibility of suffering a humiliating defeat.

That possibility remained very real as he reorganized his men for a second assault. This was glossed over entirely in his report to Gage, in which he merely said that his troops persevered and carried the rebel position, with no mention of being initially repulsed. On the left of the British line, Brigadier General Pigot had also been thrown back by heavy fire from the rebel redoubt. Casualties were mounting and the price being paid for the hill was already too high.

Across the Charles River, Clinton watched the bloody mess unfolding and took the decision to exceed his orders. Begging Burgoyne to vouch for him if Gage was angered by his crossing the river without authorization, he rushed to a boat and was rowed across to the scene of the battle. Finding confusion everywhere, he rallied a party of guards and whatever walking wounded still had some fight in them—"which, to their honour, were many"— and advanced on the rebels. According to Clinton, Howe was effusive in his thanks, admitting that he had saved the day. Howe claimed to Harvey that Clinton had not arrived until the rebels had already started to give way, but did credit him for encouraging the troops. Howe, spattered with blood following the loss of many of his personal staff, now watched his men return to the assault and, with the rebels running short of ammunition, the hill was finally taken.

But the cost was shocking. "I freely confess to you," Howe wrote to Harvey, "when I look at the consequences of it, in the loss of so many brave Officers, I do it with horror—The Success is too dearly bought." Not only had 92 officers been killed or wounded, Howe reported 160 rank and file had been killed outright, with at least 300 more wounded. Howe's figures were confused, but he also mentioned 300 men who were not injured but still "incapable of present duty," suggesting that the horrors of the battle had driven some men into a state of shock. The official number of casualties eventually settled at 1,054, the highest loss suffered by the British in a single battle through the entire war. Legend has it that at one point Howe found himself alone on the slopes of Breed's Hill, after each member of his staff had fallen. It seems remarkable that, so isolated, the rebels had failed to find him with a bullet, as officers were naturally prime targets, but returns after the battle confirm that among his staff officers Captain Sherwin was killed, along with Lieutenant Bruere of the 14th Regiment, while 10 further staff members were wounded.

Clinton quietly fumed over the affair, understandably upset that his own plan had been ignored. His disappointment spilled over into personal rancor and his relationship with Howe had suffered its first blow. In a letter back home, which Clinton considered so incendiary he wrote in such a way as to require reading through a cut-out mask of paper to reveal the letter's true message, he poured scorn on the operation and, indirectly, on Howe himself:

> "We are an army of children," he fumed, "and our officers have customs I highly disapprove. Our disposition on the 17th was one straggling line two deep, men loaded with blankets and knapsacks halting often to form the line, obliged to [close up] the front and when they arrived at the entrenchments many regiments without bayonets. If this is American disposition it is not mine."

Clinton's evidence was damning, if it can be believed. Howe had ordered his men to attack with the bayonet, so it seems unlikely that whole regiments would have gone into the battle without them. Likewise, what Clinton perceived as halts to re-form the line were reported by Howe as pauses to allow the British artillery to fire. The barbed comment about "American disposition" hints at a deep-seated mistrust between men who had learned their trade on different continents. While Howe had served in North America during the French and Indian War, Clinton had been in Germany. The stress of battle was always likely to bring such differences to the fore, and Clinton also noted that Howe had called him back ("I thought a little forcibly") when he had attempted to launch a pursuit of the fleeing rebels. The first sign of weakness in a relationship that was to be of critical importance to Howe was faintly visible.

Breed's Hill was cheated out of its place in American military folklore when it was usurped by the hill behind it, also occupied by the rebels but not attacked on June 17, 1775. Perhaps "the Battle of Bunker Hill" just tripped off the tongue in a more pleasing manner. The British, understandably shocked, attempted to get back to normality, but the aftermath of the battle was difficult to brush aside. Among the works undertaken by the Captain of Engineers, John Montresor, and duly noted in his journal, was the construction of "coffins without number." Gage was inundated with requests for consideration from officers eager to fill the gaps left by fallen comrades; battles were always the quickest route to promotion and men could not be blamed for attempting to grasp such a golden opportunity as that presented by the carnage inflicted on the British officer corps on Breed's Hill. Many junior officers relied on an obliging superior to write the all-important letter to Gage, while some wrote on their own account—there was little point in being reticent when such an opportunity might not present itself again for years.

The "unhappy day," as Howe referred to it, would have a lasting impact. The battle may have come dressed as a victory, but few had any trouble penetrating such a flimsy disguise. Hugh, Earl Percy, who had been present at Boston since the previous year and was promoted to the rank of major general in America in July 1775, commented to Harvey that "our army is so small we cannot even afford a victory, if it is attended with any loss of men." Howe saw it as the blueprint for eventual defeat, noting to Harvey (who must have been better apprised of the situation in America than any other man in England) that the rebels would try to fortify every post and wait to be attacked, "destroying as many of us as they can before they set out to their next strong Situation, &, in this defensive mode, (the whole Country coming into them upon every Action) they must in the end get the better of our small Numbers." Howe might also have heard the words of Harvey, who had written to him prior to his leaving Britain, as if they were being whispered in his ear: "… our army will be destroyed by damned driblets," he had warned. "America is an ugly job … a damned affair indeed."

Debate over the mode of proceeding in this "ugly job" continued. The dead men walking, Gage and Dartmouth, continued doggedly in their pretense of still being relevant. A week after the battle, Gage wrote to the incumbent Secretary of State for the Colonies, full of pessimism. "The Tryals we have had show that the Rebels are not the despicable Rabble too many have supposed them to be," he wrote. "Your Lordship will perceive that the Conquest of the Country is not easy and can be effected only by Time and Perseverance, and strong Armys attacking in various Quarters, and dividing their Forces. Confining your Operations on this side [New England] only is attacking in the strongest part, and you have to cope with vast numbers." In short, New England was too hot to handle and the British war effort needed to be focused elsewhere. Gage finished with a wry observation. "In all their wars against the French," he said of the rebels, "they never showed so much Conduct, Attention and Perseverance as they do now."

A month later, Gage's patience was wearing thin. He wrote of his disgust at Boston as the seat of operations, and his preference for New York, and a month later still, on August 20, he wrote to Dartmouth once more to complain bitterly about his position in Boston. The advantages of the Hudson River, offering a supply line from Canada and also making communications between the northern and southern colonies difficult, were clear. He also spoke of his suspicions that the rebellion had been in the planning for some time and was no spontaneous uprising.

Unknown to Gage, when he wrote this last letter to Dartmouth, he had already been relieved of his command, although the instruction from Dartmouth was still beating its way across the Atlantic. Dartmouth, on August 2, had ordered Gage to return to England, "in order to give his Majesty exact information of everything that it may be necessary to prepare as easily as possible for the Operations of next Year..." It was a paper-thin veil to spare Gage's blushes, but he took it in surprisingly good spirit. At the same time, Dartmouth had included a second letter, musing on the possibilities for the next campaign. The dancing around the subject of the Hudson strategy continued, as if nobody wanted to admit the simple fact that there was no alternative aside from simply withdrawing from the colonies and enforcing a naval blockade. The charade of pondering a range of potential strategies reached new levels in Dartmouth's letter, which included the alternatives of doing very little, or nothing at all. Under the heading of "Future plan of Operations of Our Forces in North America," Dartmouth pretended to seriously consider attacking the rebels in their New England stronghold. Perhaps embarrassed by the ludicrous suggestion, he dealt with this option in one sentence, before going into far more detail on option number two:

> "Whether, viewing the whole state of America, it would not be more advisable to make Hudson's River the Seat of the War, & for that purpose immediately take possession of the City of New York with a part of our Force, leaving at Boston what is necessary to secure that Post, and keep up a Diversion on that Side."

Option three suggested doing an unspecified *something* at an unspecified *somewhere*, "... which, if it served no other purpose, would at least enable you to collect a large supply of live stock for Provision, which is no trifling object in your present Circumstances." Even this seemed recklessly bold compared with option four, which suggested leaving the colonies and seeing if anybody could come up with a better idea over the winter.

The final choice, Dartmouth insisted, was Gage's—but he managed to get in one more nudge and a couple of winks by pointing out the "variety of cogent reasons" that favored the New York option—"for altho' your own knowledge and experience, aided by the advice & opinion of the able generals who assist you, will be far better Guides to your judgement than any thing I can suggest, yet it may not be altogether useless to mark out (however incorrectly) some of the Ideas of Military Men of knowledge and ability here."

Gage's "knowledge and experience," of course, was so valued that he was being invited to come back to England to share it with the King, but that awkwardness would hopefully be forgiven. For Gage's part, he handled his recall admirably, consulting with his generals on the "options" laid out by Dartmouth right up until his departure, on October 11. He also continued to correspond in friendly terms with the generals he left behind in America. Perhaps, seeing the difficult nature of the job at hand, he was so relieved at leaving the colonies that he was willing to overlook the rather clumsy manner of his recall.

––––––

The shape of Britain's response was now becoming discernible. Gage was out and Howe, in a separate letter from Dartmouth on August 2, was appointed commander-in-chief during Gage's absence. Nobody needed to have it spelled out that the absence would be permanent. Guy Carleton was to command the British forces in Canada, which presented a tricky situation that would have its repercussions; Carleton was superior to Howe in terms of seniority and would therefore become commander-in-chief if the two armies met in New York, as was the plan under the Hudson strategy. That potential awkwardness was not an immediate concern, but it would come to weigh on Howe's mind. For now, he expressed his pleasure at the promotion. "Your lordship may rely upon my utmost endeavours to forward his Majesty's service in the important department with which I am honoured," he wrote to Dartmouth, "and I enter upon it with greater cheerfulness from the knowledge I have of the superior abilities of Major Generals Clinton and Burgoyne, upon whose support and assistance I can place the best grounded confidence in every difficulty that may arise."

Howe's army was going to be substantial. Dartmouth's letter on the options for the following campaign included great detail on the army that would enact the final selection. "The desire," he wrote, "is to have an army of at least 20,000 in North America early in the next Spring." This was almost exactly the number specified by Howe in his letter to his brother. In order to reach this figure (no easy feat when the entire British Army numbered around 45,000 at the time), 22 battalions were to be augmented with two additional companies each. Company strength was to be brought up to 67 officers and men. Two regiments that had suffered during the Breed's Hill assault, the 18th and 59th, were to see their remnants absorbed into other regiments in the Boston garrison, while their officers and NCOs would return to Britain to recruit, rebuilding the units almost from scratch.

Boston could now serve no purpose for the British. On September 5 Dartmouth stressed once more, this time directly to Howe, the advantages of shifting the British base to New York, but this time he went further, saying that it "seems not only advisable but necessary to abandon Boston before the Winter." Dartmouth's letter also included the first hint of a separate operation when he suggested a "sudden & unexpected Enterprize to the southward." The seed of the disastrous "southern expedition" had been planted.

Before departing the scene, Gage was given one more reason to view his recall as desirable. His official report on the Battle of Bunker Hill drew a furious response from Clinton, who felt that his role in the affair had been belittled. Gage mentioned only that Clinton had "followed" the reinforcements over to the battle, and although he offered a robust defense, insisting he had asked Clinton about his role only to be told that it was trifling and of no consequence, Clinton was angry; a pattern was already becoming clear regarding his relationships with fellow officers. At the same time, he was giving his opinion of the options offered by Dartmouth, which had been passed on to him by Gage. Unsurprisingly, Clinton favored the New York option, although he doubted reinforcements could arrive in time to take possession of the city immediately. He was also a proponent of raids along the American coastline.

Clinton and Howe now formed a clique of two (Burgoyne had returned to London to seek employment in Canada), meeting frequently to discuss options and united, for the time being, by a dissatisfaction with Gage, who wanted to do nothing before returning to England. From home came reports of the inactivity of the North administration and its failure to properly consult with military experts. From William Phillips, an artillery officer not currently serving in North America, Clinton learned of the location of the Cabinet, scattered throughout the country, the day after news of Bunker Hill had arrived. Only the Chancellor of the Exchequer was in London at a time when serious debate was surely called for. Military preparations were left to the Secretary at War, Lord Barrington. Phillips also saw fit to weigh in with his personal recommendation of the Hudson strategy.

The Howe–Clinton conferences were not cozy affairs. The two men continued to disagree on almost every point, but they shared the feeling that something ought to be done to respond to the humiliating situation of being under siege. Both lamented the lack of forces available, but also felt that small-scale operations were possible. On September 4, Clinton suggested an expedition to Newberry with 1,000 men and complained to Howe that Gage did not think he could spare them. Howe agreed with Clinton that the plan was sound and that the men could have been found. Grumbling behind the back of a superior is easy enough, but the time was fast approaching when Howe would be elevated to that position, and then he would have no excuse for inactivity. His army was promising to be bigger than anticipated, Dartmouth informing him that negotiations were under way with Catherine the Great to secure Russian troops for the service. The Tsarina, it appeared, had promised the British as many troops as they wanted, and it was hoped to get 20,000.

More murmurings of an operation in the southern colonies continued to arrive. Governor Josiah Martin, who had been driven from his residence in North Carolina and forced to take refuge on a British ship on the Cape Fear River, believed that a small number of redcoats would allow him to restore royal authority to his colony and also neighboring South Carolina. Following the departure of Gage, on October 11, the plans began to crystallize. Viewed as a means of taking the war to the colonists in a limited form, while awaiting the build-up of the main army, an operation to support loyalist forces in North Carolina promised to provide a valuable second base for the British and hopefully subdue a number of the southern colonies, as well as acting as a launchpad for seaborne raids along the American coast. Dartmouth's letter to Howe outlining the plan, however, included an ominous sentence: "I hope we are not deceived in the Assurances [regarding the depth of loyalist support in the region] that have been given." The need for some show of decisive action was now clear. Howe was informed that, as far as the British were concerned, the colonists were now in "open and declared war. There is no room left for any other Consideration but that of proceeding against them in all respects with the utmost Vigour, as the open and avowed Enemies of the State."

Proceeding against them, however, was proving troublesome. Hopes of Russian troops quickly proved chimerical. Catherine the Great had led the British envoy a merry dance before finally admitting she had no intention of supplying the men, and the German states were now being consulted instead. At the same time, Howe's appetite for soldiers had started to grow, a common enough phenomenon among commanders-in-chief. Whereas 19,000 had seemed adequate when he was second-in-command, on October 9 he suggested that 25,000 would be more fitting. Howe also expanded upon his apparent understanding of the Hudson strategy; by establishing posts along its entire length the colonies could be effectively divided. An army of 12,000 men at New York would get the job done, with five battalions earmarked for garrison duty in the city itself while the remainder of the corps operated on the Hudson. At this early stage, it was still envisioned that Boston should be held by a defensive corps of 5,000, commanded by Clinton. Howe stated his preference, however, for using those men instead to take and hold Rhode Island. Howe's attitude to the rebel army was not entirely clear. He asserted that if posts were to be established along the Hudson, "the Reduction of the Rebels in the Province of New York must in some measure be included," but he failed to specify by how much they would need to be reduced. A force of 3,000 regulars, supplemented by Canadian and Indian units, could operate from Canada, and he added that an extra 5,000 men, evenly split between Rhode Island and Canada, would be desirable.

Then came the critical part of his letter: "The early Arrival of the destined Reinforcements in the Spring is of such material Consequence to His Majesty's Service that I am persuaded it is needless for me to trouble your Lordship with any Solicitations upon so essential a Point." Apparently oblivious to what he had just written, Howe then proceeded with just such a solicitation: "But I should hope the Troops for the Boston Division may be embarked by the Beginning of February, in which case they may be expected here about the Time I should wish the Campaign to open, in the middle or latter end of April."

Such a start date was never going to be realistic. A month later, Howe was informing Dartmouth that he was unable to evacuate Boston as planned because of a shortage of transport vessels. The disagreeable reality of remaining there for the winter had to be accepted. Howe attempted to put a brave face on matters, expressing his wish that the rebels might try some sort of action, which would draw them out from their defensive works, "to which alone they may attribute their present security." They were brave words, and Howe would have been interested to hear that the rebels' new commanding officer, General George Washington, also wished for activity to "season" his inexperienced army, but both generals were to be disappointed. Nothing happened for nearly four months.

Back in England, Germain finally took the reins as the Secretary of State for the Colonies on November 10. As Britain had inched closer to the full use of coercive methods, so he had appeared more and more the man for the job. A risible attempt to make this committed hawk a peace commissioner to negotiate with the rebels had come, unsurprisingly, to nothing; Germain was not in the mood for conciliation. Six days after taking office he sat in the House of Commons, nervous about the reception he might get with the ghost of Minden still at his elbow. During a debate on a "Bill for composing the present Troubles in America," Germain made his first comments as Secretary of State. He admitted that he had always held but one opinion of the situation in America: that the rebels must accept British supremacy. There was a hint of flexibility, however. Although he insisted upon, and would never concede, Britain's right to tax the colonies, he was willing to consider withholding the exercise of that right if an alternative means of raising the revenue necessary for their defense could be found. He was not scared of war, believing Britain to be equal to the challenge. On the subject of specific actions to be taken, he declared himself in the hands of the generals in America. Asking himself rhetorically what force was needed, he insisted that only the men on the spot could answer such a question. His responsibility was to provide what was requested. Germain was speaking, of course, in the knowledge that Howe had talked of getting the war won with as few as 19,000 men.

The pieces were now in place. The first two campaigns of the American War of Independence would be shaped and implemented by William Howe and Lord George Germain. Two men who had once seemed on irrevocably different career paths now found themselves joined in a great military struggle. Germain had no doubts that he had the perfect man in place to implement his envisioned strategy of harsh coercive action. As it turned out, his confidence was entirely misplaced.

In fairness to Howe, he was enduring a miserable introduction to the role of commander-in-chief. Space in Boston was at a premium, and although the heat of the summer had been oppressive, it had at least been possible to house the army under canvas; something like 1,500 tents had been in use in July, by which point fresh meat and provisions were reserved mainly for the sick and wounded, of whom there were plenty. As the siege drew out and the seasons changed, new deprivations had to be suffered. A shortage of wood for fires and an outbreak of smallpox and, inevitably, scurvy, left the garrison in a wretched state.

Howe's correspondence with Dartmouth remained businesslike, but in private he was sinking into something like a depression. Frequent conferences with Clinton revealed the commander-in-chief to be in a lethargic frame of mind, full of pessimism for the trials ahead and unable to rouse himself to action. Murmurs were made of prospective operations—using the frozen Mystic River to launch a raid on the rebel barracks, a descent on Rhode Island, a plan to launch a four-pronged attack on the rebel lines to possibly force them to retire—but nothing was actually put into motion.

At the same time, Howe became preoccupied with potential problems. The rebels might burn the barracks on Bunker Hill, he feared, while guilt over the burning of Charlestown tortured him. Clinton attempted to buoy up his commanding officer's mood, insisting that he also had his share of the blame to bear and had no regrets. Howe seemed particularly downcast over a letter from Dartmouth in which he declared that the only way of dealing with the rebels was "by fire and sword." He even began to see problems before they had arisen, potentially a desirable quality in a commander, but one that Howe took to extreme lengths. Imagining that the rebels might build defensive works at a position near Phip's Farm, he anticipated that driving them out would bring him no glory and be dismissed as a "victory of cannon." Perhaps shaken by such a pessimistic train of thought, Clinton insisted that any victory, by cannon or otherwise, was worthwhile.

A raid on the town of Falmouth (now Portland, Maine)—in which around 400 houses were destroyed, leaving an estimated 1,000 people homeless as winter drew near—was particularly distressing to Howe. The raid had taken place at the same time as the handover from Gage and Dartmouth to Howe and Germain, and Howe was concerned that the British public would think he had ordered it. Clinton, still trying to lift Howe's spirits, said that the raid had been justified given the colonists' lack of obedience to the Crown, and insisted it should have been carried out earlier. News from elsewhere in North America was no comfort. The Americans had launched a major offensive in Canada and at one point appeared to be close to realizing their goal. Carleton had been driven from Montreal and holed up at Quebec, resulting in the unedifying situation of two British armies under siege from the upstart colonists at the same time.

Howe was not good company during the winter at Boston, darkly muttering that Britain was "liable to attack from the whole world," and Clinton was happy to be given the opportunity of finding better weather, better company, and possibly even a little glory to the south, since he had been given command of the proposed southern expedition. He was concerned that his orders were imprecise, but having championed the concept of expeditionary warfare, he could hardly baulk at commanding one. Optimistically, naively so, it was anticipated that Clinton could meet with reinforcements from Britain off the coast of North Carolina, restore order in four colonies, and return to Howe in time to take part in the main campaign the following year. Bearing in mind that Howe had mentioned his desire of opening the campaign by the end of April at the latest, timing was always going to be tight; this was to be a lightning strike by 18th-century standards, and Clinton departed on January 20, 1776. Howe would not see him again for more than six months.

Also absent from Boston was Burgoyne, the third of the major generals who had arrived on the *Cerberus*. Having returned to London, he was at that moment pressing his ideas for the upcoming campaign, notably in a paper entitled "Reflections upon the War in America." Largely through his apparent grasp of the nature of the type of war necessary to be fought in the colonies, he was granted the position of second-in-command to Carleton in Canada. Clinton, as Burgoyne's senior, would have been given the position had he not already been engaged in the southern colonies.

In Boston, matters continued on their dispiriting course. Percy, who had struck up a strong friendship with Clinton, was not in favor with Howe. He reported to his absent friend that Howe remained passive. "We have had nothing extraordinary here since your departure," the major general wrote on February 1, "for it is not extraordinary to have three ships taken [by rebel privateers] within ten days, two of them just off the lighthouse ... With respect to me our commander-in-chief is as reserved as ever. He had about two days ago very near endeavoured to bring on a general action without my knowing anything about it. I accidentally called that morning at headquarters and so was informed about it." The impression of an army riven by cliques was once more inescapable.

Shortly after departing the scene at Boston, Clinton conjured up an ambitious and sensible plan to seize a range of fortifications being raised by the rebels in the Hudson Highlands, approximately 50 miles (80 kilometers) upriver from New York City. With control over the length of the river the keystone of the proposed strategy for the coming campaign, Clinton's plan was logical as well as having a touch of style—getting the rebels to do the hard work of constructing defensive works and then stepping in to take them over. During his voyage southward Clinton lamented the fact that he would have no way of bringing it to Howe's attention for some time. As it happened, he would have to wait two years for his plan to finally be enacted.

Stopping at New York on his way south, Clinton had the opportunity to appraise the region that was to be the springboard for the Hudson strategy. "This place might be taken without any mischief," he noted, believing that the city itself could not be fortified effectively while it remained standing. With just a small force on Long Island, he believed, the rebels could be forced to evacuate New York City. With a larger army, the British could land directly on Manhattan, or even beyond it, trapping any rebel forces on the island, leading Clinton to conclude that "... the island of New York [Manhattan] may be ours without any loss." As at Boston, Clinton saw the possibility of using the mobility imparted by a strong naval force to outmaneuver the rebels and trap them in a hopeless position. As at Boston, his advice was to be ignored.

———

In London, Germain was drawing rave reviews for the energy with which he was attacking his new job. "From the time Lord George Germain has come into office," wrote Richard Cox to Clinton, "the military business bears a much better aspect." Charles Mellish had similar tidings, having been "... told by great merchants in the city of the affability and assiduity of Lord G. in the American Department, and I have since found not a moment is lost." Francis Hastings, the 10th Earl of Huntingdon, referred to Germain as "an active as well as an able man," also pointing out that London was in a festive mood and "not in the least concerned about what is passing on the other side of the Atlantic."

Germain's appetite for the job was understandable. He had been waiting 16 years for such an opportunity. There were the inevitable sniping comments that he was driven only by the desire to expunge the disgrace he had earned at Minden (attempting "to reconquer Germany in America" in the words of Edward Gibbon), and the element of truth must have made these comments sting a little more, but the fact was that Germain was doing a good job. Howe, unavoidably out of touch with events in London, might still have been writing to Dartmouth, but it was Germain who received the letters and framed the responses.

Thus it was Germain who officially approved Howe's plans for 1776, submitted to Dartmouth the preceding October. He also accepted that evacuating Boston before the winter had not been possible and reported on the process of building Howe's army for the coming campaign. Two thousand Highlanders were to be formed into a regiment, the first new regiment to be raised in response to the American crisis. Nominally under the command of Simon Fraser, and referred to informally as "Fraser's Highlanders," the regiment was officially designated the 71st Regiment of Foot. Fraser had led a regiment in the French and Indian War, where it saw action, alongside Howe's light infantry, at the battle on the Plains of Abraham.

The 42nd Regiment, the Black Watch, was to accompany the 71st to America and it was hoped that this body of 3,000 formidable soldiers would be ready to sail by early April. There had been progress also on the question of foreign troops. Out of an anticipated 17,000 hirelings, Howe would receive 10,000, or at least he would when it had been decided where they were to come from. Germain added that supply ships en route to Boston would hopefully give Howe enough tonnage to evacuate his army. A little less than a month later Germain was in touch again. The Guards, Britain's elite infantry regiments, had demonstrated such enthusiasm for serving in America that a composite battalion, numbering 1,000 men and drawn from all three Guards regiments, was being assembled for Howe's use.

Howe felt the need to restate his plans for the coming campaign, perhaps feeling that this would compensate for the lengthy period of inactivity at Boston. If he was delivered an army of 20,000 men, he wrote on January 16, still believing he was addressing Dartmouth:

"… the present unfavourable appearance of Things would probably wear a very different Aspect before the end of the ensuing Campaign: With fewer Troops the Success of any offensive Operations will be very doubtful, the Enemy possessing Advantages that will not be readily overcome by a smaller Force."

Howe had been taught to respect the rebels from their performance on Breed's Hill and from intelligence flowing into his headquarters in Boston. "Neither is their army by any means to be despised," he insisted, "having in it many European Soldiers, & all or most of the young men of Spirit in the Country, who are exceedingly diligent & attentive to their military Profession."

Howe's desire to evacuate Boston was still strong, and he planned to move directly to New York to get the campaign under way as quickly as possible, but the number of loyalists in Boston was a problem. Unwilling to be left behind when the British withdrew, they wanted to be given safe passage—along with their possessions. Many more ships would be needed for this.

It was March before Germain was able to inform Howe that treaties had been signed with several German states for the provision of troops, and that 12,200 would soon be on their way to Howe—transports were on their way to pick up the first wave of 8,200. The Highlanders and Black Watch were not expected to sail for another month, while the Guards would sail with the Germans when they arrived in Britain. Time was slipping away and the southern expedition was now considered expendable. The troops had not even left for America until February 12 and bad weather had quickly forced many of the transports to return to port. Orders had been sent to Clinton to abandon the expedition and return to New York to take part in the main offensive.

The letter could hardly have been more indicative of the problems of running the war. The order to cancel the southern expedition never reached Clinton, while Howe's desired start date of mid-to-late April was now unattainable. Worse than this, as Germain took paper in hand he had no way of knowing that the British army was no longer at Boston. Having dithered for months about the necessary evacuation, Howe's decision had been made for him, because taking pride of place among the many things that he had not done during his first months in command was his failure to occupy the heights on Dorchester Neck.

FOUR

The Evacuation

"On the 9th of November, 1775, I received the Secretary of State's order, dated the 5th of September, to abandon that town [Boston] before winter ... The late arrival of the order, and the deficiency of transport tonnage, rendered the removal of the troops impractical till the 17th of March following, when I embarked with about 6,000 rank and file, fit for duty, and about 900 sick.

"It has not been insinuated that any disgrace was brought upon his Majesty's arms by the manner in which the town was evacuated."

Howe's narrative, April 22, 1779

IF HOWE CONTINUED AT this rate his speech would be over in a matter of minutes. Having entirely ignored the Battle of Bunker Hill and the following nine months (to the day) under siege in Boston, he was now glossing over the manner in which that situation had finally been resolved. If he thought that no disgrace had been brought upon his Majesty's arms by the manner in which the town was evacuated, he must have been capable of a very high level of self-delusion—everything about the evacuation of Boston was disgraceful and deeply humiliating to British prestige, and it was all the more so because it could so easily have been prevented.

In April 1775, in the letter to his brother, Howe had mentioned the desirability of occupying two pieces of high ground that could, if taken by the rebels, make the British position in Boston uncomfortable at best and untenable at worst. He suggested that the high ground on Dorchester Neck should be taken first, followed by the hills on the other side of town, near Charlestown. A plan had been under way to move on Dorchester when the Americans launched their pre-emptive strike, on the night of June 16.

The blood-letting on the slopes of Breed's Hill might have acted as a spur to further action regarding the other high ground from where rebels could threaten Boston, but it did not. Clinton remarked in his own narrative of the war that this filled him with foreboding: "For I foresaw the consequences, and gave it formally as my opinion at the time *that if the king's troops should be ever driven from Boston, it would be by rebel batteries raised on those heights.*" Clinton may have been crediting himself with this foreboding after the event. His plentiful notes on conferences with Howe during the long, uneventful months following the Battle of Bunker Hill are devoid of any urging on his part to occupy the Dorchester Heights. On December 3, 1775 the conversation did touch on Dorchester Neck, but only inasmuch as Clinton was musing on the possibility of the rebels setting fire to the town there. Howe assured him he did not think it likely, but there is no record of Clinton taking advantage of this opening to segue into a suggestion to occupy the high ground.

On the other hand, having no concerns over the possibility of the rebels possessing the heights would have been strange indeed. The events of June 17 suggested that the British would only drive the rebels from these positions at great cost, and the loss of another thousand men would have been disastrous. The price paid may, of course, have been even higher and a worst-case scenario would have seen the British unable to budge the rebels at all. Failing to pre-emptively occupy the heights in these circumstances seems little short of a dereliction of duty.

In Howe's defense, the Americans were in no hurry to reprise their Breed's Hill escapade. Perhaps shocked by the persistence of the redcoats on June 17, they made no move to threaten the heights on Dorchester Neck or the hard-won British positions near the smoking ruins of Charlestown. Washington, getting to grips with the job of commanding the rebel army, had his hands full dealing with deficiencies in men, engineers, tents, clothing, ammunition, and money, as well as with a worrying lack of unity between soldiers from different colonies. Concerned at the prospects of fighting off a British offensive if it came, he was in no frame of mind to consider any such move of his own. The suggestion of an ambitious plan to bottle up the entire British fleet and army by occupying a number of points, including the Dorchester Heights, were dismissed by Washington, not because he thought they were fanciful, but because "… what signifies Long Island, Point Alderton, and Dorchester, while we are in a manner destitute of cannon, and compelled to keep the little powder we have for the use of the musketry."

Howe, whatever intelligence he was receiving, could not have been sure of American intentions, and on February 13, 1776 word reached him that Washington was intending to occupy Dorchester Neck. Howe took this intelligence seriously, dispatching a body of men, including grenadiers and light infantry, to burn the houses there and thus deprive the rebels of cover. He did not, however, follow up with the obvious move when it turned out the rebels had no such plans. For now the heights remained unoccupied, spurned by both potential suitors, but the situation could not continue for long.

Washington, indeed, was tempted to launch a full-scale assault on Boston in the depths of winter, making use of the frozen waterways, but his generals, consulted at a council of war, were unenthusiastic. The American commander-in-chief was partially mollified by the suggestion that something should be tried even if a full-scale assault was too risky. The "something" turned out to be the seizure of the Dorchester Heights. Having been given more than enough time and incentive to do something about the situation, Howe was about to have the matter taken out of his hands.

———

"I am preparing to take post on Dorchester," Washington wrote to Joseph Reed on February 26, "to try if the enemy will be so kind as to come out to us." Washington's polite sentiments masked a genuine hope that occupation of the heights could have serious and important consequences. In a separate letter to the President of Congress, he explained his thinking on the matter further: "... I should think, if any thing will induce them to hazard an engagement, It will be our attempting to fortifie these heights; as on that event's taking place, we shall be able to command a great part of the town, and almost the whole harbor..." It seemed so simple it was remarkable that no prior effort had been made on either side.

Washington's eagerness to act was all the more interesting considering the fact that his intelligence suggested strongly that the British were preparing to leave Boston in any case. The baking of large quantities of biscuit and the shifting of cannon and mortars from defensive works on to ships all pointed to a British evacuation. Washington, however, was not willing to simply let the redcoats go. He was as aware as everyone else that British strategy would revolve around the capture of New York and dominance of the Hudson River and any disruption he could impose on the execution of that strategy would be worthwhile.

The move, when it finally came, caught the British by surprise, despite the fact that it was preceded by a three-day artillery bombardment and the raising of works at Phip's Farm (which Howe had expressed concern about in conversation with Clinton the previous year). "The rebels," Howe informed Clinton, "made a strong and very extensive work at Phip's Farm without our being able to prevent it by the cannon from Boston's Point, or a possibility of dislodging them." On the morning of March 5, 1776, the British discovered that under the cover of these diversionary actions a sizable force of rebels had occupied the Dorchester Heights. "We were much amazed in the morning," Howe admitted, "with the forwardness of their works, having a strong abbatis round them..." Perhaps attempting to deflect from the embarrassment of having been caught flat-footed, Howe insisted that the extent of the works must have required the labor of 12,000–14,000 men. However many it had taken (and it was certainly far fewer than that), the rebels were now in possession of dominating high ground, and if the British were to remain in Boston, or at least leave it at a time of their own choosing, they would need to remove them. Nine months after the Battle of Bunker Hill, the British found themselves in a disturbingly similar situation.

Howe had little alternative but to launch an assault on the new rebel positions, which was exactly what Washington had hoped for. In informing the Congress about his audacious move, Washington confided that "I flatter myself, from the posts we have just taken and are about to take, that it will be in our power to force the ministerial troops to an attack ... I think from these posts they will be so galled and annoyed, that they must either give us battle or quit their present possessions."

Preparations were made for an immediate assault. "The Ardor of the Troops encouraged me in this hazardous Enterprize," Howe informed Dartmouth, but his plan hinted at uncertainty. A force of something more than 2,000 men (Howe specified 2,200 to Clinton, but 2,400 in correspondence with Lord Dartmouth) was assembled and ordered to cross the river to Dorchester Neck. Howe had learned his lesson from Breed's Hill, and rather than simply ordering his men to rely on the bayonet, he forbade them from loading their muskets at all; the aim was to dislodge the rebels as quickly as possible and avoid another horrific casualty list. The unauthorized firefight the grenadiers and light infantry had been drawn into at the fence on Breed's Hill was obviously a painful memory.

Howe was clearly concerned as his men moved out to launch their attack, but the assault never took place. Bad weather intervened, with adverse winds making it impossible to land the men where they were needed—several landing craft ran aground. The bad weather continued through the next day and night, giving the rebels time to strengthen their position and bring up more cannon, until Howe was forced to accept, on March 7, that any assault was by then far too risky. "I could promise myself little Success by attacking them under all the Disadvantages I had to encounter," he wrote to Dartmouth, but the consequences of his failure to move the rebels were immediately clear. The British would have to evacuate Boston immediately, ready or not.

———

By the time he stood in front of the House of Commons three years later, Howe had convinced himself, or merely chosen to believe, that there was no disgrace in the manner in which the British had left Boston. At the time, the ministry had attempted to downplay the affair, insisting that the army had left Boston "… with the greatest order and regularity, and without the least interruption from the rebels." They might have got away with such a gross distortion of the truth were it not for the fact that private letters carried very different versions of the affair. On May 10, 1776 George Montagu, the 4th Duke of Manchester, expressed his disgust at events in America in the House of Lords, referring to "the deepest stain on the glory of British arms" and "no veil but that of silence to cast over the disgrace." Angry exchanges drew others to reveal what they had heard in private correspondence, the Marquis of Rockingham revealing that he had been reliably informed that the British had only been allowed to leave Boston unmolested because they had threatened to burn it to the ground if attacked.

Equally distressing was the fact that Howe headed north-east after leaving Boston, rather than south-west. The disorganized withdrawal had forced him to make yet another painful decision. The army could no longer move directly from Boston to New York; it would need to go first to Halifax, Nova Scotia, to reorganize and prepare for the opening of the planned offensive. The decision would cost Howe months of the campaigning season.

The commander-in-chief attempted to put a brave face on these events both at the time and retrospectively. In his narrative, he commented that:

"the army by going thither [to Halifax] received great benefit, not only from necessary refreshments, but from the opportunity of being exercised in line, a very material part of discipline, in which we were defective at that time. I might also add that the troops performed very essential service at Halifax, by constructing redoubts, and other strong works, for the defense of the town and dock, which could not have been executed by the garrison."

At the time, Howe admitted that he would have preferred to have gone directly to New York. Two months before the evacuation of Boston he had expressed his belief that Clinton's southern expedition should have been called off, in order to concentrate British strength for the move on New York. There were 2,500 men, with transports and warships in proportion, with Clinton, and the addition of such a corps to the main army just might have made it possible to move directly to New York. It is more likely, however, that Howe would still have moved to Halifax first. The extended period of confinement in Boston had reduced the fighting qualities of his army and it was true that Halifax promised breathing room, more plentiful provisions, and a release from the peculiar mixture of monotony and stress that would have marked a period under siege.

At the same time there were worrying signs that Howe was losing focus and that it was simply beyond his abilities to deliver the vigorous prosecution of the war that Germain had counted on. Having settled into quarters at Halifax, Howe wrote again to Clinton, passing on the news that Hessians were to be hired rather than Russians. Howe appeared disappointed by this, suggesting that Russian soldiers would have been more willing to serve than Germans (he also made reference to the fact that Clinton had served with a corps of Russians in 1774, referring to them as "your northern friends"). More importantly, he passed on the news that recruitment in Britain was going slowly and added the shocking assertion that no plan of operations had yet been settled upon.

The numerous letters Howe had submitted, detailing his thoughts on the coming campaign, as well as his desire to open it in April, must have escaped his memory. If he was waiting for direct orders then he was already falling short of the type of commander Germain had been looking for. At a distance of 3,000 miles (4,800 kilometers) from London, he would have to be able to make up his own mind on how to proceed—Germain had already made it clear that he had no time for a general who would not "venture to take a single step beyond the letter of his instructions."

Howe's letter had a profound effect on Clinton. The southern expedition, which had already been canceled by Germain although his order appears never to have reached Clinton, had been shorn of its primary purpose in February. Expecting the British force to arrive imminently, the loyalists of North Carolina had risen up prematurely, to be soundly thrashed by patriot forces at Moore's Creek Bridge on February 27. Clinton did not arrive on the scene until March 12 and the force he was to operate with did not start to arrive from Britain until more than a month after that. It was not complete until May 31. By any reckoning, this was a miscarried expedition, but just when Clinton might have been expected to call the whole thing off and return to the north, he received Howe's letter. There was, apparently, no fixed plan for the campaign, and recruitment was going slowly. Perhaps, therefore, Clinton might be able to do something worthwhile with the small corps at his disposal. Howe's letter went further, suggesting that Charleston might be worth attention. Clinton needed no further encouragement.

On June 15, he wrote to an unknown correspondent, explaining how a letter written on April 12 left him, more than two months later, "totally at liberty for a few days at least." His commander's letter, Clinton reasoned, "seems not to call upon me; nay, I know not where to find him if I should seek him." Clinton must have been aware that events can move quickly in wartime. Pointing to a letter written two months ago as an excuse for inaction was a dangerous game and Clinton was about to be caught out, because by May 22 Howe had changed his mind. Having received Germain's letter detailing how the southern expedition had been canceled, Howe had asked Clinton to return to New York as quickly as possible. Clinton was authorized to leave no more than one or two regiments behind in the south, and only "if you think it may answer any essential purposes."

It is not always feasible to be certain when a letter was received in the 18th century, especially one sent via ship in a war zone, but in this case it is possible to make an educated guess. On June 15, Clinton felt "totally at liberty." On June 18, in a note to Brigadier General Sir John Vaughn, he was "impatient to get to the Northward." By then an attack on the unfinished fort guarding the approach to Charleston harbor was going badly and Clinton suddenly seemed under pressure: "Time is precious," he confided to Vaughn. "I heartily wish our business was done, and we on our way to the North." It does not seem unreasonable to suggest that Howe's recall instructions had arrived sometime between June 15 and June 18.

The attack on Sullivan's Island achieved nothing. The American defenders comfortably fended off the naval assault of Commodore Sir Peter Parker, while Clinton failed to even bring his men into action. A stretch of water believed to be shallow enough to wade through turned out to be 7 feet (2 meters) deep and the redcoats were forced to watch helplessly as the navy pressed the attack without support. A frigate was lost before the shambolic mess was finally brought to an end. More important than the military humiliation, however, was the damage the affair did to the relationship between Clinton and Howe. Clinton was able to bear a grudge for years, and with the slightest provocation. He felt let down by the unfortunate timing of Howe's communications, and his embarrassment over the failed southern expedition warped into resentment of both Howe and Sir Peter Parker. The Commodore was to be the recipient of angry communications from Clinton for years, while Howe was to find his second-in-command in prickly mood when he finally returned from his misadventure in the South.

Shortly after arriving at Halifax, Howe became aware that Germain had replaced Dartmouth as Secretary of State for the

Colonies, receiving a letter on March 26 that had been written the preceding November. Perhaps seeing no reason to speed up what had already been a luxuriously slow process of communication, Howe did not bother replying for another month. It is hardly surprising, therefore, that dilatory communication was to be one of the charges leveled at him.

When he did finally write, however, he told Germain exactly what he wanted to hear. Reporting that the rebels were fortifying New York City and Rhode Island, Howe stated that both were worthwhile objects for attention, but that New York was the more important. It was crucial, Howe stressed, to "check the spirit which the evacuation of Boston will naturally raise among the rebels," and he seemed to suggest that he was awaiting only a sufficient supply of provisions before moving on New York. Once there, he believed he would be able to bring the rebels to a major engagement, while they were "flushed with an idea of superiority." This, the destruction of the rebel army, was to be his principal aim: "... nothing is more to be desired or sought for by us, as the most effectual means to terminate this expensive war; and I have the greatest reason to be sanguine in my hopes of success, from the present health and high order of the army." In a second letter, written the day after, Howe remembered to offer his congratulations to Germain on his new position, throwing in a little flattery for good measure. "Being conscious I cannot find words to express how sensibly I feel your goodness to me," he wrote, "permit me to say that in my pursuits for carrying your Lordship's plans into execution, every nerve will be stretched to attain the accomplishment of them; and I beg leave to add that the whole army rejoices in the idea of acting under your Lordship's auspices..."

Germain may have felt a warm glow of satisfaction as he read Howe's letters, having received them on June 4, but one phrase might have caused him to frown. Howe had written of "carrying your Lordship's plans into execution," yet surely the plan for the 1776 campaign had been submitted by Howe? Was the commander-in-chief already trying to distance himself from the formulation of the official British strategy? More suggestion that Howe was doing just that was to be found in a third letter received on June 4, in which he mentioned that he had not yet received his official orders for the campaign. If Germain was troubled enough by this to look for further points of concern, he would have been able to find one in Howe's first letter. Immediately after stating his intention of seeking a decisive victory, Howe had gone on to explain why such a victory might be hard to achieve. If such a decisive battle could not be brought on early in the campaign, he argued, "it is most likely that they [the rebels] will act upon the defensive, by having recourse to strong intrenched situations, in order to spin out the campaign, if possible, without exposing themselves to any decisive stroke." Here, then, was the blueprint for rebel success that Howe had seen vividly on the slopes of Breed's Hill—a drawn-out, defensive war, inflicting casualties on the British for every yard of ground they occupied. The tortuous nature of communications with America may now have given Germain cause for concern. Before he had received these letters from Howe, Germain had written to the general in America advising him to be patient. He commended Howe for his "spirit and vigour" in planning for an early strike on New York, but cautioned that it might be better to wait until his reinforcements had arrived before making his move. As such large reinforcements were on the way, Germain had argued, "your force may be so increased as to render your success more certain." That letter, making its ponderous way across the Atlantic, would soon arrive and advise Howe to wait when the general himself had just spelled out the potential consequences of failing to move quickly. Germain may well have experienced a sinking feeling in his stomach.

It would have been a feeling similar to that afflicting Clinton as he tried frantically to disengage from the fiasco at Charleston. On July 8 he wrote to Germain to shift the blame for the interminable delay in rejoining Howe onto that general and Sir Peter Parker. By July 17 he was practically begging Parker to hasten preparations to return to the North, going so far as to suggest he would be willing to sail without an escort of frigates, which would have been foolhardy in the extreme. Fearful of opinion back home, he sent his private secretary, Richard Reeve, to London, in order to defend his actions as forcefully as possible. On July 25, Clinton wrote a distinctly cool letter to Howe, essentially blaming the commander-in-chief's lack of clear instructions for Clinton's delay. In short, Clinton had worked himself up into a lather, but he had little reason to fear a reprimand from Howe, whose resolve to open his campaign quickly had steadily weakened, if it had ever really existed in the first place.

The stopover in Halifax had proved useful. The soldiers had mostly been confined to quarters on their transport ships, but they were ordered ashore for drill, with special attention given to the light infantry companies. Parades were sometimes held after drill days in order to further sharpen the men's discipline. After a brief period of centralized training, Howe left the matter in the hands of the individual regimental commanders. By April 26, however, he felt confident enough to refer to "the present health and high order of the army" in his first letter to Germain. The 18 light infantry companies were then formed into two composite battalions, while the 18 grenadier companies were similarly divided, with the addition of a company of marines to each battalion. It was still a small army, of course, and Howe's desire to take the war to the rebels dissipated as the promise of substantial reinforcements tempted him to wait even before he received Germain's letter suggesting that he do exactly that. His steady retreat into caution played out over the course of his correspondence with Germain. Six weeks after informing the American Secretary that he desired nothing more than a decisive battle with the rebels, his ardor had cooled, and he could only bring himself to say that "should the enemy offer battle in the open field we must not decline it." This creeping passivity created a steadily escalating concern on the part of Germain that nothing appeared to be happening in America. There was also a worrying sign that Howe was uncertain about the main strategy for the year. The question of Carleton's seniority had obviously been troubling the general, and he artlessly raised the matter now. Howe attempted to disguise his misgivings, asking if Germain might write to Carleton to assure him there was no need to be concerned about the "delicacy of interfering with my command" when the two armies met on the Hudson. Having assured Germain that he had no problem with Carleton assuming control of both armies, Howe went on to demonstrate that he had plenty of problems. Would it not be possible for the two armies to remain in separate camps after the junction? Would he not be able to retain all the usual responsibilities of a commander-in-chief even when Carleton was on hand? And surely Carleton would not be able to cherry-pick units from Howe's army without his permission?

Germain, eager to remove any impediments from Howe's path, took the decision to install Burgoyne as commander of the northern army in response to these concerns, with Carleton staying at Quebec. Howe would therefore have been the senior officer upon a meeting of the two armies. But Germain's letter never reached Carleton. As events played out, it was a moot point anyway.

By June 7, Howe was awaiting favorable weather before finally setting off for New York to get his campaign under way. He was planning to land on Long Island, "in order to secure the Passage of the shipping into the Harbour, which can only be effected by the Possession of a commanding Height near Brooklyn, said to be fortified." Howe also suggested that he might be willing to take New York when Clinton joined him with his corps, whether or not further reinforcements had arrived from Britain. The following day, the first reinforcements arrived, a portion of the Highlanders of the 42ⁿᵈ and 71ˢᵗ regiments reaching Halifax as Howe prepared to leave. In what was to become a defining feature of Howe's correspondence, he now made a rash comment, in the form of a declaration of gratitude to Germain. "I cannot take my leave of your Lordship," he wrote, "without expressing my utter amazement, at the decisive and masterly strokes for carrying such extensive plans into immediate execution, as have been effected since your Lordship has assumed the conducting of this war, which is already most happily experienced by those who have the honour of serving here under your auspices." It was a heartfelt expression of gratitude, but it left Howe with nobody else to blame if things did not go according to plan, and there were reasons for genuine concern.

The delay in shifting from Boston to New York had given the rebels time to fortify New York, and intelligence had been rolling in steadily concerning their efforts. As early as February, reports had come in that the rebel general Charles Lee, formerly a British Army officer and therefore reviled as a turncoat while simultaneously respected as an opponent, was surveying New York and preparing defenses. By early June, a detailed breakdown of "forts, batteries and breastworks erected about the city of New York and Hudson's River" was in British hands. By the time Howe's ship, HMS *Greyhound*, reached Sandy Hook on June 25, Long Island was also fortified. Having met with Governor Tryon and other "fast friends to Government," Howe felt obliged to rethink his plans. As he explained to Germain, the rebels were "numerous and very advantageously posted with strong Entrenchments both upon Long Island and that of New York, with more than 100 pieces of Cannon for the Defence of the Town toward the sea, and to obstruct the Passage of the Fleet up the North [Hudson] River."

Howe still intended to land his army directly on Long Island, at Gravesend Bay, but further intelligence reached him concerning a ridge of high ground, the Gowanus Heights, running across Long Island, some 2 miles (3 kilometers) in front of the main rebel defensive lines at Brooklyn. Reasoning that this ridge, which was easily passable in only four places, could be quickly defended by the rebels, Howe changed his plan. He would instead land his army on Staten Island and wait for reinforcements. The bulk of his fleet arrived from Halifax on June 29, after which he updated Germain on his progress. "I propose waiting here," he informed the American Secretary, "for the English Fleet, or for the arrival of Lieut. General Clinton, in Readiness to proceed." It was another delay, but Germain was probably getting used to that by now.

Whether or not the colonists had been encouraged by the lackadaisical British response, the nature of the dispute was also about to change, dramatically. Just a day after Howe disembarked his troops on Staten Island, the colonies declared their independence from Great Britain. Rather than merely fractious subjects, the Americans now viewed themselves as a completely different country. Convincing them otherwise would not be easy.

———

New York was not a promising position for the rebels. Thanks to the presence of two major rivers, the Hudson (or North River) and the East River, it was tailor-made for the Royal Navy to exert its dominance, landing troops wherever it wanted and threatening to cut off regiments, divisions, or even whole armies. Lord Howe was on his way to America to act as joint peace commissioner with his younger brother, as well as to take command of naval forces. More importantly, he was bringing thousands of reinforcements for the army and hundreds of ships. The British fleet would eventually number more than 400, including 30 ships of the line, the most terrifying weapons platforms of the day.

New York City was a relatively minor place in 1776, occupying the bottom tip of Manhattan, or York Island. Without shipping, the only way off Manhattan was via two bridges at its northernmost tip. It was therefore a potential deathtrap for an army without substantial naval support. Making matters more complicated was the fact that the city was dominated by high ground across the East River, on Long Island. The Brooklyn Heights could perform exactly the same job at New York as the Charlestown and Dorchester Heights had at Boston—render the city untenable. The rebels proved they could learn from their enemy's mistakes when they quickly occupied the Brooklyn Heights, which made it possible to at least defend the approach to Manhattan via the East River, though how effective such a defense could be remained to be seen. The problems for the rebels did not end there, however, because the Brooklyn Heights in turn were vulnerable to an approach from their landward side on Long Island, so a system of defensive works was constructed across the neck of the Brooklyn peninsula. The ridge of high ground running across Long Island to the south of this line was yet another position the Americans would decide to fortify before the opening of the 1776 campaign.

Washington had severe doubts that New York could be held, but he recognized the importance of it, and the harm that would be done to the patriot cause if it were simply handed over to the British. Charles Lee's report on the defensibility of the place was an equal mixture of pessimism and optimism—he doubted the city could be held, but did think it would be possible to force the British to mount a series of costly assaults on prepared defenses, bleeding them white before they could claim their Pyrrhic prize. Not only did this fit into the successful pattern established on Breed's Hill, it might be the only way in which the rebels could effectively resist the British juggernaut. Washington reluctantly accepted that his men were unlikely to stand and fight in a conventional battle on open ground. Work had therefore begun to turn Manhattan into a redcoat's nightmare. The only questions to be answered were whether Howe would be obliging enough to ram his head against prepared defenses again and again and, if he did, whether the rebels would stand long enough to exact the maximum toll. This proposed defense in depth also posed a very serious problem for the rebel army. It would need to be split into many small units in order to man the several defensive positions at the same time. Without knowing where the British would eventually strike, they had to be as close to ready as possible in all quarters at the same time.

Washington had expected the British to make their move on New York sooner. When Clinton departed to command the southern expedition, it was believed he was heading for New York (he did drop in, but only while en route to the South). "No place so likely for his destination as New York," Washington had commented on March 3, "nor no place where a more capital blow could be given to the interests of America than there." Six days later, he had doubted intelligence that suggested the British would make for Halifax after leaving Boston, believing that New York was the actual (and obvious) destination. Washington had anticipated a race to reach New York in time to defend it from a British invasion, and he worried that bad roads would make his progress slow. The British were not the only ones to see the benefits of the Hudson strategy; Washington also feared its implementation. "For should they get that town, and the command of the North River," he had written on March 14, "they can stop the intercourse between the northern and southern colonies upon which depends the safety of America."

By the middle of April, while Howe was drilling his men at Halifax, Washington was at New York, where he found "many works of defence begun, and some finished." By April 20 he was establishing lookout posts to signal when the British fleet appeared, not realizing that it would be more than two months before they would oblige. It was an agonizing wait, with the tension cranked up by reports that German troops had been taken into British pay and were on their way to quell the rebellion. News of the failure of an American offensive against Quebec was also a blow to morale. From the British perspective it opened up the possibility of pursuing the Hudson strategy in full, with armies operating on both ends of the Hudson at the same time.

Canada, however, was a worry for somebody else and when Washington was called to Philadelphia to report to Congress, he left detailed instructions for Major General Israel Putnam to follow as commander at New York in his absence. Most importantly, the works on Long Island were to be completed "as expeditiously as possible," along with works on Manhattan and Governor's Island. If these were completed before Washington returned, or if there were enough men and tools to start on other sites at the same time, planned works at Paulus Hook and the Narrows were mentioned. Washington's instructions hinted at the difficulties of fortifying a living, breathing city. Barricades had been erected across the streets leading from the waterside through the city and Washington ordered that wherever these had been torn down, presumably by a populace eager to get on with its regular routine, they were to be repaired and not "meddled with" in future.

In Washington's absence, the fortifications at New York gradually took shape. Five forts or redoubts were included in the string of works across the neck of the Brooklyn peninsula on Long Island, linked by entrenchments. From left to right, as the defenders looked south across Long Island, were an unnamed redoubt, Fort Putnam, an oblong redoubt, Fort Greene, and finally Fort Box. The road from Brooklyn into the heart of Long Island ran through the entrenchments linking Fort Greene with the oblong redoubt and both flanks of the line were secured by marshland. The progress of the work was charted by Captain Jeduthan Baldwin, an engineer in the Continental Army, who knew a thing or two about constructing defenses—he had helped build the works on the Dorchester Heights that had forced the British out of Boston. The Americans initially hoped that this would be their main line of defense. It would need to be an impressive one to resist the army that was gradually assembling on Staten Island.

———

Although the build-up of British force was inexorable and still promised great things, correspondence between Howe and Germain was becoming increasingly disjointed. Playing chess by mail is a laborious affair. If the pieces on the board constantly move independently, it becomes impossible. Germain could not impose direct orders upon Howe and was reluctant even to jolly him along when it began to seem like his campaign would never open. On June 21 he was hopeful that Howe might already have taken possession of New York. By August he was backtracking on his earlier advice to await reinforcements, claiming that he had only meant that Howe should wait for one of the groups of reinforcements (Clinton's corps, the Highlanders, or the main fleet from Britain, which included the Hessians), not all of them. He tried a none-too-subtle jab in the ribs by referring to Howe's "tedious detention at Halifax."

For Germain, the lack of action was becoming seriously disturbing. It was not simply a matter of his wanting to smash the rebellion, although he undoubtedly did, it was also a fact that the expense of the war was already enormous, and he wanted it to be reduced as soon as possible. In June he had mentioned to Howe that the transports bringing his reinforcements should be dismissed from the service as soon as possible, in order to cut costs. It is possible that Germain began to regret not being more explicit in his wishes for the war to be ended with one gigantic effort. True, he had written a letter to a general declaring that he "should be for exerting the utmost force of this kingdom to finish this rebellion in one campaign," but the general in question was his closest friend, Sir John Irwin, not Howe. Not once to the commander-in-chief of the army in North America did Germain clearly express a desire for the war to be finished in one campaign, and that must have been playing on his mind as summer turned to fall and news of a dramatic victory stubbornly refused to arrive in London.

Howe was not entirely inactive while awaiting his reinforcements. Two ships, the *Rose* and the *Phoenix*, were sent up the Hudson River on an exploratory mission, both to test out American defenses and to look into the possibility of cutting off the supply line to the American army on Manhattan and Long Island. On July 12 they blazed their way upriver while the American defenses thundered back at them, with no evidence of any serious damage being done on either side, although a few shots from the British ships landed in the city and prompted a mild panic. The major American work guarding the Hudson, Fort Washington, was still incomplete. It would eventually be twinned with a second fort on the opposite bank, and a great chain would be strung across the river, along with sunken vessels intended to block it, but for now at least, the river was very much open to the British.

It would have been a sobering realization for the men of Washington's army who, just three days earlier, had been informed of their newly independent status. Amid their celebrations they had pulled down a statue of George III in the city and planned to melt it down to make musket balls. Now their hold on New York seemed tenuous at best. Matters only worsened as British reinforcements began to arrive. The first transports appeared on July 1 and a steady stream brought more men and supplies over the following days. Lord Howe himself, aboard his flagship, the *Eagle*, arrived on July 12, determined to make a serious effort to end the war before it went a step further.

What would today be called the "peace process" had never been given much of a chance in the build-up to war. An institutional failing to understand the scale of colonial grievances had led to the British authorities believing that nothing more than a stern glance ought to be enough to bring a rowdy minority back to heel. Steadily escalating violence had persuaded them that stern glances needed to be accompanied by stern actions, but still there was an unwillingness to offer any meaningful concessions, hence the disastrously restrictive terms available to the Howe brothers in their roles as peace commissioners.

Germain had remained watchful after Lord Howe had been appointed as peace commissioner. The careful courtship the admiral had engaged in, using his brother's letters from America as the pretext for contacting Germain, had been effective in persuading the American Secretary to re-evaluate his opinion of the elder Howe, but it had not removed all doubts. He remained suspicious of the idea of making the admiral the sole peace commissioner, feeling that his conciliatory nature might lead to him offering excessively lenient terms to the colonies. He wanted to tie Lord Howe to a fellow commissioner, someone with a more hawkish attitude, but the admiral was resistant to that. Finally, eager to have such a respected figure serving in the colonies (and aware that many other qualified generals and admirals were sitting on their hands when volunteers were asked for), Germain settled upon a compromise. Lord Howe would have to accept a joint peace commissioner, but it would be his own brother. Germain hoped that he had read the general correctly, and that he would act as a check on his older brother's leniency.

With the admiral came Henry Strachey, the designated secretary for the peace commission. Strachey recorded how the Howe brothers opened their instructions on July 12. Lord Howe, Strachey recorded, seemed more sanguine than his younger brother about their chances of brokering a peaceful solution to the situation. He was keen to meet with Washington, but William doubted that the general would even do this, reckoning that he would insist they address themselves to Congress, which would run the risk of inadvertently legitimizing the body. Their instructions included a proclamation to be delivered to the colonists. After reading it over, William declared he did not think it would have any effect, as the colonists had already declared their independence, but he was at least satisfied that it would not cause any embarrassment. The brothers dined together the following evening and resolved to at least try for a meeting with Washington. It was always likely to be a forlorn hope. Germain had ensured that the terms the Howe brothers could offer were almost certain to be rejected; the rebels effectively had to surrender before Great Britain would deign to listen to their grievances. Events at Boston had shown that the Americans were more than capable of resisting military force and there was little chance of them now giving up their struggle. Washington was unimpressed with the scope of the peace commission, commenting dryly, "Lord Howe is arrived. He and the General, his brother, are appointed commissioners to dispense pardons to repenting sinners."

In contrast to the restrictions placed upon his role as a peace commissioner, Lord Howe was encouraged to throw himself whole-heartedly into the military side of his duties. Rebel ports were to be blockaded or raided, while privateers were to be hunted down and destroyed. Shutting down trade with the outside world was intended to force the colonists to rethink—but there was also the obvious risk that it would force them ever further from their mother country.

———

On July 31, Henry Clinton arrived at New York with the force of a naval broadside. Seething over his failure at Charleston and in a state of agonized suspense over the reception his secretary would receive in London, he was also burning with indignation over the part Howe had played, in Clinton's mind at least, in the debacle. Had Clinton been in a calmer frame of mind he would quickly have recognized the fact that the commander-in-chief was in no hurry to open the campaign and was, in fact, now waiting for all of his reinforcements to arrive. Clinton's absence had not delayed the campaign by so much as a single day and he could have quietly taken up his position as second-in-command without worry.

Instead, he felt compelled to start pressing his advice on Howe, as though it would somehow prove that any subsequent delays were not attributable to him. In his retrospective account of the war, he acknowledged that this may have created friction: "My zeal," he admitted, "may perhaps on these occasions have carried me so far as to be at times thought troublesome..." At the time he did not seem to have any such awareness, or perhaps he was insensible to it while focused entirely on his own worries. He had already suggested a means of proceeding at New York, having dropped in there to gather intelligence on his way to North Carolina. Now he had more ideas to offer, and they were more ambitious in scale. By landing troops at Spuyten Duyvil, he reckoned the British could seize control of King's Bridge and trap the rebel army on Manhattan and Long Island. In his account of the war he made pointed reference to the fact that Howe had "nearly 10,000 troops in high health and spirits," suggesting that it was about time he made use of them.

However, Howe was committed by now to awaiting all of his reinforcements. The delay meant that Washington's army was given more time to prepare its defenses, but it also meant that a potentially bigger prize was on offer when Howe attacked: the more reinforcements the rebels brought into the area, the more could be bagged if operations went well. On August 6 Howe informed Germain that he had enough men to open the campaign, but that he was now "detained by the Want of Camp Equipage, particularly Kettles and Cantines, so essential in the Field, and without which too much is to be apprehended on the score of Health, at a Time when Sickness among the British Troops was never more to be dreaded."

Howe had a point. Around 8,000 of Washington's army were out of commission due to camp sicknesses, and Howe was aware, after his experience at Havana in the previous war, of the toll disease could take on an army, but this still smacked a little of looking for yet another excuse for inactivity. Certainly when German received the letter, on September 28, his reply had more than a touch of sarcasm to it, saying that he was "too well convinced of your zeal and alertness to suppose that there will be any unnecessary delay in your operations." When Germain wrote this last letter (and it is easy to imagine him slumped in his chair in resignation), it had been six months since Howe had left Boston and a scarcely credible 15 months since the British army in America had last acted against the rebels. He was not to know that while Howe's letter had been making its slow progress across the Atlantic, the man who had written it had finally made his move. Howe had not exactly done this quickly, that simply was not in his DNA, but he had received his final reinforcements (as well as the camp equipage) by August 15, on which date he informed Germain that "no Time will be lost in proceeding upon the Operations of the Campaign."

Probably oblivious to the irony of this comment, Howe prepared to open the campaign.

FIVE

The Pass

"I hasten to the action at Bedford, on Long-Island, the
27th of August, 1776..."

Howe's narrative, April 22, 1779

*L*ISTENING TO *HOWE'S SPEECH*, *Germain may well have
allowed himself a rueful smile. Had Howe hastened to the action on
Long Island it would have taken place long before August 27. Still, after
paddling about in the shallows, Howe was venturing into deep water for
the first time; the first serious questions about his command were about to
be addressed. The Battle of Long Island had once seemed to be everything
Germain had hoped for. In his unbridled joy at news of the encounter he had
been rash enough to describe it as "the first military operation with which
no fault could be found." He would later have cause to revise that opinion,
and Howe would have to deal with the reasons why if his speech was to
retain credibility. He did not waste any more time getting to the heart of
the matter. "A paragraph in my public letter of the 3rd of September," he
continued, "has been quoted against me as a violent charge."*

*It was indeed a violent charge. Many believed that Howe had failed
to make his victory on Long Island decisive, that he had allowed the
rebel army to slip through his fingers when it was at his mercy. Reasons
offered for this perceived failure were plentiful and varied, ranging from
incompetence and laziness to outright treason. Criticism of Howe's
conduct after the battle was particularly strong because many well-
informed observers recognized that such a perfect opportunity might
not come again. Almost three years later, as the war with the colonists
dragged on, no similar opportunity had yet presented itself.*

The battlefield on Long Island had been waiting for 17,000 years, since the great ice sheet that once sat on the land a thousand feet thick had started to retreat. As well as putting Howe's unhurried progress into some sort of perspective, the slowly receding ice left behind a terminal moraine, which just happened to run along much of the length of Long Island. For thousands of years the area had been a habitat for mastodons, a hunting ground for indigenous people, and the site of spectacular lakes until the trapped waters behind the moraine eventually escaped into the Atlantic. At its tallest point, the moraine was around 400 feet (120 meters) high and as water, animals, and humans moved over it, pathways became defined. By 1776 the ridge was known as the Gowanus Heights and the steep slopes and heavy vegetation made the ridge impassable to large bodies of soldiers except through a number of passes. It was a natural defensive line, as formidable as anything men could have built, and by the time Howe started to move his army it was in the hands of the Americans.

Having received his reinforcements, his camp equipment, and his brother's ships, Howe had faced delays from other causes. The Hessians, under the command of Lieutenant General Philip Leopold von Heister, had arrived at the same time as the thousand-strong contingent of Guards, but although the British troops declared themselves ready for action immediately, von Heister insisted his men needed time to recuperate after their voyage. To be fair to the Germans, they had endured an unpleasant journey just to get to Britain in the first place, before being shipped out along with the Guards, but Howe was unimpressed. It was a bad start to his relationship with von Heister, and things were not to improve. Exasperated, Howe decided to move without the Hessians and prepared his army to once more take to the water. This time, thankfully, the voyage would be short. It was just a quick hop from Staten Island to the designated landing points on Long Island.

Howe had reached out to his opposite number, Washington, in a heartfelt letter on August 1, in which he had expressed "the deepest

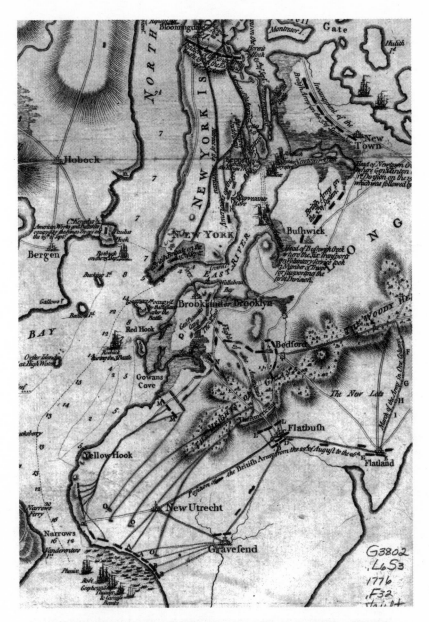

'A Plan of New York Island with part of Long Island, Staten Island & East New Jersey.' Details of the Battle of Long Island, including Howe's lengthy flanking march, are shown. Faden, W. (1776). London. (Geography and Map Division, Library of Congress.)

Concern that the unhappy State of the Colonies, so different from what I had the Honor of experiencing in the Course of the last War, deprives me of the Pleasure I should otherwise have had in a more personal communication." As veterans of the French and Indian War, it is easy to imagine Howe and Washington chewing the fat over a bottle of Madeira had circumstances been different. Instead, as Howe failed to address the general by his official title, the letter was returned unopened.

The date for moving to Long Island was set as August 22, with Clinton having the honor of leading the first troops ashore, but proceedings had to wait while a spectacular storm ripped through the area on the preceding night. Eyewitness accounts of a circulating mass of dense cloud suggest this was a terrifying spectacle, and several of Washington's soldiers were killed by lightning strikes. Superstitious types could have read their choice of message into the tempest.

The next day's landings were unopposed. Denyse's Ferry saw the first contingent arrive—4,000 men coming ashore in flat-bottomed boats. Gravesend Bay was soon welcoming another 5,000. When the boats had finished their work there were 15,000 troops on Long Island, along with 40 cannon. A corps of Hessians under Colonel Carl von Donop accompanied the British troops, but the bulk of the German contingent remained on Staten Island with von Heister. Those rebel troops who witnessed the spectacle fired a few defiant shots before retiring, burning buildings and crops as they went so that plumes of smoke climbed into the air as the redcoats advanced. The landing might have been opposed by the rebels, but the number of warships at the Howes' disposal would have made that a costly affair. Instead, the Americans put their faith in the defenses they had built over the spring and summer months.

Howe had recognized the importance of moving quickly after landing and had ordered that the troops were to carry nothing but their muskets, 60 rounds of ammunition per man, a blanket and three days' worth of rations—1lb (450g) of bread and 13.5oz (380g) of cooked pork per man per day. Canteens were to be filled with grog (rum mixed with water) and officers were to ensure their men made this last as long as possible.

The American army was divided into five divisions, under the command of Major Generals Israel Putnam, William Heath, Joseph Spencer, John Sullivan, and Nathanael Greene. Eight regiments were posted on Long Island on the day of the British landings, with the bulk of the army dotted around Manhattan. Carefully watching the British moves, and with intelligence suggesting that Howe's force could number up to 35,000 men (it was actually around 28,000), Washington fed just 1,800 reinforcements into the Brooklyn lines, unsure as yet whether this was to be the main British effort. American strength on the island stood at around 5,400, but Washington was also unsure of exactly how many troops the British had landed. Reports suggested it might have been as few as 9,000.

The original commander on Long Island, Nathanael Greene, had been taken ill and was replaced by John Sullivan just two days before the British landed. It was Sullivan who had recognized the need to occupy the Gowanus Heights, putting between 500 and 1,000 men each at the Narrows Road (also known as Gowan's Road), Flatbush Pass, and Bedford Pass. As Howe had suggested when considering his options after reaching Staten Island, the ridge of high ground was too obvious a position for the Americans to fail to occupy it, and they had done so just in time. There was a flaw to their disposition, however, and it was to prove a fatal one. Sullivan had done well to spot the need to occupy the Gowanus Heights, and it was possible that the troops he had placed in the three defended passes could inflict serious casualties on the British, who would presumably be forced to mount a frontal assault.

But there were four passes through the Gowanus Heights.

Washington expected the hammer to fall at any moment. "I consider that the city of New York will in all human probability very soon be the scene of a bloody conflict," he wrote to the New York Convention on August 17, and after landing on Long

Island, Howe shared his sentiments. There seemed to be no alternative to launching a full-scale assault on the rebel positions along the Gowanus Heights, and that carried the threat of repeating the bloodshed seen on Breed's Hill more than a year previously. However, a new option was soon to be presented to the commander-in-chief.

Clinton had spent part of his childhood on Long Island, while his father had been governor of New York in the 1740s. How well he remembered the area 30 years later is debatable, but whatever knowledge he still possessed convinced him that he had special insight to offer. British forces had taken a firm grip on the land below the Gowanus Heights. After landing, Charles, Earl Cornwallis had pushed forward to the Flatbush Pass but, upon finding it manned, he had withdrawn to the village of Flatbush. Three days after the main landings, the Hessian commander, von Heister, had stirred himself and come over to Long Island with two of his three brigades, the third remaining to defend Staten Island in case of a surprise rebel attack. While the build-up continued, Clinton undertook a reconnaissance of the area, which uncovered the weakness in the rebel position—the unguarded fourth pass through the Gowanus Heights.

The Jamaica Pass cut through the ridge roughly 2½ miles (4 kilometers) from Bedford Pass, which marked the left flank of the rebel position. It did not take a genius to see the opportunities offered by such a route into the enemy's rear and Clinton was no fool. "The position which the rebels occupy in our front may be turned," he realized, "by a gorge about six miles from us ... That, once possessed, gives us the island; and in a mile or two further we shall be on the communications with their works at Brooklyn."

The first Howe heard of the idea was when one of his subordinates, Sir William Erskine, handed him a message from Clinton. Erskine had been part of the scouting party with Clinton and would have been able to offer his own first-hand advice to Howe. The fact that Clinton chose him to act as a go-between was indicative of the strain in his relationship with Howe. Clinton's sensitivity since returning from the southern expedition, along with his constant advice and attempts to hurry Howe along, had become grating to the commander-in-chief. Still, here was solid intelligence that could not be ignored. The rebels had made the sort of mistake that might be expected of amateur soldiers and a path to a simple victory had opened up. Howe had ignored Clinton's advice before, when it might have offered a bloodless solution to the rebel occupation of Breed's Hill and Bunker Hill. The proposed move to Spuyten Duyvil, promising to quickly and painlessly bottle up the rebel army, had also been discounted. Clinton no doubt felt anxious while awaiting news of how his latest counsel would be received, but he must also have felt hopeful.

Howe's response was shocking. Other officers present had apparently poured scorn on the idea, dismissing it as "German jargon," a derogatory reference to the European theatre of the Seven Years War, where maneuver had been more important than in North America. Erskine also reported that Howe had made a clumsy joke, suggesting that as the rebels had no idea what a flank was, turning it would have no effect on them.

Howe had obviously had enough of his subordinate's advice, but it was part of the role of a second-in-command to offer alternatives. The cliquish response was certainly unbecoming of a commander-in-chief, but there were deeper forces at play. As usual, Clinton had been less than tactful in his approach. Had he simply informed Howe of an unguarded pass through the Gowanus Heights, then the news might have been more welcome. Howe would undoubtedly have been able to see the opportunity it offered. Instead, Clinton could not resist going further, offering a plan that was so detailed as to be very close to insulting: "The corps which attempts to turn this flank," he had continued, "must be in very great force, for reasons too obvious to require detailing. The attack should begin on the enemy's right by signal; and a share taken in it even by the fleet, which (as the tide will then suit) may get under way and make every demonstration of forcing by the enemy's batteries in the East River, without, however, committing themselves." It is easy to imagine Howe's hackles rising at the mere tone of Clinton's letter, which even presumed to tell his brother how to operate his ships as part of the attack, but Clinton was far from done, spelling out the need for diversionary actions along the line of the Gowanus Heights and finishing up by adding: "I beg leave also to propose that this corps may begin to move at nightfall, so that everything may be at its ground by daybreak; and that light infantry and chasseurs may cover its left flank in such strength as to effectually prevent the enemy's patrols from forcing them and thereby making a discovery of our intentions."

Clinton's plan was sound and sensible, but it left no room for Howe to claim any of the credit if it succeeded. Howe's response was therefore driven as much by the peeved realization that Clinton was stealing everyone else's thunder as by genuine contempt. There was nothing contemptuous in the idea itself, which was proved the next day when Howe quietly instructed Clinton to enact his plan. The commander-in-chief may have been sensitive, but he was not going to jeopardize his campaign just to teach Clinton a lesson in tact.

The situation for the rebels was dire. On August 8, Washington had reported that he had just 10,514 men present and fit for duty out of a total of over 17,000. He desperately called for reinforcements, but even double his numbers would have made little difference. "Our posts are too much divided," he had informed Congress, "having waters between many of them, and some distant from others Fifteen miles." Nothing in the layout of the region had changed since Charles Lee had reported, back in March, on the difficulties of holding the city, but the presence of Howe's army was focusing minds. Four days after Washington's bleak assessment of his situation, reinforcements had arrived in the shape of a battalion of Marylanders and two battalions of Pennsylvania riflemen. Militia units were also coming in, but were contracted to stay for just a few weeks. Still, Washington was in a better frame of mind by the time the British landed on Long Island, and a small act of defiance had been made by the launching of fire ships against the *Phoenix* and *Rose* on August 16. The attack did not damage the ships, but did persuade them to drop down the Hudson once more to rejoin the main fleet. Fire was very much the topic of conversation. A rumor had started to circulate that authority had been given for the city of New York to be put to the torch if the Americans should be forced to abandon it. Washington strenuously denied issuing any such order and pointed out that many patriot civilians remained in the city, making such an act self-defeating.

Having carefully fed reinforcements over to Long Island in response to the landings, Washington remained convinced that the British plan was more complex than it appeared. "My opinion of the matter is, that they mean to attack our works on the Island and this city at the same time," he wrote from New York, on August 24, "and that the troops at Flatbush are waiting in those plains till the wind and tide (which have not yet served together) will favor the movement of the shipping to this place." At the same time, he had to consider the possibility that the only British assault would come on Long Island. "This also being very probable," he admitted, "I have thrown what force I can over, without leaving myself too much exposed here." He just did not have enough men to be secure everywhere.

The following day, Washington changed the focus of the rebel defense of Long Island. Israel Putnam replaced Sullivan as commander on the island, and the carefully thought-out strategy of offering a defense in depth was abandoned. Instead of the Gowanus Heights being merely an important layer of the defense of the island, it became the dominant element. The intention was no longer to inflict the maximum number of casualties on the British before falling back to the next line of works, across the neck of the Brooklyn peninsula—it was now to stop the British in their tracks. To facilitate this, Washington ordered that Putnam place his best men in the positions along the Gowanus Heights, leaving the militia to man the Brooklyn lines. Washington's instructions were explicit, insisting that Putnam's "… best men should at all hazards prevent the enemy's passing the wood, and approaching your works."

It simply was not realistic to expect the defenders of the passes through the Gowanus Heights to resist the British and Hessian troops that were preparing to storm them. Approximately 2,800 rebels were divided between the three positions, while Howe could call on more than 20,000 men. Nor were the Americans unaware of the Jamaica Pass, but they seemed to think that either the British would fail to discover it, or that it was too far away to be important. Colonel Samuel Miles, with the Pennsylvania State Rifle Regiment (also known as the First Regiment of Riflemen and comprising two battalions), was given the difficult duty of patrolling the left flank of the American position. This included responsibility for keeping an eye on the Jamaica Road, which was 2½ miles (4 kilometers) from the left-most position on the Gowanus Heights, at the Bedford Pass. It was a lot of ground for one regiment to cover. Additionally, a patrol of five horsemen was ordered to watch the area and report if the British approached the pass. It was inviting disaster; if Washington genuinely hoped that the Gowanus Heights could be made impenetrable, then leaving open a route for the British to bypass them completely was a spectacular gamble.

By August 26, the American general was finally convinced that Howe was not playing any sort of elaborate game. The steady build-up on Long Island was not a bluff or a diversion—this was where the "grand push," as Washington termed it, would start. With Washington freed from his concerns about the need to defend multiple areas at the same time, the Americans could now send more men into their Long Island works. Somewhere between 7,000 and 9,000 men were present by the evening of August 26 (the paper strength of the regiments in place was around 9,500, but Washington himself admitted that he could not get accurate returns).

Washington remained on Long Island until night fell on August 26, convinced that the British must move soon.

Clinton's plan had been adopted almost to the letter. Substantial diversions were mounted at two of the defended passes. Major

General James Grant was instructed to press the defenders at the Narrows Road, on the extreme left (from the British perspective) of the Gowanus Heights. His force was comprised of 3,000 redcoats and 2,000 marines. Grant's orders were to feign a serious assault, starting at 2 a.m. on August 27. As well as attracting attention, it was possible he might draw reserves from the rebel lines at Brooklyn, but he was not to press too firmly and risk unnecessary casualties in what was, after all, only a diversion. The second diversion was to be staged by the Hessians under von Heister, who were to press the Americans in the Flatbush Pass.

The real work, however, was to be undertaken by a 10,000-strong flanking column, with orders to set out at sunset on August 26. The vanguard would be comprised of the elite light infantry battalions, while the only mounted troops available to Howe, the 17th Light Dragoons, patrolled on the fringes of the column to keep prying eyes at a safe distance. Any civilians encountered were to be temporarily imprisoned while the march passed by; any sounding of the alarm would obviously undermine the entire operation. As well as the lights, the grenadier battalions also formed part of the column, along with the Guards and the 33rd Regiment, itself reckoned to be one of the finest in the army. In short, Howe had placed almost all of his best units in the flanking column. A circuitous route would hopefully carry the troops safely around the fringes of the American positions to the Jamaica Pass, but it would be a lengthy, stressful, and tiring march in the dark. One officer reported that it "… dragged on at the most tedious pace from sunset till 3 o'clock in the morning, halting every minute just long enough to drop asleep and to be disturbed again in order to proceed twenty yards in the same manner. The night was colder too than I remember to have felt it, so that by daybreak my stock of patience had begun to run very low."

The intention was to reach the village of Bedford, firmly in the American rear, by 9 a.m., when two cannon shots would signal that the march had been completed. The two diversionary actions were then to be pressed more forcefully as the flanking column moved up behind the rebel positions. It promised to be nothing short of a total rout, if things went well.

Things did go well for the British. In fact, they went better than could have been hoped. Around 2 a.m. the column reached Howard's Inn, near the Jamaica Pass. Clinton, commanding the vanguard, ordered a patrol of light dragoons forward to check that the pass was still unguarded. On their way to the pass, the patrol ran into and captured the five horsemen who represented the only chance the Americans had of discovering the flanking march. Clinton questioned the men and then forced the owner of Howard's Inn and his son to act as guides, approaching the Jamaica Pass carefully and gratefully taking possession of it unopposed. To all intents and purposes, the battle was already over.

On the westernmost point of the Gowanus Heights, Grant put his diversion into operation on schedule. There had been a brief skirmish two hours previously, when British soldiers, bored and hungry, had wandered into a watermelon patch under the noses of American pickets, but nothing more than a few random shots had been fired and peace had quickly returned. Now, as the clock ticked down to his appointed start time of 2 a.m., Grant prepared to send 300 men along the road to initiate the diversion. The defenders here had originally been Continental infantrymen, but after the brief skirmish at the watermelon patch they had been replaced, exhausted after four days on duty. Militia battalions from New York and Pennsylvania took their place, which weakened the position considerably. Washington would have been unhappy to learn that his order to place the best men in the advanced positions and leave the militia to man the interior lines had been ignored on this occasion.

Grant's advanced party sent the militia scurrying. A few shots were fired and word was sent to the main lines at Brooklyn that the British were attacking. The American response was immediate. First to leave the main lines to reinforce the Narrows Road was Colonel Samuel John Atlee. Half of his regiment of Pennsylvanians was already part of the defensive corps that was falling back before the British and he now hurried with the remainder of his men to join them. Putnam also called Brigadier General William Alexander (who claimed the title of Lord Stirling), ordering him to take the nearest regiments down the road toward the location of the British attack. Stirling set off as quickly as possible with the men of the Maryland and Delaware regiments, the best American soldiers on Long Island at the time and possibly the best in the entire Continental Army. Two further regiments soon followed Stirling, bringing the total reinforcement to around 1,600 men. By dispatching his best troops, Putnam was belatedly adhering to Washington's orders, but also limiting his options if the British should launch a simultaneous attack elsewhere.

Had Grant been on a mission to penetrate the rebel lines he might have marched along the Narrows Road before the reinforcements could arrive. The American defenders present were in a state of confusion and unable to mount an effective resistance. With the arrival of Stirling, however, the Americans at least had an opportunity to reorganize. "I desired Colonel Atlee to place his regiment on the left of the road," Stirling later reported to Washington, "and to wait their [the British] coming up, while I went to form the two regiments I had brought with me, along a ridge from the road up to a piece of wood on the top of the hill; this was done instantly on very advantageous ground."

The ground may well have been advantageous, but this was not the sort of position Washington had envisioned defending. Rather than being ensconced behind formidable defensive works, his troops were standing in the open and British musketry and cannon fire began to take their toll. But the anticipated assault did not come. "One of their brigades formed in two lines opposite our right," Stirling recalled, "and the others extended in one line to the top of the hills in the front of our left; in this position we stood cannonading each other till near eleven o'clock."

This was battle in "true English taste," as one Marylander exulted, the first time Continental had stood against redcoat in the open field. Grant, perhaps frustrated at not being able to press his advantage due to orders, quickly ran through his supply of artillery ammunition and had to send for more, while the rebels replied via a two-gun battery of their own. Stoically holding their ground, the Americans had no way of knowing at this point that British and Hessian soldiers were already advancing toward them from behind.

Howe, with the main body of the flanking column, caught up with Clinton's vanguard shortly after the Jamaica Pass had been secured. After a brief stop for refreshments, the march toward Bedford continued. The battalion of Americans under Colonel Samuel Miles discovered the vast column only as it completed its march through the pass, having initially been drawn toward the sound of firing at the opposite end of the American defenses. Miles later claimed to have warned General Sullivan of the likelihood of the British advancing through the Jamaica Pass, but he had been taken unawares when they finally moved. The last hope of an early warning had gone, as Miles was unable to do anything with his small body of men and did not possess any horses to send word back to Brooklyn. A warning was sent, but it traveled by foot and eventually arrived at the Brooklyn lines just moments before the British themselves.

Clinton would later claim that Howe had been in a dour mood throughout the march and that he did not appear to realize when they had reached Bedford. Being unfamiliar with the territory, it would not be surprising if Howe did not recognize the village, and he was a notorious late riser, so staying awake the entire night would undoubtedly have dampened his spirits. The first British troops reached Bedford around 8:30 a.m. and the signal cannons were fired, on schedule, at 9 a.m. Although the march had been tiring, it had been a complete success. With the benefit of a little luck, the British were now behind the positions on the Gowanus Heights without the rebels (outside of the captured patrol and Miles' helpless battalion) having any idea they were there.

At the Flatbush Pass, the Hessians under von Heister had proved better able to restrain themselves than Grant. Although also ordered to mount a diversionary attack, they had failed even to push in the American pickets when General Sullivan arrived to inspect the position shortly before 9 a.m. Aware at the time that Stirling was heavily engaged on the extreme right of the line, Sullivan was understandably eager to know if it was to be the only British assault of the day. After arriving, he found the Hessians in lethargic mood and might have dared to hope that Grant's attack was to be the only one. If that was indeed the case, then further reinforcements could be sent and the American plan might just be working perfectly. Had such a hope formed in his head, it would shortly have been interrupted by two cannon shots. Rather than the regular booming to be heard from the direction of the Narrows Road, however, these two shots came from behind, from the direction of Bedford.

Soon after this, firing broke out as British units, notably the light infantry battalions and light dragoons, were unleashed on the rear of the American line. Miles' battalion was discovered trying to get back to Brooklyn and, after a brief fight, was forced to surrender. As well as these worrying developments in the rear, the Hessians suddenly seemed more interested in pressing forward. It did not take Sullivan long to realize what was happening. The Flatbush Pass was now fatally comprised and, with it, the entire line along the heights. If the British were not to cut off the entire advanced defensive works, with 3,000–4,000 men, then the retreat needed to be general and it needed to be swift. Sullivan claimed to send word to Stirling on the right flank that he was retreating, and then found his hands full as Hessians advanced in front and British closed in from behind. The defensive works that might have taken a toll on the ponderously advancing Hessians were largely abandoned by the time the German troops, with flags waving and drums sounding, reached them. By then, the Americans had turned to face the British, attempting to fight their way through and reach the safety of the Brooklyn lines. Some managed to get through but many more were captured, killed, or driven back to their defensive works, where the Hessians were now waiting. The German troops had a fearsome reputation and some reports suggested that they lived up to it here. There were even suggestions that British officers had done their best to arouse the Hessians by informing them that the rebels had declared they would show them no mercy if captured. "The Hessians and our brave Highlanders gave no quarter," one officer gloated, "and it was a fine sight to see with what alacrity they dispatched the Rebels with their bayonets after we had surrounded them so that they could not resist." Few officers would have taken pleasure at such a pitiful and barbaric scene, but it played out at numerous points during the chaos of battle. American riflemen, feared because of their legendary accuracy but hamstrung by the inordinate amount of time it took them to load their weapons, were to be found skewered to trees by bayonets, while others trusted to their speed to escape the marauding British and Hessian troops. "In one thing only," noted Lord Howe's personal secretary, Ambrose Serle, "they [the redcoats] failed—they could not run so fast as their Foes, many of whom indeed [were] ready to run over each other."

The noise of the battle had alerted the city of New York that the British had finally opened their campaign. Washington had quickly crossed to Long Island, as well as ordering several regiments to follow him over as reinforcements. In one of the units was a young private called Joseph Plumb Martin, who would go on to write (more than 50 years later) one of the most colorful memoirs of the war. Ordered with his regiment to cross to Long Island, he had returned to his quarters to grab his equipment, taking the opportunity to climb to the top of the house, which offered a view over to Long Island. "I distinctly saw the smoke of the field artillery," he claimed, "but the distance and the unfavourableness of the wind prevented my hearing their report, at least but faintly." It was a remote and muted battle, then, to which Martin found himself marching, but it quickly became more real after reaching Long Island, when he encountered the stream of wounded men returning from the front, "some with broken arms, some with broken legs, some with broken heads. The sight of this a little daunted me…"

Men were streaming back from the Bedford and Flatbush passes, but as yet the bulk of the men along the Narrows Road, under Stirling, were standing their ground. They should not have been. Sullivan's order to retreat (assuming one had been sent) had not reached Stirling, and two hours after the British flanking column had fired its signal cannons, the men under Stirling were still facing up to the overwhelming numbers of Grant's force. The best men in the rebel army were about to be cut off from any possibility of retreat as redcoats and Hessians closed in from behind. Stirling recognized the danger at the last possible moment, as redcoats from the 71st Regiment and a battalion of grenadiers closed in, commanded by Cornwallis. The road back to Brooklyn was already blocked by the British, but there was a chance of escape, although it was a hair-raising one at best, across the marshland that anchored the right flank of the Brooklyn defenses. Even so, something would need to be done to fend off the British while the men did their best to escape. With Grant now pushing more forcefully, Stirling took the decision to take half of the Maryland Regiment and hold off Cornwallis, while the rest of the men under his command took their chances in the marshland. The order to retreat was given, but did not reach the Pennsylvanians of Colonel Atlee, who stood their ground and were cut off. A handful of Atlee's men managed to escape, and a party of more than 20 hid and made it back to the lines at Brooklyn the following morning, but the rest were captured.

With around 260 men, Stirling marched up the Gowanus Road to confront Cornwallis. The mismatched opponents met at a stone house. Redcoats had already taken possession of the house by the time the rebels arrived, pouring fire into the American lines as they prepared to attack. It was a hopeless task, but the Marylanders earned their place in American military lore with their bravery. Only nine escaped back to the rebel lines, the remainder either killed or captured by British and Hessian troops, but the multiple charges they launched against Cornwallis had held the British up long enough for the bulk of Stirling's command to escape. Stirling himself, realizing the game was up, sought out a Hessian officer to surrender to.

For the men wading, stumbling, and sometimes swimming through the marshland at the Gowanus Creek, it must have seemed very much like a defeat. Upon its arrival on Long Island, Martin's unit had been pushed out toward the creek in order to help cover the retreat. He recorded how British field pieces sprayed the retreating rebels with canister shot and grapeshot, until the Americans managed to drag a 12-pounder through the mud and force the British gunners to withdraw. Even so, the marshes were dangerous enough without the threat of enemy action and several men drowned in the desperate escape. Those who reached safety were badly shaken. "There was in this action a regiment of Maryland troops," Martin noted, "all young gentlemen. When they came out of the water and mud to us, looking like water rats, it was a truly pitiful sight. Many of them were killed in the pond, and more were drowned. Some of us went into the water after the fall of the tide, and took out a number of corpses and a great many arms that were sunk in the pond and creek."

From all points along the Gowanus Heights, rebel troops were now fleeing for the Brooklyn lines, pursued closely in many instances by British and Hessian units. Those who won the footrace were able to scramble through the outer defenses and into the main works. Some of those who were cut off managed to lie low until nightfall and creep into the lines under cover of darkness, but many, inevitably, were captured. The critical moment of the battle was now at hand. Howe's orders had called for nothing more than had already been achieved. The men in his flanking column had express orders not to approach the string of five fortifications across the neck of the Brooklyn Peninsula. In the excitement of battle, and with a broken enemy fleeing before them, some men could not resist doing just that.

At Fort Greene, Colonel Moses Little reported British infantry and cavalry approaching to within musket range before being driven off, "being met with a smart fire from our breast works." Lieutenant Colonel Daniel Brodhead, who was among those who escaped from Miles' regiment, had only just got into the lines near Fort Putnam when the British pursuing him approached, clearly intent on storming the position. "I had no sooner got into the Lines," he later wrote to an unknown correspondent, "than the Enemy advanced up to them and kept up a brisk fire on us, but only one man killed in the Lines." The redcoats in question, the 33rd Regiment and a battalion of grenadiers, were watched indulgently by Clinton, who knew full well that they were exceeding their orders. "I must confess that (notwithstanding I knew the Commander in Chief's wishes) I had permitted this move," he wrote in his account of the battle, "and I had at the moment but little inclination to check the ardor of our troops when I saw the enemy flying in such a panic before them." Clinton, believing that the momentum of the troops and the disorganization of the rebels promised to bring further success, hoped his commanding officer would see things the same way. "I was also not without hopes," he explained, "that His Excellency, who was on a neighboring hill and, of course, saw their [the rebels'] confusion, might be tempted to order us to march directly forward down the road to the ferry, by which, if we succeeded, everything on the island must have been ours."

Howe did not see things the same way. Unwilling for his orders to be exceeded, he dispatched a rider to halt the attack. With the men in full cry the order had to be repeated several times before they begrudgingly turned away from their quarry. Brodhead believed that it was defensive fire from the Americans that drove the British away: "as soon as we returned the fire with our rifles and musquetry, they retreated," he claimed, "and if we had been provided with a field piece or two, of which we had a sufficient number elsewhere, we might have killed the greater part of their advance party."

In fact it was the orders of Howe that put a stop to the assault. Displaying a shocking lack of prudence, he then wrote candidly about the incident in his official report to Germain. It was to prove the basis for the "violent charge" he would later refer to during his speech to the House of Commons: "... the grenadiers and 33rd regiment being in the front of the column," he reported to Germain, "soon approached within musket-shot of the enemy's lines at Brooklyn, from whence these battalions, without regarding the fire of cannon and small arms upon them, pursued numbers of the rebels that were retiring from the Heights so close to their principal redoubt, and with such eagerness to attack it by storm, that it required repeated orders to prevail upon them to desist from the attempt." It was risky to admit to stopping an army in pursuit of a broken enemy, but Howe obviously did not see the dangerous territory he had wandered into. He then made it even more perilous by adding, "Had they been permitted to go on, it is my opinion they would have carried the redoubt..."

Howe's letter was nothing short of a hostage to fortune, something to be used against him if the war should go badly from that point. Perhaps he could not envisage a scenario in which he would fail to end the rebellion, having won such an easy victory in his first major action. His decision, however, ensured that the victory was only a partial one. The rebels had been outflanked and outclassed and were badly shaken, but the bulk of their force on Long Island was still intact. At the time, Howe explained that he believed the lines could be captured by conventional siege works "at a very cheap rate," and that he did not want to risk the loss of men that might follow a storming of the lines. Although the preservation of his own men was an important responsibility, the force of this argument would ultimately rest on the strength of the lines in question. Could they have been assaulted successfully or had there been a risk of the redcoats being repulsed with heavy losses?

Shockingly (though unknown to Howe on the day), having had months to perfect their positions, and having staked their entire strategy on exacting the maximum number of casualties if the British chose to attack, the lines at Brooklyn were not as strong as the works thrown up overnight on Breed's Hill more than a year before. In fact, as the battle opened on the morning of August 27, they had not even been finished.

———

The earliest mention of a string of fortifications at Brooklyn had come from Charles Lee, when he surveyed New York in early March. Describing Long Island as of greater importance even than the city of New York itself, he proposed "a camp, fortified by a chain of redoubts, mutually supporting each other…" This camp was to be manned by 4,000–5,000 men, with 8,000 in total for the defense of Long Island. This line appears, however, to have been originally planned to lie close to the East River. Work had just begun on the proposed defenses when Lee was called to the south, to oppose Clinton's expedition, but it would continue under a different overseer.

Captain Jeduthan Baldwin had arrived in New York in March, in fine spirits having recently received $116.75 for his service as an engineer in the Continental Army. Part of Baldwin's money was spent on a new horse and saddlebags for his journey from Boston to New York and by March 25 he was dining with Lord Stirling at King's Bridge. The following day he inspected the state of New York's defenses, both around the city and on Long Island (at the time, Fort Stirling was the major work on Long Island, built on the Brooklyn Heights and intended to defend against shipping moving along the East River). Showing as great an appetite for spending his newfound wealth as for his work, Baldwin proceeded to dart from location to location. On March 29, he started preparations for a barracks at Fort Stirling and also spent $16.50 on a cutlass. On April 2, he reported another visit to Long Island, in which he "Laid out & proposed several works there." The following day, as well as spending another $15 on a new coat and jacket, plans for two more works on Long Island were drawn up.

Baldwin's proposals went much further than Lee's. Red Hook, Governor's Island, the city—all were visited and plans laid out for defensive works. The line of redoubts at Brooklyn was now pushed further inland, to drape across the neck of the Brooklyn peninsula from Wallabout Bay to the Gowanus marshes. By the end of the month Baldwin's services were needed elsewhere and he was ordered to Canada, but his journal shows that extensive work had been under way on Long Island since early April, giving the Americans almost four months' grace before Howe launched his offensive.

Responsibility for the defenses now fell to Colonel Rufus Putnam, the brother of Israel. Promoted to chief engineer, he continued the work that had been started by Lee and Baldwin. Putnam claimed that work went on without pause ("... my whole time was taken up from daylight in the morning until night in the business"), yet the defenses were still not complete by August. The largest planned fortification on the island, between Fort Stirling and a small structure atop Cobble Hill, had not even been started. Its dimensions had been laid out on the ground and it was to be linked with Cobble Hill and Fort Stirling by entrenchments, but it was actually constructed by the British after they took control of the island.

Failure to complete all of the proposed works was no disgrace, and the frequent additions to plans meant that there were always likely to be some unfinished structures when the war finally awoke from its extended hibernation, but the Brooklyn lines were the heart of the rebel plan right up until the middle of August, when they were superseded by the Gowanus Heights. Surely these lines were complete? The Connecticut native Colonel Gold Selleck Silliman found otherwise when he was sent over to Long Island with his regiment shortly after the British landed. On August 24 he wrote to his wife, explaining that his regiment had been employed that day in completing breastworks in the Brooklyn lines.

After the battle had started, on the morning of August 27, further reinforcements were sent over. Among them was Brigadier General John Morin Scott, who took his place in the lines, awaiting an expected assault from the British. Of the lines he wrote: "They were unfinished in several places when I arrived there, and we were obliged hastily to finish them, and you may imagine with very little perfection, particularly across the main road, the most likely for the approach of the enemy's heavy artillery." Not only had the lines been unfinished on the day of the battle, Scott went on to claim that they were badly sited, with dominating high ground within 40 yards (37 meters) of them. He estimated that a man standing on this high ground would have been able to fire over the breastworks and under the belly of his horse.

Whatever the actual state of the lines, they could still have created an impression of strength, especially in the heat of battle, where decisions have to be made quickly and under intense stress. Many of the opinions voiced by British officers on their strength were written with the benefit of hindsight and, in many cases, an opportunity to inspect the works in detail. Years later, after reading Howe's narrative in its published form, Clinton commented that the lines were "an unfinished ditch without pickets or abbatis." Charles Stedman, a commissary with the British, believed that they could not have resisted an attack, particularly considering the fact that Howe's troops had not yet been heavily engaged in fighting, while the Americans were in disarray. The engineer John Montresor (also one of Howe's aides-de-camp on the day) testified at the Howe inquiry that the lines were complete and protected by strong abbatis, while a Hessian officer, who may have been drinking, saw a series of lines reaching back to the sea when there was in fact only one, and claimed they could only have been successfully stormed by an army of 50,000. Major General James Robertson, who claimed to have approached within 150 yards (137 meters) of the works during the battle, declared that the lines were not even fully manned, and that only 300 rebel soldiers were present as the British advanced upon them.

It is perhaps surprising that a non-military man presented the most balanced opinion on the lines. The Howes' secretary, Henry Strachey, wrote: "The works on Long Island were so numerous and strong, that had they been properly defended, the taking of them must have cost us very dear, both as to men and time." Strachey's reasonable assessment (the lines were neither insignificant nor impregnable) included the critical phrase "had they been properly defended." Perhaps even more shocking than the idea that the lines were not completed until the day of battle is the evidence that suggests they were thinly manned as well. Robertson's assertion that only 300 men were in the lines as the British closed in on them is the most extreme claim, but others echoed the sentiment. Clinton believed that only one section of the entrenchments between the five major works was manned, and that the fort targeted by the 33rd Regiment and grenadiers was the only one out of the five forts or redoubts to actually be occupied (which begs the question, why didn't the British soldiers target an empty section of the lines instead?). By the time he came to write his account of the war, he was convinced that this had become common knowledge, writing: "... it has since, indeed, been very well known that the rebels had not at that very moment above 800 men behind the great extent of line (which would have required at least 6,000 to defend the different works along it)."

Washington had indeed downgraded the importance of the Brooklyn lines at the last moment, insisting that the best men be placed along the Gowanus Heights, and Captain Stephen Olney recorded that the lines were "poorly manned with sick and invalids." Numbers, however, would not have been a problem—Washington had between 7,000 and 9,000 men on Long Island on the morning of the battle, and brought more over before the British arrived at Brooklyn. With something less than 3,000 men along the Gowanus Heights, there were thousands available to man the lines even after the reserve troops had been drawn off to the fighting on the Narrows Road. If only 800 men were manning the forts, redoubts, and entrenchments at Brooklyn, what on earth were the remainder of the corps on Long Island doing? Brigadier Scott, who reported on the hasty efforts to complete the lines after his arrival on Long Island on the morning of the battle, also noted that the three battalions he was with were positioned behind the breastworks that defended the road down to the Brooklyn ferry. Furthermore, since early June the Americans had been routinely manning their works. While Nathanael Greene had commanded on Long Island he had stipulated that 15 companies should be posted in Fort Box, Fort Greene, and Fort Putnam (five in each), with three more in each of the two unmanned redoubts.

Common sense would suggest that the Americans would not have left their lines unmanned, especially when a stubborn defense was the basis for their entire strategy. Even allowing for the fact that it had been hoped the British could be stopped dead along the Gowanus Heights, by the time men started to stream back from those positions it would have been clear that this gambit had failed. Failure under those circumstances to order regiments to take positions in the forts and behind the breastworks, however insubstantial they may have been, would have been incompetence on a grand scale.

However many opinions there were on the state of the American defenses, and whoever held them, only one opinion mattered—that of Howe himself. The carnage of Breed's Hill is often advanced as a reason for his recall of the assault on the lines at Brooklyn, but even without that cautionary experience there is reason enough to respect his decision. There was no way for Howe to be sure of the strength of the works, and he had no reason to believe they would be anything other than formidable, having twice witnessed what the Americans could do in a matter of hours at Boston. He also approached the lines close enough to get a feel for their construction—if he had not been close he would not have been able to issue the order to recall the 33rd Regiment and grenadiers in time.

Furthermore, the assault was unauthorized, and Howe was a stickler for obedience during battle. His plan had gone as far as he had intended it to; the rebels had been dislodged from a very advantageous position along the Gowanus Heights with little loss. There seemed no point in risking all that had been gained by an assault on a defensive work unless he could be absolutely sure of its strength. Clinton, free of the burden of command, instinctively felt that the risk was worthwhile. Howe instinctively felt that it was not. In fact, as rebel resistance crumbled and they were forced back behind their defensive works, cut off from Manhattan by the East River and with Royal Navy ships dominating the waterways, Howe could have been forgiven for thinking that the Americans had no means of escape. Regular siege works would soon force Washington to surrender the entire corps on Long Island, dealing a potentially crippling blow to the patriot cause.

So when Howe came to deal with the decision during his narrative, almost three years later, he should have been on firm ground. He had made a choice, as commander-in-chief, not to risk the lives of his men when the battle appeared to have been won. Instead of sticking to this safe, and frankly obvious, approach, he instead tackled the controversy in another way—by attempting to mislead the House on the layout of the American defenses: "I am at a loss to know," he said during his narrative, "from whence it has been supposed, that carrying the lines would have been followed by the defeat of the rebel army." Anybody who had seen one of the freely available maps of the battle (such maps were quickly reproduced and sold for the titillation of the general public, as was the case with any significant victory) would have had no doubt that taking the lines at Brooklyn would have resulted in the capture of all rebel troops on Long Island. But Howe was not done. He continued:

"The facts are these; the rebels had a body of men posted in front of the lines [presumably Howe was referring to the positions along the Gowanus Heights], to guard against an attack from Flat-Bush, and from the lower road upon their right. These troops were defeated with considerable loss. The remainder of the corps was posted behind the lines, the main army being then on York-Island [Manhattan]; so that admitting the works to have been forced on the day of action, the only advantage we should have gained would have been the destruction of a few more men, for the retreat of the greatest part would have been secured by the works constructed upon the heights of Brooklyn, opposite to New York…"

Although terribly muddled, Howe seemed to be claiming that even had the assault on the rebel lines been successful, the corps of the rebel army on Long Island would have been able to retreat under cover of further works behind the lines. Such works simply did not exist. Cobble Hill housed a mere four guns, while Fort Stirling had been built to protect the East River, not to withstand an assault from its landward side. Howe could theoretically have advanced this as supporting evidence for his decision on the spot, and it is possible he believed that there may have been more defensive works behind the Brooklyn lines (a major fort had, after all, been marked out for construction and Clinton had snipingly offered the suggestion that Howe may have received faulty intelligence that influenced his decision). But having examined the lines after the battle, Howe would have been clear that there were no substantial works behind them and that no organized retreat would have been possible.

Howe had clearly taken pains over this passage of his narrative, making it remarkable that it was still so unclear—unless that had been his intention. In its final form he concluded that not recalling the men would have been "criminal." The draft of his speech, however, reveals that he had originally intended to say, "I should have been deemed a madman had I encouraged the attack in question." He had also included the following: "But for a moment to admit none of these men [the Long Island corps] had escaped, the rebel army would only have been weakened by that small number in comparison with the whole, which I am confident would not have had the least effect towards a conclusion of the war." Howe wisely chose to omit this passage. The "small number" of rebels on Long Island comprised half of their army and included their commander-in-chief. Howe's critics in the House of Commons may have stirred in their seats as his speech reached this point. He had failed to deal convincingly with the first crisis point in his command and had left himself open to attack from numerous directions. If the narrative continued in this vein, he was in serious trouble.

At any rate, the recall of the unauthorized assault on the Brooklyn lines ought to have been nothing more than a footnote, an interesting "what if" for armchair generals to ponder. It might even have been lost entirely amid the back-slapping and relief over the collapse of the rebel war effort, because surely, penned in at the edge of Long Island, with 1 mile (1.6 kilometers) of water between them and the safety of Manhattan, there was no way Washington could extricate his army. Having suffered an embarrassing defeat in the field, and having been given a lesson in professional soldiering, the corps on Long Island could now await only the certainty of surrender as the British siege lines closed in on their hopeless position.

If that had happened, of course, Howe would not have been standing in the House of Commons three years later.

SIX

The Escape

"In this instance, from the certainty of being in possession
of the lines in a very few days, by breaking ground, to
have permitted the attack in question, would have been
inconsiderate, and even criminal."

Howe's narrative, April 22, 1779

*T*HE *HONOURABLE* *MEMBERS* *LISTENING* to *Howe might*
still have been trying to digest his confusing depiction of the
layout of the defenses, in some cases probably trying to reconcile it
with their own knowledge gleaned from maps or correspondence with
eyewitnesses, but Howe was determined to move on. However, as with
the Battle of Bunker Hill earlier in his speech, he was about to pass
over a major event. A lawyer might have looked on Howe's words with
a certain respect at this point. He talked of "the certainty of being in
possession of the lines in a very few days," and that is exactly how
events had played out. The British had indeed gained possession of the
lines, on the morning of August 30. But by then the rebel army was no
longer in them.

Washington brought more men over to Long Island on the
morning of August 28. Given the situation, this was a reckless
move and merely put more of his army at risk of capture. The new
arrivals brought his strength to around 9,500, still far inferior to
the army opposing them, but sufficient to make a determined stand
if the British would oblige by attacking. As the men waited in their
defensive works, the heavens opened. It would rain solidly for the

next two days. "You may judge of our situation," wrote Brigadier Scott, "subject to almost incessant rains, without baggage or tents and almost without victuals or drink, and in some part of the lines the men were standing up to their middles in water." And the British were not going to be obliging; during the night of August 28, they began to construct siege works, the "regular approaches" alluded to in Howe's letter to Germain.

In the early hours of August 29, Washington wrote to Congress, apparently content to hold his position, but as dawn broke the situation changed dramatically as the British siege works gradually became visible. The Americans understood perfectly what it meant—rather than risk a frontal assault, the British were going to approach using the scientific certainties of siege warfare. There was no means of stopping such an approach if carried out with determination and skill. Sallies from the defensive lines could disrupt the advance of the trenches, but the end result was inevitable. It was just a matter of time. On the morning of August 29, the British approaches were within 600 yards (550 meters) of the American lines; another day would see them move within striking range and the rebels' position would be hopeless, if it wasn't already. Washington called a council of war, which concluded, inevitably, that a retreat was the only possible salvation for the army. The reasons cited for the retreat were remarkable, especially as several of the circumstances listed had existed prior to the battle. Among these was the fact that the division of the army enforced by the defending of so many areas simultaneously was inherently dangerous, and the fact that the British might get ships into the East River and trap the entire corps on Long Island.

Especially interesting, given the debate that was about to erupt over the strength of the Brooklyn defenses, was the sixth reason forwarded in support of the need to retreat:

"Tho our Lines were fortified with some strong Redoubts, yet a great part of them were weak being only abbattied with Bush, and affording no strong cover, so that there was reason to apprehend they could be forced, which would have put our Troops in confusion, and having no retreat, they must have been cut to pieces, or made prisoners."

The exhaustion of the men and the demoralizing effect of the battle two days previously were also cited. No mention was made of the siege works that had prompted the council of war in the first place.

The decision to evacuate was sensible and even obvious. It was one thing, however, to recognize the need to withdraw. It was an entirely different matter to actually accomplish it. An evacuation of the island would be a desperately dangerous affair with the large British army encamped so close. Not all of Washington's officers approved of the decision. Brigadier Scott, for one, instantly opposed the plan, being unwilling to give the British ground without making them fight for it, but reason prevailed.

However, any suggestion that an evacuation was in progress would surely draw a rapid response. Washington therefore attempted to make the evacuation as quiet as possible and went to great lengths to disguise his intentions. A great number of boats would be needed to ferry the troops across the East River, but Washington issued the order to collect them under the pretext of ferrying more men over to Long Island. The gathering of any vessel that could hold a number of men has drawn comparisons to the British evacuation at Dunkirk, but although it was a stressful affair, the Americans were able to proceed without interference from their enemy. Far from keeping a sharp watch over the rebel lines, British observation was lax and nothing was suspected as Washington's men began to file off by battalion and march down to the Brooklyn ferry.

The Americans had little to be proud of up until this point, except for the spirited resistance along the Narrows Road on the morning of August 27, but now they managed to evacuate their lines, along with most of their artillery, from under Howe's nose. Disaster nearly struck when one regiment left the lines prematurely, but the men calmly returned to their posts when informed of their mistake and no panic broke out. Benjamin Tallmadge called it "one of the most anxious, busy nights that I ever recollect," and noted that it was the third consecutive night in which the men had enjoyed little or no sleep. Joseph Plumb Martin recalled: "We were strictly enjoined not to speak, or even cough, while on the march. All orders were given from officer to officer, and communicated to the men in whispers." The soldiers had no idea where they were going, and some imagined they were marching to outflank the British and launch an offensive.

Evacuating nearly 10,000 men, however, is a time-consuming affair, and as dawn broke on August 30, several regiments were still in the lines awaiting their turn to move. At precisely the right moment, a thick fog descended over Brooklyn, covering the retreat of the last men from the rebel army. Romance and folklore is always likely to take an interest in such an event, and the story of a black slave sent to warn the British by a sympathetic loyalist may be merely apocryphal. Whether he existed or not, the legend states that he ran into a party of Hessians, who could not understand what he was trying to tell them. More certain is the fact that a British patrol, led by Montresor, discovered an unmanned section of the lines, but nothing seems to have been done about the discovery, at least not quickly enough. British troops only awakened to the situation when the last rebels were already in boats and being rowed across the East River to safety. A few defiant shots from the redcoats was all that could be offered in response.

Howe dealt with the matter briefly in his report to Germain, noting only that the rebels had evacuated their lines on the night of August 29, "with the utmost silence." His brother painted a more dramatic picture, claiming that they had "retired with great precipitation across the East-River." Many British officers were shocked at the turn of events and some were openly scornful of Howe for letting the rebels escape. "The having to deal with a generous, merciful, *forbearing* enemy," wrote sir George Collier, captain of the *Rainbow*, with vicious sarcasm, "who would take no unfair *advantages*, must have been highly satisfactory to General

Washington, and he was certainly very deficient in not expressing his gratitude to General Howe for his *kind* behavior towards him." Surprisingly, Clinton, who was acquiring a taste for criticizing his commanding officer, resisted the temptation to do so in his account of the war, commenting only that the rebels had "wisely evacuated" their lines and had "very ably effected the retreat of their whole army over the East River."

The British would now need to follow them, but before that Howe had a job to complete—the dismantling of the Brooklyn lines. This was done with such haste that some believed he was embarrassed, having had the chance to inspect them closely, by their weakness.

October 1776. Summer had come and gone in England and Germain's plans for the campaign appeared to be in tatters. It had once been hoped that it might have opened in the spring, but everything had slipped, and slipped again. Fall had arrived, but there was still no word of any offensive action at New York. For a man of Germain's energy, not to mention impatience, this must have been torture. He had painstakingly put together an army with one goal in mind—a swift and merciless crushing of the rebellion. His hopes of resurrecting his own reputation now seemed faint. There was only one glimmer of hope—that something dramatic had happened in America and a ship was even now struggling across the ocean with the good news. Germain must have been wondering if such a ship would ever arrive when, miraculously, it did.

On October 10, the *Hyde* reached Britain, carrying a letter from Howe detailing the victory on Long Island. Germain's response was extraordinary, even taking into account how long he had been waiting for the news. It appears to have taken him more than a week to calm down, because he did not reply until October 18. Even then, his joy was overflowing, and the letter strongly expressed his satisfaction at having recognized Howe's abilities and at not having been let down. "Those who," he wrote to Howe, "in the early part of your life, from an observation of the inborn courage and active spirit which you manifested in inferior situations, were led to form favourable conjectures, relative to your future exploits, will, with me, be happy to find their expectations so fully answered." Howe, Germain claimed, had surprised everyone with how quickly he had matured into a formidable commander, "by thus uniting to the fire of youth all the wisdom and conduct of the most experienced commander." In a separate letter written on the same day, Germain informed Howe that the King was also delighted and had decided to confer upon him membership of the Order of the Bath—a knighthood.

Anyone reading Germain's effusive congratulations might have believed Howe had actually won the war, but the American Secretary was not yet finished. He wrote another private letter to Howe on the same day, in which his praise was even more effusive. "The service you have done this country is of the utmost consequence," he opened. "The anxiety with which the account was expected, and the satisfaction with which it was received, sufficiently prove the importance of it." He went on to point out the importance of keeping European noses out of the affair, and told of how they were carefully watching the war to see if any opportunity for mischief might present itself. Then it was back to effusive praise. "I cannot sufficiently admire the disposition you made," he enthused, "nor the manner in which it was executed in every part. It is the first military operation with which no fault could be found in the planning of it, nor in the conduct of any officer to whom you entrusted a command." Howe may have blushed at such praise, but may also have felt a pang of annoyance. The perfect plan to which Germain referred had, of course, come from Clinton.

Even what little criticism Germain had to offer was palatable. Both the King and Germain believed that Howe had been too brave during the battle, and should not have exposed himself to so much danger. This was "wrong in a man who had upon so many occasions shewn his personal bravery, and who ought now to consider how much the publick would suffer by the loss of a General who had gained the affection of the troops, and the confidence of his country." Germain's euphoria tempted him to muse on a possible early end to the war. The rebel army might simply dissolve after such a thrashing and Howe might be able to pay a visit to Philadelphia for the purpose of "punishing that seat of the Congress." If the war was to go on, he hoped Boston would be targeted in retribution for having started the whole thing in the first place.

Success had brought Germain's hawkish nature to the fore, including an unpleasant appetite for punishing the colonists who had dared to defy their sovereign. He made no mention of the decision to halt the assault on the rebel lines at Brooklyn, nor of the subsequent evacuation of Washington's army. They may have seemed minor quibbles considering the fact that the revolutionary war effort appeared to be on its knees. From Percy, he had heard that "the Rebels have severely felt the blow, and I think I may venture to foretell that this business is pretty near over." Percy also described the battle as "ably planned and nobly executed."

Germain would have recognized a discordant note, however, within a further letter from Howe, in which he stated that a second campaign would most likely be necessary. Germain certainly had not planned on that, but he would have drawn some comfort from the fact that Howe did not seem to think he would require extensive reinforcement. In fact, he asked for just 800 further Hessian jägers—members of the elite German light infantry—as well as 100 hussars, to be provided horses in America. Germain was well aware of Howe's regard for light infantry and would have understood his enthusiasm at the thought of having a corps of jägers 1,000 strong to work alongside the English light infantry. As Howe pointed out, such a corps "would be of infinite service in covering the march of the army, and would prevent much loss and fatigue to the main body."

Germain could afford to agree instantly to this modest demand, stating that Howe would receive the men quickly enough to make an early contribution to the next year's campaign, while also hoping that they would not be necessary. If the good weather in America held, there were potentially several months of campaigning conditions left, and the rebels were no doubt reeling from the blow dealt on Long Island. Germain waited for his next information from Howe, no doubt dreaming of more successes and the collapse of the rebellion.

———

Back in America, Howe had shown no urgency to follow up his victory. In fact, after administering a severe blow, the time seemed right to consider a diplomatic solution once more. One of the American prisoners, General Sullivan, believed he might be able to broker a peace agreement with Congress if allowed to inform them of the terms the Howe brothers were able to offer. It is difficult to see how he could have come to such a conclusion, given the paltry terms on offer, but it is likely that Lord Howe allowed Sullivan to believe he had more discretion than he actually did. While waiting to see if Sullivan could set up a conference, the Howes laid down their plans for the invasion of Manhattan.

It was a potentially dangerous operation; the rebels had been constructing defensive works on the island for months. However, the same had been said about Long Island, and American resistance there had proved weak at best. Tides would need to coincide with darkness in order for the British to assemble their ships for a landing on Manhattan, and this is the most likely reason for the delay in the progress of the campaign at this stage, although Howe would go on to prove that he did not need any excuse for moving slowly.

There was good reason for acting swiftly, if possible. The Americans were in the doldrums after their drubbing. Washington reported that members of the militia were leaving in droves, sometimes almost by whole regiments, after their first taste of battle. Morale was so low that Washington felt "obliged to confess my want of confidence in the generality of the troops." Later in the same letter he went further: "Till of late," he confided, "I had no doubt in my own mind of defending this place; nor should I have yet, if the men would do their duty; but this I despair of. It is painful, and extremely grating to me, to give such unfavorable accounts; but it would be criminal to conceal the truth at so critical a juncture." The American commander was doing his men a disservice here. Placed in an impossible situation on Long Island, they could not have been expected to do more. It was leadership, rather than the common soldier, that had let down the patriot cause on Long Island. The clear knowledge of this, in fact, was one of the main demoralizing influences on the American army. Daniel Brodhead wrote: "Upon the whole, less Generalship never was shown in any Army since the Art of War was understood," and he was not alone in thinking that the British had given the Americans a harsh lesson in the realities of professional soldiering.

Sullivan, meanwhile, had presented his case to Congress, and although there was little hope of a peaceful resolution, it was considered worthwhile to at least make sure of the terms the Howe brothers could offer. A conference was arranged for September 11. Although, given the limited scope of American interest, it would today be described as "talks about talks," the conference did present an opportunity for key figures to exchange opinions face to face. Lord Howe was not about to let such an opportunity pass by and he chose to mount a deliberate charm offensive. On Staten Island he prepared a conference room with all the care of a bowerbird, transforming a house that had been used as a billet by draping branches and moss around the room and preparing an elaborate meal. There was even a guard of honor outside the door awaiting the American delegates, but the choice of Hessians was not the most diplomatic, given the Americans' disdain for the use of hired troops.

The three Americans sent to the conference were John Adams, Benjamin Franklin, and Edward Rutledge. Adams commented that the room prepared by Lord Howe was "romantically elegant," and the refreshments offered were welcome. On the British side, Lord Howe was joined by the secretary for the peace commission, Henry Strachey, but his younger brother was absent. As joint peace commissioner, this was curious, and William's desire to find a peaceful solution was sincere. Given his lack of sophistication in official correspondence, however, his older brother may have considered him to be a liability in diplomatic talk.

As the men got down to business, it quickly became apparent that Lord Howe's rather ponderous approach was no match for the quick wit of Franklin, who danced around the admiral with ease. To Lord Howe's protestation that, "... if America should fall, I should feel and lament it like the loss of a brother," Franklin replied, with a smile, "My lord, we will use our utmost endeavors to save your lordship that mortification." The stolid admiral deserved better treatment, but the conference had nowhere to go. It became bogged down immediately on the issue of whether the Americans were in attendance as private citizens, or as representatives of the Congress. Lord Howe fretted that he was not even meant to acknowledge the Congress's existence, let alone meet formally with its representatives, but then the real stumbling block was encountered, even though every man in the room had known it was there all along. Lord Howe was unable to do anything unless the Americans first withdrew their declaration of independence. "It is desirable," Lord Howe insisted, "to put a stop to these ruinous extremities, as well for the sake of our country as yours ... The question is: Is there no way of treating back this step of Independency, and thus opening the door to a full discussion?"

Franklin's response was as categorical as possible: "We cannot now expect happiness under the domination of Great Britain," he replied. "All former attachments are obliterated." Adams pointed out that he was only authorized to talk to Howe as a representative of independent states, while Rutledge tried a different tack, suggesting that Britain would be far better served by recognizing American independence and embracing them as a new and powerful ally and trading partner. It was left to Lord Howe to pronounce the conference dead. "If the colonies will not give up the system of independency," he stated simply, "it is impossible for me to enter into any negotiation."

The talks about talks had failed. Britain would now need to resort once more to force.

———

Rumors had been swirling about the Americans' intentions ever since they had evacuated Long Island. Intelligence suggested their army was in disarray, and on September 1 Howe had received news from multiple sources that the rebels were planning to evacuate Manhattan as well. He alerted Clinton that he was preparing to occupy the city quickly if that was indeed the case. Getting his men away from Long Island was important, and not only because the campaign needed to move ahead. Tents and huts left behind by the rebels on Long Island had been burned in an attempt to prevent the camp diseases that were raging through the American army from contaminating the British, but outbreaks were inevitable. Redcoats took to calling dysentery "the Yanky," and Loftus Cliffe, an officer with the 46th Regiment, informed relatives back home that it had "reduced my thigh to the thickness of my leg, and my leg to a grenadier's musquet barrel." It was rumored that there were 4,000 rebel soldiers sick in New York, which may have been a conservative estimate, and it was generally assumed that Washington would have left the city already if it weren't for his vast numbers of invalids. There was also word that the rebel commander was worried that inter-colonial tensions might lead to fighting, especially between New York troops and those from New England, if the city was abandoned to the British. Henry Strachey noted wryly that such an event might end the war and "save us a great deal of trouble."

The summer had proved mercifully mild, which was a relief to the troops. Strachey reported to his wife that temperatures on Long Island had been almost uniformly between 70 and 74°F (between 21 and 23°C) and had never exceeded 83°F (29°C). The fine weather was expected to last as late as December. "Preparations are making for our crossing the river to the eastward of the city," he added, on September 3. This included the provision of rations for the men, which escalated steadily over the following week. On September 8, each man was to have one day's worth. The following day this was increased to two days' worth, and on September 12 four days' worth was issued to the troops.

Something was clearly afoot, but exactly what had been the subject of debate. No doubt flushed with the successful adoption of his plan of attack on Long Island, Clinton had once more been free with his advice, and once more it had been sound. He had suggested landing men behind the rebel positions on Manhattan and seizing King's Bridge. Following the shocking evacuation of Long Island it could no longer be assumed that trapping the Americans would inevitably lead to their surrender, but it would at worst force them to find a way off Manhattan, across the Hudson, and this would result in New York falling into British hands at no cost whatsoever. This time, however, the commander-in-chief was not in the mood for Clinton's advice. "[T]he arguments adduced for landing on York Island proved, however, most prevalent," Clinton recorded in his account of the war, glossing over the disappointment he felt at being ignored.

Howe still wanted input from his second-in-command, but he also wanted to chart his own course. Repeatedly following plans submitted by Clinton would have been embarrassing and, eventually, humiliating. Clinton insisted that when he gave advice he "spoke it with candor and without warmth," but Howe may have been able to sense the underlying frustration in his subordinate. Still, on September 14, Howe asked Clinton to meet to discuss plans for landing on Manhattan. Howe had also received some good news; reinforcements were on their way and could be expected to arrive at any moment. The second division of Hessians, the 16th Light Dragoons, remounts for the 17th Light Dragoons, and 400 recruits for the first division of Hessians were on their way. Already greatly superior to the force defending Manhattan, Howe's army was about to get even bigger.

SEVEN

The Landings

"The necessary preparations, and effecting batteries, to facilitate the landing upon the island of New-York and battering the enemy's works at Horens-Hook, occupied us till the 15th of September, when the possession on New-York was effected ... From that time until the 12th of October we were employed in fortifying the heights from Macgowan's Pass to North River..."

Howe's narrative, April 22, 1779

*T*HIS WAS A MOST *peculiar speech. Howe was alternating excruciating (and confusing) detail with lightning-fast summaries, skating over months at a time and ignoring important events. In the space of a few lines the House of Commons had been whisked from August 29 to October 12, the taking of New York mentioned in passing as though it were of little consequence. It was, in fact, the initial goal of the campaign and should have fired the starting pistol for a full implementation of the agreed-upon strategy for the year.*

Instead, Howe was describing another delay, while fortifications were made to resist a rebel army that seemed to be disintegrating; an entire month, it seemed, had been filled with the construction of these defensive works. And had the taking of the city really been as easy as Howe's narrative was suggesting? The answer, surprisingly, was "yes."

Clinton had no doubts that Howe's plan for the capture of New York was risky. In a private memo he detailed his thoughts. "In short, I like it not," he wrote. "No diversion, no demonstration but what a child would see through, little prospect of victory without buying it dear, some apprehension of receiving—what we might have given—a defeat *en détail.*" The "demonstration" referred to so disparagingly in Clinton's memo involved Major General Robertson and Sir William Erskine making a diversion at Hell's Gate. Clinton's growing contempt for the commander-in-chief, as well as his pique at having his own plan rejected, was clear in his memo, but he was also aware of an important fact. He would be leading the landing on Manhattan, and it is possible that if things went badly, he wanted a scrap of evidence to hand proving that he had been opposed to the plan all along. Clinton jotted down his little note on September 15, as he prepared to lead the assault.

Landing troops on a shoreline with prepared defenses has always been a hazardous undertaking. Clinton noted that the strength of the rebel entrenchments was significant, believing that they could not be bombarded by British warships. He also believed that rebel batteries could pound the Royal Navy ships and the longboats ferrying men to shore. It is easy to imagine the scene of destruction dancing in Clinton's mind, and he was not alone in his concerns. Cliffe wrote of "large columns" of American soldiers moving between their various works on the island and also believed their breastworks were too strong for a naval bombardment to destroy. The rumor was that Howe expected to lose at least 500 men in the landing.

If the rumor was accurate, Howe gave no such indication. Whether he was putting on a brave face for his men is unclear, but he informed them that they had little to fear. Reminding the British and Hessian soldiers of their "evident superiority" as demonstrated on Long Island, he informed them that "they [the Americans] now place their security in slight breastworks of the weakest constructions of which are to be carried with little loss by the same high spirited mode of attack." The men were to rely on their bayonets once more. Howe must have been painfully aware that he had over-estimated the strength of the

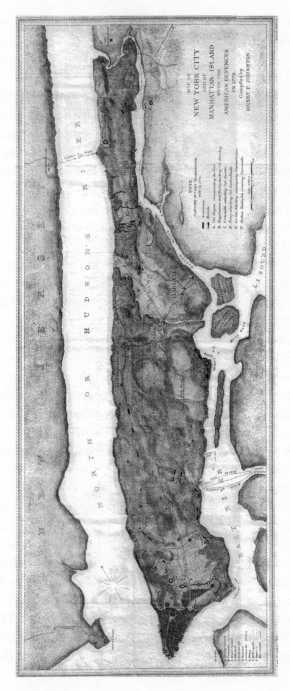

'Map of New York City and of Manhattan Island with the American Defences in 1776.' Detailing American defensive works in and around New York City, the Harlem Heights and Forts Washington and Lee. Johnston, H. P. (1878). Brooklyn. (Wikimedia Commons.)

rebel lines at Brooklyn and was not about to make the same mistake again.

It was not at all certain that there would be any American soldiers in New York by the time the redcoats finally showed up. Ever since arriving on the night of August 29, Washington had been agonizing over whether or not to defend the city. The Brooklyn Heights had been considered essential to its safety, which was why they had been defended by such a substantial corps of the army. Their loss surely was as damaging to the rebel position as the loss of the Dorchester Heights had been to the British at Boston. If the British wanted, they could bombard the city from the same fortifications erected by the rebels to defend it.

The possibility of abandoning the city raised another difficult question, one Washington alluded to in a letter to the President of Congress on September 2: "If we should be obliged to abandon the town, ought it to stand as winter-quarters for the enemy?" The idea of razing the city was unpalatable, but so too was the idea of granting the British a comfortable base for future operations. With the Hudson strategy well understood, and feared, by the rebels, there was a strong case to be made for denying the British such a base. "… I dare say the enemy mean to preserve it, if they can," Washington continued. "If Congress, therefore, should resolve upon the destruction of it, the resolution should be a profound secret, as the knowledge of it will make a change in their plans."

Washington only hinted at destroying the city, but Nathanael Greene was more forthright. "We have no very great reason to run any considerable risk for its [New York's] defense," he informed Washington. "I would give it as my opinion that a general and speedy retreat is absolutely necessary, and that the honor and interest of America require it. I would burn the city."

Congress debated this option, and quickly decided to send Washington reinforcements. If forced to withdraw from the city, however, he was to ensure that "no damage be done to the said city by his troops on their leaving it; the Congress having no doubt of their being able to recover the same, though the enemy should for a time obtain possession of it."

Once more, the wealth of options available to the British was torture for Washington, who feared exactly the sort of operation that Clinton had suggested, trapping the rebels on Manhattan by landing beyond King's Bridge. His uncertainty was such that he was considering evacuating the city without a fight, but in the meantime he was forced once more to split his force to prepare against all of the possible routes of attack. Reorganizing his army into three divisions, he placed Putnam in the city itself, with orders to protect both it and an approach from the East River. Joseph Spencer's troops continued the defensive line along the East River, while the final division, commanded by Heath, stood guard around King's Bridge. It was too much territory for such a small, inexperienced, and badly shaken army to defend, which Washington eventually accepted. In an agonized letter to Congress he made it clear that it was impossible to deny New York to the British, declaring that "nothing seems to remain but to determine the time of their taking possession." He reorganized his men once more, withdrawing the bulk of his army to the Harlem Heights, with a garrison of 5,000 men remaining in New York. Although the city itself was not to be destroyed, even though British occupation was a certainty, the infrastructure of Manhattan was not afforded the same consideration. Heath was ordered tear up the roads from King's Bridge to the city to make them impassable. Church bells in the city were to be removed and melted down for the production of cannon.

Howe's ponderous progress had not undermined his campaign to this point. In fact, if anything it had helped it, as Washington had gathered more men around New York, increasing the potential scale of victory for the British. Now, however, the Americans were slipping from his grasp, albeit in slow motion. While Howe finalized his plans for a landing at Kip's Bay, on the eastern side of Manhattan, Washington had already removed the bulk of his men to positions further north, around the Harlem Heights. Only the 5,000 men in New York were still threatened by the chosen landing site, and on September 12, Washington acted again. It had taken several days, but the absurdity of retaining a small corps in New York had been recognized. A party of officers had requested a council to reconsider the decision to leave troops in the city, and the necessity of abandoning it completely was finally accepted. Putnam's men began to withdraw, but it was a slow process. Great quantities of stores had been left in the city and now needed to be removed. On September 14, Washington confided to Congress that it would take a couple of days to complete the withdrawal. He hoped the British would defer their attack for a while longer.

Washington was not to get his wish. Whether, as Joseph Plumb Martin suggested, the British always preferred to open operations on a Sunday, when the prayers of the nation were behind them, or whether it had more to do with tide times, the landings on Manhattan began the following morning. Howe's initial intention had been to land in two divisions, at both Kip's Bay and Horn's Hook, but various difficulties had led to the concentration of all forces at Kip's Bay. Still hoping to stage some sort of diversion, three ships were sent up the Hudson River, on the western side of Manhattan, as far as Bloomingdale, hoping to catch the rebels' attention.

Surveying the proposed landing site at Kip's Bay from the deck of the *Roebuck*, Clinton's gloom deepened. Extensive entrenchments, well-manned, appeared ready to hurl the redcoats back into the river and he noted how, once the landing boats had delivered their cargoes, fire support from the naval vessels would no longer be possible. The infantry would be on its own and high ground above the landing area was suitable for enemy artillery emplacements.

From the other side, the Americans' position appeared far less formidable, echoing the situation at Brooklyn. Upon first seeing them, Martin had dismissed the lines as little more than a ditch with the earth thrown up toward the British. The rebel soldiers had been watching the deliberate British preparations with some interest over the preceding days. Five ships, including the *Roebuck* and the *Phoenix*, were loitering with intent, but the landing site was still in doubt. Washington was further north, anticipating a landing there. Once more, he was attempting to defend more ground than he could possibly hope to.

The morning of September 15 immediately promised developments. Martin awoke to find that the British frigates had moved closer to shore during the night and now lay at anchor within musket range, while the arrival of packed landing craft (which Martin described as appearing like "a large clover field in fill bloom") left no further doubt that the British were coming. Confusion immediately engulfed the Americans, who believed that the long boats were aiming for a different part of the shoreline and began to move; from his vantage point, Clinton recognized this as a major opportunity. At least some troops had remained in the defensive line, because Martin recalled how, bored with the slowness of developments, he had wandered away from his post to explore an old warehouse nearby. While he was rummaging through the debris in the building, the battle began.

Clinton, seeing that the rebels had realized their mistake and were attempting to hurry back to their Kip's Bay positions, requested naval fire to prevent their return. At the same time, the main bombardment to support the landing began. It was, by all reports, a thing to behold. Martin's perusal of the contents of the warehouse was rudely interrupted by "such a peal of thunder from the British shipping that I thought my head would go with the sound." A Hessian officer involved in the landing wrote of "the thundering rattle of five men-of-war," while the American militia officer commanding the rebel defenses, Colonel William Douglas, reckoned it to be "as heavy a cannonade perhaps as ever was from no more ships." Douglas perhaps had reason to describe the bombardment in such terms, since his command was about to disintegrate without offering any resistance, but the naval fire was undeniably beneficial. Howe was more restrained in his report, but he did refer to the effectiveness of the five warships: "The fire of the shipping being so well directed, and so incessant," he informed Germain, "the enemy could not remain in their works, and the descent was made without the least opposition." Martin, who had scrambled back to the relative protection of the lines as soon as the bombardment had begun, had no choice but to keep his head low for as long as possible, but with the British guns leveling the fortifications, the order was given to withdraw.

It took a special kind of bravery to leave the lines and cross the level area behind them, exposed, as Martin reported, to grapeshot and langrage (scraps of metal enclosed in a case and primarily used for damaging the rigging on an enemy ship, but equally adept at damaging men) as they ran. The Americans dispersed under the fire, heading in whatever direction promised to end the torment most quickly. When finally out of the range of the guns, Martin had just two other soldiers with him. More than 300 men had been taken prisoner.

The landing force, with a first wave comprising British light infantry and the best of the Hessian troops, lost little time in moving inland, soon catching up with muddled parties of rebels looking for a route to safety. Confusion led to Martin's trio approaching a group of Hessians, thinking they were the remnants of their regiment. Hastily changing direction, they found a party of their comrades, only to see them fired upon by British troops advancing through a cornfield. It was a scene of utter disorder.

His visions of carnage having mercifully failed to materialize, Clinton had ordered four battalions of Hessian grenadiers to penetrate inland, while using the bulk of his first wave to secure the high ground (known as Inclenberg Hill or Heights) that dominated the area. Once more, he had orders from Howe not to proceed further and, this time, he was unwilling to press his luck. At Breed's Hill and Brooklyn he had attempted to push on to achieve a more complete victory and on both occasions Howe had been displeased. Twice bitten, Clinton could be forgiven if he was now shy, and the minor skirmishes with retreating rebels represented the only fighting of the day. Had the full situation on Manhattan been appreciated, he may yet have chanced his arm, because the New York garrison was at that very moment attempting to flee to the north and rejoin the bulk of the army around the Harlem Heights. Once more, a sizable portion of Washington's army was vulnerable, if the British could just move quickly enough, but when Howe arrived on the scene, around 2 p.m., he made no move to throw men across the island to trap the Americans streaming northward along the shore of the Hudson River. The second wave of troops landed three hours later and Howe contented himself with sending men northward to feel out the extent of rebel positions around the Harlem Heights, and southward, to secure the city. New York had fallen, and the confidence of Congress regarding how easily they would be able to take back the city would prove misplaced. The British would remain there for the next seven years.

Washington had ridden to the sound of the guns and arrived in time to witness the disintegration of the American position at Kip's Bay. He apparently tried to rally his troops, without success, and legend has it that he was so dispirited that he fell into a sort of daze and was nearly captured by British troops. It is difficult to see how much more could have been expected of the Americans, given the confusion caused over where the British landing craft were aiming and the lack of effective leadership. The men who bore the brunt of the British assault were militia rather than regular infantry, and there was little or no experience of battle to draw upon, while the ferocity of the naval bombardment would have terrified new recruits; "... the demons of fear and disorder seemed to take full possession of all and every thing on that day," Martin noted. In addition, he witnessed rebel troops dropping almost everything they carried—muskets, hats, canteens, coats—in order to flee the advancing British more quickly. Martin also had strong words on the failure of the American officer class. "The men were confused," he claimed, "being without officers to command them—I do not recollect of seeing a commissioned officer from the time I left the lines on the banks of the East River, in the morning, until ... the evening. How could the men fight without officers?"

British opinion of the American soldier, never high, was sinking ever lower. Loftus Cliffe took the time to write to a relative from New York to declare that, prior to the Battle of Long Island, he had believed the Americans to be a respectable enemy. Since then, however, "... they have shown the greatest pusillanimity that can be imagined from men who pretend to fight for liberty and independence." At Kip's Bay he believed the rebel defenses had been far stronger than Martin reported, insisting that the Royal Navy ships could never have destroyed the breastworks. The British, according to Cliffe, had been amazed when the rebels had fled without putting up any resistance. New York also was a favorable position. It was "... by nature extremely tenable and every advantage nature gave had been improved to the best by these scoundrels, who if they could fight as they work might defy any power in the world."

Alongside a growing disrespect for the fighting qualities of the Americans, there was also recognition of the peculiar nature of the war. Fighting foreigners was one thing, and a redcoat needed little motivation to tackle a Frenchman or a Spaniard, but orderly books found in New York presented an uncomfortable reality. "In their returns," Cliffe noted sadly, "we find almost every name that's among us." The records also made clear the plight of the rebel army. As well as detailing the wholesale desertion of troops, including entire companies, after the British had landed on Long Island, there were reports of disciplinary measures, including officers punished for cowardice on August 27.

The war was repeating itself. Washington had withdrawn to new positions and Howe had failed to take another opportunity to deal a more severe blow to the enemy. Few could have any doubts, however, that the British were winning. The Americans had been utterly routed in the only two serious actions so far and once more found themselves awaiting a British assault.

Howe remained reluctant to throw his men against prepared defenses. When putting together his narrative nearly three years later, he struggled over how best to express this. A draft of the speech includes a passage repeatedly crossed through and amended, in which he tried to strike the right tone. "I am free to own," he started, "I would never hazard the assault of lines..." Recognizing that this was too strong, he tried "... if I could remove an enemy from a very advantageous situation without the hazard of an attack I should certainly embrace it." This was wrong as well—a general should not embrace an opportunity to avoid attacking the enemy. As his words became more torturous he tried "... if I could remove an enemy from a very advantageous situation without the hazard of an attack, where the object to be carried was not adequate to the cost of men to be expected from an assault upon strong lines, I should certainly embrace it in the hopes of meeting him upon more equal terms." This was almost right, if clumsy, but "embrace" had reappeared. He substituted "adopt that cautionary conduct" instead. Howe, always ham-fisted with words, might have simply stated that he was unwilling to risk losing more men than absolutely necessary to achieve his goals. His speech would have been shorter and would have caused fewer headaches among those listening to it.

Poor oratory did not invalidate Howe's motives, of course, and his underlying thinking on the subject was reasonable. His caution won approval from at least some of his men, who no doubt did not relish the idea of storming defensive works. "General Howe is determined to make regular approaches," Cliffe reported, "and not run our heads against their works, which is what they have all along hoped for." Howe had no intention of fighting the kind of war Washington was trying to draw him into. Where he saw no alternative to a frontal assault, as had been the case with the landing at Kip's Bay, he was willing to take the risk. Where a less costly alternative offered itself, such as at Brooklyn, he would take that. It kept Washington off balance and denied him a series of Bunker Hills that would have eventually left Howe with a uselessly small army. Howe's deliberate, steady approach was threatening to strangle the rebel cause with minimal losses on either side, which would also make reconciliation easier after the inevitable military victory. Washington's only prayer, at this stage, appeared to be for some sort of miscalculation on the part of the British. His prayer was answered the next day.

Howe's men had belatedly spread themselves across Manhattan, from Horn's Hook on the east side to Bloomingdale on the west. Fort Washington, toward the northernmost tip of Manhattan, was the centerpiece of the new American defensive position, but further works had been constructed on the Harlem Heights and at Kingsbridge. The morning after the landing, Washington was understandably anxious to get a more complete picture of the situation, calling upon some of his best troops, around 120 Rangers, to reconnoiter the British position. The Rangers, volunteers from the New England Continental regiments, were resourceful and steady men, the equivalent of the British light infantry and Hessian jägers. Commanded by Lieutenant Colonel Thomas Knowlton, they were soon advancing carefully under the cover of woodland. They encountered the British about 1 mile (1.6 kilometers) out from the American lines.

The response was swift. Two light infantry battalions, along with the 42nd Regiment, moved out to confront the small American force, which held its nerve and its ground, firing from behind the cover of a stone wall before withdrawing calmly. It had only been a minor skirmish up to this point, but the Rangers had already lost ten men. Continuing to withdraw toward the safety of their own lines, the Rangers were pursued by around 300 light infantry. The British were confident that the rebels would once more panic and run, and bugle horns were sounded as if they were engaged in nothing more dangerous than a fox hunt.

Washington, alerted to the skirmishing, saw the opportunity to secure a small victory, something that might restore the morale of his army. Ordering the Rangers to attempt to get behind the advancing British, he pushed 150 volunteers forward to hold the redcoats' attention. Knowlton's Rangers began their flanking move, reinforced by 120 Virginians commanded by Major Andrew Leitch. The light infantry, over-confident, advanced toward the small body of men in front of them and prepared a firing line, unaware that the Rangers and Virginians were moving around their right flank. The rebels' diversionary force opened fire, and although the range was too great for the fire to be effective, it concentrated the attention of the British soldiers.

What appeared to be a perfectly unfolding plan was then undermined. The trap was sprung too quickly and the British found themselves attacked in the flank, rather than the rear. Although alarming, it gave them the opportunity to withdraw. It was a fighting withdrawal, as proved by the fact that both Knowlton and Leitch were fatally wounded while pursuing their enemy. Still, the Americans had seen the backs of those famous red coats and were in no mood to call off their pursuit. Washington poured more reinforcements in, Marylanders this time, as the number of Americans engaged swelled to around 1,800 men. For the first time in the war, Washington and Howe now faced each other directly, the British commander having been alerted to the action in the same way as his American counterpart. Like Washington, Howe fed more men into the developing battle. What had started out as a brief and small-scale skirmish was threatening to turn into a serious engagement. The 42nd Regiment, jägers and Hessian grenadiers, as well two field pieces, were moving into action on the British side.

Still the rebels pushed forward, forcing the British to give ground once more. The main British camp was now threateningly near, and the arrival of yet further reinforcements, including the 5th Regiment of Foot, convinced Washington that enough had been risked for one day. The battle, which had blown up like a dust devil, now dissipated as the Americans carefully disengaged, making sure to give a concerted whoop, perhaps in response to the light infantry's insulting use of their bugles.

There was no doubt that the Americans had gotten the better of what became known as the Battle of Harlem Heights. Howe was furious that such an unplanned engagement had been allowed to develop and was especially displeased with Brigadier General Alexander Leslie, the commander on the spot during the battle. "General Howe has been a good deal hurt at this," Loftus Cliffe reported, "as before so much had been done with so little loss and as he declared it his intention not to lose the finger of a single man wantonly, he says he did not deserve it." Howe had reason to be displeased. He had lost around 150 men in killed and wounded, while American losses were probably below 100. Determined to prevent such an escalating engagement from breaking out again, Howe ordered pickets to allow neither officers nor men to pass them in pursuit of the enemy.

The British might now have reconsidered their opinion of the rebel soldiers, but Cliffe was not to be swayed easily. "Every one of the enemies killed and wounded," he declared, "stunk infamously of rum, their canteens still contained the remains of sheer spirits, even their officers were in this manner urged on." This, according to Cliffe's ready wit, demonstrated "the difference of British and American *spirit.*"

Washington, unsurprisingly, took something rather different from the battle. At the very moment it had erupted he had been writing to Congress on the "disgraceful and dastardly conduct" of his men at Kip's Bay. He may have reconsidered his words after returning from witnessing the bravery of the soldiers at the Harlem Heights, but his secretary, unsure of when the commander-in-chief would return to his letter, had sent it on without a signature; it was read in Congress the following day. By then, Washington was singing a different tune, or at least writing one. "I have the pleasure to inform you our men behaved with bravery and intrepidity," he informed Nicholas Cooke, Governor of Rhode Island. Washington's orderly book also included praise for the men, who would have been delighted to hear: "The General most heartily thanks the troops ... The behavior of yesterday was such a contrast, to that of some troops the day before, as must shew what may be done, where Officers and Soldiers will exert themselves."

Washington should also have been aware that he had been handed a new blueprint for tackling the British. Repeated attempts to make them attack prepared defensive positions had failed; Howe was simply not going to play that game again. But small-scale engagements, in which the Americans could use their knowledge of the country and keep the redcoats at arm's length, promised success. They would never lead to crushing victories, but an army 3,000 miles (4,800 kilometers) from home could ill afford to lose 150 men in protracted skirmishing. Faced with massed ranks of enemy infantry, or the thundering gunfire of Royal Navy ships, the green American soldiers would break and run. Facing a few hundred redcoats in the woods was far less daunting and at least offered a chance for the Americans to land a few blows of their own before withdrawing. It seems obvious, but Washington was soon to show that he had not yet learned the lesson.

He was also still not used to Howe's method of operation. Four days after the Battle of Harlem Heights, the American general believed that a further British move was imminent. "The Enemy are forming a large and extensive Encampment," he informed the President of Congress on September 20, "... and are busily employed in transporting their cannon and Stores from Long Island. As they advance them this way, we may reasonably expect their operations will not long be deferred." It was almost as if he had never watched Howe at work before.

Far from planning to swiftly follow up his landing on Manhattan, Howe was determined to make the city safe from a possible rebel counter-attack, and embarked upon an extensive series of fortifications. In the short term this was certainly unnecessary; Washington's men were in no fit state to contest the British occupation and would have to go through the bulk of the British army just to reach the city. In the long term, if sizable corps were to be detached from the region, then fortifying the city would be necessary. Howe was clearly thinking, therefore, of a prolonged campaign, but was he thinking of the Hudson strategy? The first stage of that beguilingly simple plan, the occupation of New York, had been accomplished with relative ease, if not perhaps as quickly as some would have hoped. Would the British commander-in-chief now start to move forces up the Hudson River? Any such thoughts were to be rudely interrupted.

"Between the 20th and 21st," Howe informed Germain on September 23, "a most horrid attempt was made by a number of wretches to burn the town of New-York, in which they succeeded too well, having set it on fire in several places, with matches and combustibles that had been prepared with great art and ingenuity." Howe had no doubt that the fire that destroyed a quarter of the city had been started deliberately, and given the musings on the part of Washington on whether the town should have been left intact for the British, there was circumstantial evidence to support the suspicion. Many men were arrested on the night, most to be released almost immediately, but several were summarily executed. Washington claimed to have no idea how the fire began, and it is possible it was started without explicit orders. It was feared that further attempts would be made to finish the job of destroying the city, and tensions ran high for the next few days.

Howe continued his deliberate progress, capturing the rebel position on Paulus Hook on September 23. The Americans had once more quit their position on the approach of British troops, and the rebel batteries were taken without any resistance. Many in the British army began to assume that the war was drawing to a close. Cliffe reckoned that a timely appearance from Burgoyne, who was hopefully making his way southward, would finish the job. "If he comes upon the enemy's rear at King's Bridge," he surmised, "and we in front of them, I believe he will have little more disagreeable than their stink to stand against."

Edward Braddock falls during the disastrous Battle of the Monongahela, July 9, 1755. Native American warriors can be seen making use of cover while firing on the hapless redcoats. (Anne S. K. Brown Military Collection, Brown University)

Britain loses another general, this time in a moment of triumph. James Wolfe lies dying on September 13, 1759, while William Howe, in his unconventional attire, points to the victory unfolding on the Plains of Abraham. (Wikimedia Commons)

George Washington raises his hat to the fledgling Continental Army as he takes command on July 3, 1775. As was usual for a Currier & Ives lithograph, liberties were taken with the depiction of uniforms worn on the day. (Anne S. K. Brown Military Collection, Brown University)

Alonzo Chappel's interpretation of the 'Battle of Bunker's Hill' keeps its distance from the action, but still conveys a sense of the chaos and carnage of the British Army's bloodiest day of the war. (Anne S. K. Brown Military Collection, Brown University)

William Howe personally oversees the destruction of cannon prior to the evacuation of Boston, while his men are crammed onto the waiting transport ships. (Anne S. K. Brown Military Collection, Brown University)

The uniforms are all wrong in this depiction of the Battle of Harlem Heights, but the Americans did force their red-coated adversaries to retreat, boosting morale at a critical moment in the 1776 campaign. (Anne S. K. Brown Military Collection, Brown University)

A very colourful New York City burns on the night of September 20, 1776. While some try to rescue valuables from their houses, others are intent on punishing suspected arsonists. (Anne S. K. Brown Military Collection, Brown University)

Charles Lee's dreams of taking command of the Continental Army are interrupted by a party of British light dragoons on December 13, 1776. The former British officer had been deliberately slow in his movements to link up with Washington's corps. (Anne S. K. Brown Military Collection, Brown University)

Washington scores a knockout on Boxing Day 1776, rescuing the campaign with his audacious and brilliant attack on the Hessian outpost at Trenton. (Anne S. K. Brown Military Collection, Brown University)

American troops fire a volley into advancing British ranks at the Brandywine, September 11, 1777. Howe's last chance for a decisive victory followed a familiar pattern, with the Americans defeated, but not destroyed. (Library of Congress)

"The Conference between the Brothers HOW to get Rich". This satirical cartoon suggests the Howe brothers (advised by the Devil himself) were deliberately prolonging the war to fill their own wallets. (Library of Congress)

Lord George Germain (formerly Sackville) never quite shook off the whiff of shame from his court martial, but he tackled the job of subduing the rebellious colonies with enormous energy. (Anne S. K. Brown Military Collection, Brown University)

William Howe seemed a solid choice for commander-in-chief, given his experience in the French and Indian War and expertise in light infantry tactics. (Anne S. K. Brown Military Collection, Brown University)

Richard, Lord Howe, provided valuable support for his younger brother while commanding British naval forces in North America, although some would later depict him as offering little more than a taxi service for the army. (Anne S. K. Brown Military Collection, Brown University)

George Washington came close to disaster on numerous occasions, especially in the tumultuous 1776 campaign, but bounced back from repeated defeats to somehow keep an army in the field. (Anne S. K. Brown Military Collection, Brown University)

Given the ease with which Howe had taken each target he had set his sights upon, his next letter to Germain was curious and must have been read with some alarm by the American Secretary when it arrived in London, on November 2. Written on September 25, the letter effectively declared the 1776 campaign to be over. "Upon the present appearance of things," Howe wrote, "I look upon the further progress of this army for the campaign, to be rather precarious..." He went on to list a series of excuses; the campaigning season was coming to a close, the second division of Hessians had still not yet arrived, and Carleton seemed to be making slow progress from Canada. Without Carleton adding pressure on Washington's army from the north, Howe felt that any risk on his part was unwarranted, "as a check at this time, would be of infinite detriment to us."

Why Howe feared a check is uncertain. Washington's army had proved unable to stand its ground on multiple occasions. Now, however, Howe believed their positions on the Harlem Heights were too strong to assault. "The enemy is too strongly posted to be attacked in front," he argued, "and innumerable difficulties are in my way of turning him on either side..." The American positions may well have been strong, but the rivers that flowed on either side of Manhattan not only secured Washington's flanks from a turning move, but they also made it possible to bypass the rebel positions altogether. Or had Howe forgotten that he had his brother's fleet to hand?

Howe's letter also contradicted itself. Having mentioned that he could not be sure that Carleton was making any progress, Howe reported rumors that Burgoyne, with a separate detachment operating in the Mohawk River, was fast approaching Albany. "If he [Burgoyne] gets possession of Albany," Howe admitted, "it will, no doubt, facilitate General Carleton's movement to that place, and will be attended with favourable consequences." Howe actually believed that the northern army might be making very significant progress indeed. On the same day he wrote his pessimistic letter to Germain, Howe was informed by Sir William Erskine that the Americans on the Harlem Heights appeared to be on the move. Howe asked Clinton to look into the matter and suggested that news of Burgoyne approaching Albany might be behind the Americans' restlessness. Despite this, he insisted to Germain that "I have not the smallest prospect of finishing the contest this campaign..." His lack of care in communications with his political master was at times baffling. Howe seemed completely oblivious to the need to present an image of himself as a driving, forceful commander, ready to take every opportunity to advance the cause of restoring peace to the colonies. Caution had its place, but Howe admitted to far more than was advisable. More baffling still was the fact that at the same time that he was informing Germain that he could not hope to outflank the Americans, he was contemplating doing exactly that.

Finally, Henry Clinton's idea of landing behind the Americans was being seriously considered; as a means of forcing the Americans from their strong positions, it was a sound strategy. Howe would later botch his own defense during his narrative, when making the meek assertion that he had gathered intelligence on the lie of the land beyond Manhattan "upon a supposition that the enemy should remove from King's-Bridge." The draft of his narrative included a far more robust and proactive statement, stating that he had gathered information "on the country to be possessed for the removal of the enemy from Kingsbridge and to bring them to action deprived of the defense of their strong works there." Not for the first time, nor the last, Howe was his own worst enemy.

Clinton bemoaned the fact that his original landing site, Morrisania, was no longer viable due to the concentration of rebel forces at the Harlem Heights. He suggested New Rochelle ("having first given the enemy every jealousy for Jersey") as a suitable alternative, but attention instead came to focus on Throg's Neck, apparently at the suggestion of Erskine. Clinton was unimpressed: "If you don't want to attack them you are too near," he advised Howe, "if you do want to attack them you are too far off." But, perhaps feeling that he was disagreeing with everyone else too frequently, Clinton went along with the plan. Once again, he was to lead the advanced troops. Once again, he had fears of suffering a defeat, if the rebels reacted quickly to the British movement and brought enough troops to contest the landing. The stage was set for what Clinton would later describe as "a tweedledum business."

In contrast to the landings on Long Island and Manhattan, where enemy action was the only thing to be feared, the transit to Throg's Neck involved passage through the ominously named "Hell Gate." About 1 mile (1.6 kilometers) long, the stretch of water featured hazardous rocks and a huge whirlpool. At the end of the following century, dynamite would clear many of the obstructions that made the passage of water so dangerous, but in 1776, only the skill of the Royal Navy's sailors and officers, and of Admiral Howe in particular, could prevent a disaster. Clinton's plan to land at Morrisania had envisioned the army marching along Long Island before embarking upon transports, *after* the ships had been taken through Hell Gate. Under the plan to land at Throg's Neck, the ships would be full of troops. Most expected the British would lose several ships, and potentially hundreds of men. In the event, despite a thick fog making the passage even more perilous, on October 12 Lord Howe got all but two of his ships through unscathed. An artillery crew was lost, along with their guns, but that, almost miraculously, was the only loss. Around 8 a.m. Clinton and his men arrived at Throg's Neck and prepared to land.

For the British second-in-command, what followed must have triggered unpleasant memories of his farcical southern expedition. The landing site, as had happened at Charleston, proved to have been poorly chosen. In fact, some observers claimed that had they tried to find the worst possible place to land, the British could not have done better. The piece of land became an island at high tide and rebel troops had removed the planks on the only bridge to the mainland. A party of around 25 riflemen was waiting to welcome the British column when it arrived, and stood there, wondering what to do next. A narrow strip of land that the British might also have used was defended by a rebel emplacement and no further progress could be made. The British troops had landed, but could not move inland, and Clinton's embarrassment was deepened by a stream of instructions from Howe, which Clinton found both unnecessary and condescending. The victim once more of poor reconnaissance, Clinton and his forlorn force waited on Throg's Neck until they could be extricated, six days later. A tweedledum business indeed.

The days wasted at Throg's Neck gave Washington a lifeline. He did not grasp it instantly, but during a conference with his officers on October 16 he took the decision to move the bulk of his army off Manhattan. The American commander was already wrestling with the problem of how to keep his militia engaged. Enlistments were due to expire at the end of the year and although Washington had severe doubts about their quality ("To place any dependence upon militia is assuredly resting upon a broken staff"), he simply could not manage without their numbers to bulk up his army. The only thing worse than having thousands of militia troops, it seems, was not having them.

Howe's intentions had remained a mystery right up until the landing at Throg's Neck. Washington had feared that Philadelphia might be a target, or even the southern colonies. Revealingly, Washington reckoned that just 2,000 redcoats could safely hold New York, which raises questions about Howe's caution. The Hudson River remained open, despite the rebels' strenuous efforts to close it through the sinking of ships and laying of chevaux de frise. On October 9, in the latest demonstration of the futility of trying to keep the Royal Navy from operating on the river, warships again sailed past Fort Washington with impunity, the sunken obstructions doing nothing to impede their progress. Washington's army was clearly within the jaws of a trap, but the jaws were closing with imperceptible speed. On October 13, a decision had to be made. Washington's orderly book recorded that, "It being necessary since the late movement of the enemy [to Throg's Neck] to form some plan, the General proposes a meeting of his General Officers this day, at twelve o'clock, at or near King's Bridge." Three days later, the council of war was nearly unanimous (only Brigadier General James Clinton dissented) in the need to abandon Manhattan. The British position at Throg's Neck was not considered dangerous ("The grounds … are strong and defensible, being full of stone fences, both along the road and across the adjacent fields, which will render it difficult for artillery, or indeed a large body of foot to advance in any regular order…"), but if the British did break out, or if they shifted their troops to a new position, the main army on Manhattan could find itself trapped. Surprisingly, Fort Washington was to be held. The fort had already proved inadequate to stop British shipping from sailing up the Hudson River and could not hope to withstand a siege or serious assault with the reduced number of men that were to be left as a garrison. Not for the first time, however, a strongpoint was considered impregnable. It would not take long for Howe to prove otherwise.

Two days after the Americans held their council of war, Howe was able to extricate his men from their embarrassing position at Throg's Neck. Pell's Point was a more promising landing spot, but the Americans were ready to defend it in force, with around 750 men, under Colonel John Glover, in prepared defenses. Glover hoped to buy time for the bulk of the army to relocate to White Plains, where a stand was planned. Lord Stirling was already leading a brigade to the area to secure the ground, held at the moment by just a few hundred militia. If the redcoats could beat Washington's army to the battleground, it might prove decisive. Howe, with his unerring ability to fail to recognize a race, even when he was taking part in it, would probably have struggled to match Washington's pace, but in any event Clinton found it difficult to advance from Pell's Point as Glover's men staged a highly effective delaying action.

Clinton had detached Cornwallis, with the light infantry, grenadiers, and Hessian jägers, to cover the right flank of the advancing British column. Around 4,000 troops had been landed at Pell's Point, with more flowing in throughout the morning, but

Glover's men managed to delay their advance for a precious day, inflicting significant casualties; estimates ranged from 200 to a scarcely credible 800. No more credible was Clinton's estimation of the number of men opposing him, which he put at 14,000. Glover's men could have received no higher praise.

The following day, after the arrival of Howe, the British took possession of New Rochelle, which must have struck Clinton as ironic. It was the point he had long suggested as a suitable landing spot and could have been taken days earlier, putting Washington in a far more precarious position. Still, Howe was ready to move out on October 25 and Clinton moved forward to scout out the situation at White Plains. The race, which Howe had never shown appetite for, nor even awareness of, had been lost. Washington's army was in position on a ridge of high ground, but there was a silver lining. The new American position was far less formidable than the one at the Harlem Heights, and Washington was once more offering battle. This time, Howe was ready to accept.

EIGHT

The Hessians

"On the 28th of October the engagement at White-Plains took place. But it has been asserted, that, by my not attacking the lines on the day of action, I lost an opportunity of destroying the rebel army ... Sir, an assault upon the enemy's right, which was opposed to the *Hessian* troops, *was* intended. The committee must give me credit when I assure them, that I have political reasons, and no other, for declining to explain why that assault was not made."

Howe's narrative, April 22, 1779

*H*OWE'S FAILURE TO LAUNCH *a full-scale attack at White Plains was one of the vital points of his command, and one for which he had received the most vociferous criticism. Members of the House of Commons may have inched further forward on their seats as Howe came to this point. He had not managed to deal satisfactorily with any of the other debating points covered so far; failure to tackle the White Plains controversy head-on might bring an end to the patience of the House.*

Howe, finally, did not disappoint. The delivery of his speech, with its emphasis on the key words "Hessian" and "was," made it clear what had happened. To scotch any remaining uncertainty, Howe added that further details on the affair would "in no degree affect my *honour or* my *conduct." Nobody listening could be in any doubt. The Hessians had refused to go into battle. Howe's "political reasons" were nothing more than an unwillingness to criticize men who were still fighting alongside British troops in North America. Howe had played his ace well, managing to clearly convey his meaning without inelegantly*

139

apportioning blame. The general, beloved of his army, was refusing to openly criticize any part of it, even foreigners. He was being generous. He was being noble. And he was lying through his teeth.

The participation of Hessian troops in the war had been controversial from the start. It was a time-honored practice, but many colonists were repelled by the idea that their mother country would bring German hirelings across the ocean to fight them. The reputation of the Hessians, in particular their reputed fondness for relying on their bayonets, resulted in them being viewed as objects of dread. In much the same way as the redcoats were in awe of the legendary American riflemen, rebel soldiers dreaded encountering the mustachioed, blue-coated soldiers from states including Hesse-Cassel and Brunswick. For Britain, there had been little option but to resort to hiring troops. Recruitment was never going to provide enough men and in any case, new recruits would take time to be trained. The Hessians may not have been the first choice, but they were experienced soldiers and could be relied upon to do their job.

There was no doubt that the soldiers who were provided would be effective, but Howe had revealed from the start that he was concerned about the officers who would command them. In a quite remarkable letter to Germain in April 1776, he had suggested that a bonus could be offered to the Hessian officers, which would be dependent on them receiving a favorable report from Howe. It may well have been considered insulting by the professional officers concerned, but Germain smoothed things over by offering reassurances that the officers supplied would be of a high quality. For the most part, that turned out to be so, but it was not the case in the most important instance of all, the Hessian commander-in-chief, General von Heister. Howe and von Heister disliked each other from the moment the elderly German officer stepped ashore on Staten Island. At the age of 69, he was "a stiff and completely militarily minded general" according to the Hessian liaison officer

Friedrich von Muenchhausen. This was a poor match for Howe's easy-going, informal nature; the two men were never going to bond over a late-night game of cards and a bottle of claret. If they had tried it would have been a strange affair, since they shared no common language.

Von Heister also displeased Howe by insisting his men needed time to recover from their long journey to Britain and then across the Atlantic. Having previously had no difficulty in finding reasons to delay opening his campaign, Howe was suddenly affronted by being offered another and he rather huffily prepared to press ahead without the Hessian contingent that he had waited so long for. There had been nothing to complain about in the Hessians' conduct during the Battle of Long Island, but further friction between the two commanders was not long in coming. Wanting the rebel lines at Brooklyn to be razed, Howe had asked the Hessian troops to do the work. Perhaps feeling that his men were being treated as workhorses, von Heister had insisted they should receive extra pay for the manual labor. Howe instead had put British troops to work and made another mark on von Heister's card.

Although disliking the commanding officer, Howe was delighted with the small contingent of Hessian jägers present in the first wave. These were exactly the sort of troops Howe dreamed of turning his own light infantry into. Referred to as "chasseurs" or "greencoats" by the British, they instantly took their place in the vanguard of the army, alongside the British lights and grenadiers, and when Howe made his first tentative request for reinforcements, he had asked for 800 more jägers.

Off the battlefield, there were problems. Howe was never able to get a grip on looting and pillaging and the Hessians were among the worst offenders, sometimes appearing to see America as a personal larder, to be plundered at will. "They slaughter milch cows for meat," reported Loftus Cliffe, "depriving everyone of milk and butter. All houses are 'damned rebel houses,' especially if there is a good cellar." Despite such depredations, and their fearsome reputation, the Hessians gradually earned a more favorable reputation among the Americans and many prisoners declared they received better treatment from the Hessians than from the British.

As Howe's army prepared to move to confront Washington at White Plains, the second wave of Hessians finally arrived, nearly 4,000 strong, including a 125-man company of jägers. Howe was pleased to get the extra troops and delighted to have more jägers at his disposal. The commanding officer of this corps was the 60-year-old Lieutenant General Wilhelm von Knyphausen. Howe may have suppressed a groan when he saw that another old man had been sent out to him, but von Knyphausen was to prove a far more effective and energetic commander than von Heister. Also stepping off the transports after the arduous journey was a jäger captain, Johann Ewald. A compact man with a soldierly posture, he was a stickler for protocol but in no way an unthinking martinet. He was one of the most imaginative soldiers in America at the time, with the priceless ability to size up the lie of the land quickly and grasp which ground could be held and which attacked. Just 32 years of age when he joined Howe's army, he had already been a soldier for half his life and had fought in the Seven Years War. His most serious injury, however, had come during a drunken brawl with friends in which he lost his left eye and took over a year to recover fully. He was to become a firm favorite of every British officer he served under, including Howe, who reminisced with the young German officer about his own days as a light infantry commander in the previous war.

The crossing from Britain had been an ordeal (fresh provisions had been exhausted almost a month earlier and scurvy had broken out) and the bemused Hessians had then encountered the eerily quiet streets of New York. With a quarter of the houses destroyed by the fire and many others deserted and ransacked, it was a ghost town and the men were happy to be transported up the East River on October 22, to join the main army. The following day, Howe and Ewald met for the first time. Seeing something of himself in the German captain, Howe complimented Ewald on the appearance of his men and put him to work straight away.

Ordered to scout out the rebel positions, Ewald and his men joined with the 1st Jäger Company and advanced. Ewald declined the invitation to mix his troops with the more seasoned troops of the other company, declaring that he needed to get to know his men. He was given the perfect opportunity within minutes, as heavy firing broke out on his left flank. Ewald's company had stumbled into an engagement with several battalions of Americans and required rescuing by British light infantry. It was an inauspicious start, costing the lives of six of his men, and Ewald received a sharp telling off from von Heister once back at camp. Partly out of his personal dislike of von Heister and partly due to his instinctive respect for Ewald, Howe took the trouble to reassure the Hessian captain and commended the bravery of the jägers in general orders the following day, referring to their "spirited behaviour."

Ewald quickly proved himself to be a man of action and relished the opportunity to put his theories on partisan warfare ("which I had acquired through much reading") to the test. On October 26 he learned of a large enemy supply depot and suggested an operation to capture it. With the support of a light infantry battalion and the 17th Light Dragoons, the depot was captured, earning Ewald another commendation from Howe. The Hessians were therefore very much on the credit side of Howe's ledger as he prepared to advance upon the rebel lines at White Plains.

Henry Clinton, as ever, was full of ideas. He suggested to Howe that he should pretend to withdraw his army back to New Rochelle, threaten an attack in a different direction, and then suddenly swing back to attack Washington at White Plains. Howe had already shown his lack of appetite for such shenanigans and Clinton should not have been surprised at being ordered instead to advance on White Plains on the morning of October 27 and make a full report on the strength of the rebel position. His report was uncharacteristically cautious: Clinton could not recommend an assault on the Americans, believing their flanks to be secure and suspecting that a clear route of retreat was available to them if pressed. Despite this, Howe decided to attack the following day.

Clinton's relationship with Howe was by this point under intense stress. Not only was his advice consistently disregarded, there is every reason to believe that Clinton had recently received two very worrying letters from London, which raked up the details of the embarrassing southern expedition all over again. Germain had written to Clinton on August 24, explaining how he was "extremely disappointed and mortified to learn by your letter of the 8th of July that you were still in the South." Three days later, Clinton's secretary, Richard Reeve, who had been dispatched to London to argue his case over the shambolic operation at Charleston, had sent a very gloomy report. Reeve had met with Lords North and Germain as well as General Harvey. Germain, according to Reeve, was "a good deal dissatisfied at your going to the southward," while Harvey "expressed regret that Clinton had gone to South Carolina in the first place." It is not possible to be certain when these letters reached Clinton, but communications from Germain to Howe, written at the same time, reached America on October 23. It is feasible, indeed likely, that as the Battle of White Plains unfolded, Clinton was fuming once more over the sorry affair at Charleston.

Unhappy over the decision to attack at White Plains in the first place, Clinton suggested that if it must go ahead, it might be best to advance in two columns, offering to command one of them. This Howe could agree to, and Clinton was given command of the right column, with von Heister commanding on the left. Von Heister encountered the enemy first. Once Washington saw the British move, he sent 1,000 men to slow the advance of von Heister's column. The regular stone walls in the area made ideal defensive positions, and the rebels were able to fire from cover on the advancing column, made up of Ewald's jägers, a battalion of light infantry, two English brigades, and two Hessian regiments, as well as part of the 17th Light Dragoons. The column numbered around 6,000 men and was too strong to be delayed for long by the rebel skirmishers, who steadily withdrew, taking up a position with more American defenders on top of Chatterton Hill, on the extreme right of the American line. Clinton had declared the American flanks to be secure, but Chatterton Hill was exposed and vulnerable. Separated from the rest of the American line by the Bronx River, it could not easily be supported. Howe decided to concentrate his initial efforts there.

On the right, Clinton was making slow progress. Believing that the rebels would withdraw from their position as soon as they saw him, he attempted to get around their flank without being discovered. From the left, Ewald watched his slow progress with puzzlement; "... why he [Clinton] did not move forward and resolutely attack the enemy is a riddle to me," he recorded in his diary, "for he had no more difficulties to overcome than the left flank had." Howe was unconcerned, believing that his first job was to clear the rebels from Chatterton Hill. With this in mind, he spoke to von Heister. What happened next is not clear. Without a common language the men could not speak directly to each other and von Heister would later complain that he often received orders written in English that he could not understand. The absence of a liaison officer to facilitate communication between the generals was a startling omission, one that was not put right until the following month, when von Muenchhausen was appointed to the critical role. On Chatterton Hill, close to 2,000 rebel soldiers waited, comprised of a mixture of steady troops and nervous militia, while the British and Hessian generals talked. In a deleted section of his narrative, Howe detailed what happened next. "The attack being intended upon the enemy's right which was opposite to the Hessian troops," he wrote, "I purposed the attack to General Heister whose consent I could not obtain and on that account it was deferred." Howe's words were ambiguous. Had he been unable to make von Heister understand what was required of him, or had there been a more definitive refusal on the part of the German commander? A point of the finger at von Heister followed by a gesture toward Chatterton Hill ought to have been enough to get the general idea across, and the draft of Howe's narrative contains a further intriguing hint that von Heister had been uncooperative rather than uncomprehending. "I purposed the attack to General Heister," he had started, "who would not..." But Howe crossed this out and substituted the far milder "whose consent I could not obtain." Still, there was little room for doubt. "I mentioned General Heister's dissent to General Clinton," Howe continued, "and my intention of making it [the attack] with the British under his direction."

After his abortive conference with von Heister, then, Howe had traipsed across the battlefield to find Clinton and ask him to lead the assault. This, clearly, was the event alluded to in Howe's speech. He had ultimately decided to omit the explicit passage detailing von Heister's "dissent," confident that he could get his point across perfectly well without it, but the speech declared that this was the reason why the American lines had not been attacked. It could not have been, since the refusal of von Heister to lead his men against the hill only delayed the assault.

In fact, by the time Howe and Clinton returned from the right flank, the attack on Chatterton Hill was under way. The British had displayed indiscipline before, on Breed's Hill, before the rebel lines at Brooklyn and on the Harlem Heights. Here they displayed it again, commencing the attack without orders from their commanding officer. Once more, the indiscipline proved costly. Four British regiments, the 28th, the 35th, the 5th, and the 49th, crossed the Bronx to storm Chatterton Hill, but their initial advance was repulsed with heavy loss. Clinton, watching the affair unfold in the company of both Howe and Cornwallis, blamed the commanding officer, who fired his musket at the Americans while climbing the hill and then stopped to reload, robbing (in Clinton's opinion) the advance of its momentum. Whatever the reason for the repulse, the British quickly returned and Hessian units became involved as well, whether under orders from von Heister or out of shame at being left on the sidelines. British troops jeered as their German comrades struggled to cross the Bronx (having picked an unfortunately deep point for their crossing, one of their color-bearers was nearly swept away), but if their progress was slow, it was also dogged. Colonel Rall in particular played an important role in the fighting, attacking the Americans in their flank and helping to drive them from the hill. The rebel soldiers, featuring once more men of the Delaware and Maryland regiments, withdrew to the main American lines. Losses were fairly even, with British casualties numbering around 200 and the Americans losing around 175. It was a very steep price to pay for the occupation of a hill.

The blaming of the Hessians demands further investigation. Unless Howe had simply forgotten the details of the day by the time he came to prepare his narrative, he must have been aware that he was doing the German troops a great disservice. Yes, von Heister had clearly baulked at the idea of leading the attack on Chatterton Hill, but the attack had gone ahead anyway and Hessian troops had eventually played an important part in it. Howe was also bypassing the real controversy, which swirled around the fact that, having taken possession of the hill, no further attempt was made to assault the rebel lines. This was the attack that did not happen, and this was the decision for which Howe's critics were demanding an explanation. The Hessians made for convenient scapegoats, but in reality Howe had no reason to resort to such underhand methods. There had actually been solid reasons why a further assault had not been made.

Following the capture of Chatterton Hill, Howe had considered his options for the remainder of the day, before deciding to launch a full assault the following morning. The rebels put the time to good use, strengthening their defenses to the extent that Howe believed reinforcements were needed if he was to tackle them. Percy was called up and duly arrived, on October 30, with men from the New York garrison. The attack was scheduled for the next day and Howe once again asked Clinton for his opinion. Clinton's response was surprising to say the least. He was opposed to the attack and provided an exhaustive list of reasons to support his position, including, "… the strength of post, the difficulty of approach, the little protection from cannon, little chance of making a blow of consequence, the risk after a tolerable good campaign of finishing it by a cheque, the moral certainty of a junction with Burgoyne next year." Clinton was not one for throwing compliments around, and Howe should have been well pleased with being credited with mounting a "tolerable good campaign," but grudging praise aside, it was clear that Clinton had little appetite for anyone's ideas but his own. He suggested that the British might limit their ambitions to the taking of another hill on the American flank in an attempt to force them from their lines.

Howe had made maneuvering Washington out of prepared defenses into his personal hobby, but this time he wanted more. To Clinton's surprise, the commander-in-chief was determined to press on with his full-scale assault. Not even heavy rain could deter him and at 2 a.m. on the morning of October 31 he ordered the reluctant Clinton forward. It was too late. The Americans had withdrawn from their lines and taken up an even stronger position about an hour's march away, at North Castle Heights. For two days Howe watched the American lines as the worsening weather hinted at the end of the campaigning season—frost now covered the ground in the mornings. Criticized as an overly cautious commander, Howe had fully intended to attack Washington at White Plains, but had delayed pulling the trigger for too long. On November 3, he turned his army away and marched back toward Manhattan. The Battle of White Plains had never properly started, but it was to claim one more casualty. Commanding the rearguard during the withdrawal, Clinton changed the order of march only to be informed by one of Howe's aides-de-camp that he was to make no deviation from his orders. Seeing this as a petty interjection, Clinton lost his temper and blurted out that he would rather be in a detached command of just three companies than serve directly underneath Howe. The outburst brought into the open Clinton's disdain for his commanding officer, and if Howe heard about it, then the two men might no longer be able to work together. Unfortunately for Clinton, he had been heard by Cornwallis.

Howe had been frustrated at White Plains, and he declared to Germain that the Americans were proving to be unwilling to stand and fight. This was plainly not true, but Howe must have been aware that he was repeatedly failing to deliver the knockout blow he had talked about so freely in the build-up to the campaign. The change in the weather suggested that time was running out to finish the job in one campaign, and the taking of Rhode Island, long considered, may well have been the only move remaining for Howe before going into winter quarters. It would have made for a fairly anticlimactic end to the campaign, but a serious mistake by the Americans was about to hand him something much bigger. In fact, it was to give him his greatest success of the war.

The Americans left behind at the Harlem Heights were now completely isolated and the only sensible course of action would have been to evacuate them as quickly as possible across the Hudson. On the other side of the river, Fort Lee was by now complete and offered an obvious stronghold for the men to move to. At precisely the wrong moment, the American leadership decided to indulge in a game of passing the buck. Nathanael Greene, based at Fort Lee, asked Washington what he thought should be done. The number of men available to him fell between two stools: "If we attempt to hold the ground, the garrison must be reinforced," he reasoned, "but if the garrison is to be drawn into Fort Washington, and we only keep that, the number of troops on the island is too large." Washington, making one of his biggest blunders, insisted that Greene must make the decision since he was the man on the spot. Washington also stressed the importance of holding Fort Washington to prevent British shipping from sailing up the Hudson, a dream that had already been conclusively dispelled. There were nearly 3,000 men still on Manhattan Island, and time was running out to extricate them.

Washington was not oblivious to the danger. After Howe's army turned back toward New York, he claimed to be unsure what the British commander had in mind. He did not believe the campaign was over, but was most fearful of a movement toward Jersey. News of British preparations for the capture of Rhode Island were dismissed by the American general as misinformation; Washington believed an expedition to the southern colonies was far more likely. As for Fort Washington, he believed the enemy would "invest it immediately," but he made no comment of taking any action to counter this or to remove the men. Washington had an instinctive understanding that Howe would be feeling the pressure to achieve something more before the end of the year ("He must attempt something on account of his reputation; for what has he done as yet with his great army?"), but seemed to miss the point that the capture of nearly 3,000 men at Fort Washington would fit the bill nicely. Again, the specter of the British rampaging through Jersey was more troubling. In a letter to William Livingston, governor of Jersey, Washington advised him to prepare his militia and to pursue a scorched-earth policy; any forage that could not be safely removed was to be destroyed to prevent it from falling into the hands of the British. To help motivate Livingston, Washington painted an apocalyptic picture of the progress of the British troops: "They have treated all here without discrimination," he warned. "The distinction of Whig and Tory has been lost in one general scene of ravage and desolation."

As had happened repeatedly, Washington appears to have awakened only slowly to dangers that ought to have been obvious. By November 8 he was feeling his way toward an order to abandon Fort Washington, citing the failure of the fort to impede British shipping on the Hudson. "If we cannot prevent Vessels from passing up," he wrote to Greene, "and the enemy are possessed of the surrounding country, what valuable Purpose can it answer to hold a Post, from which the expected Benefit cannot be had?" Rather than taking this line of reasoning to its obvious conclusion, however, Washington backed away at the last moment. "I am therefore inclined to think," he continued, "that it will not be prudent to hazard the Men and Stores at Mount Washington; but, as you are on the spot, leave it to you to give such orders, as to evacuating Mount Washington, as you may judge best." It was a shocking abrogation of responsibility, but everything Washington had seen of Howe up to that point would have convinced him that a direct assault was the last thing on the

British general's mind. An attempted siege was by far the most likely course of action.

Howe would need no further invitation. General von Knyphausen, with six battalions of Hessians, had been dispatched to Kingsbridge on October 28 and had been encamped on Manhattan since November 2. By November 12, British forces were concentrating in the area. Howe explained his decision to attack the fort to Germain, explaining how it "kept the enemy in command of the navigation of the North River." It did no such thing, and Howe also mentioned that it was covered by strong ground and "exceeding difficult of access." In short, it was just the sort of position that had deterred him on several occasions, and was a prime candidate for the sort of siege he had tried to implement at Brooklyn. Although hailed by some as impregnable, the fort was actually vulnerable, having no source of fresh water within its walls. A brief siege would see the cramped garrison surrender with little or no loss to the British.

Instead, Howe planned an ambitious assault. Tellingly, he originally intended it to be a Hessian-only affair, although British troops were later incorporated into the plan. Evidently feeling that the Germans needed to shoulder more of the burden, Howe was perhaps proving a point as much as anything else. Von Heister, whose stock with Howe was at an all-time low, was not involved; the Hessian troops were to be led by von Knyphausen. The addition of British troops also might have opened the door to Clinton's involvement. He had led the way on Long Island, at Kip's Bay, and at Throg's Neck, and Howe had turned to him when von Heister had refused to charge at White Plains. At Fort Washington, however, there was no place for Clinton, suggesting that Howe might already have heard about his petulant outburst during the retreat from White Plains. Clinton had been given command of the planned descent on Rhode Island, but there was time enough for him to take part in the attack on Fort Washington, had Howe wished it.

Nathanael Greene was unconcerned in the face of the obvious preparations and believed the fort could stall the British for a considerable amount of time. He accepted that it could not prevent British shipping from moving along the Hudson, but argued, "I cannot conceive the garrison to be in any great danger," adding that "the men can be brought off at any time." The commander at Fort Washington, Colonel Robert Magaw, was confident that he could hold out until the end of the year, but what that would actually achieve was not specified. Washington himself arrived on the scene, although his primary purpose was to get troops into Jersey to counter the anticipated move there. He and Greene consulted on the situation on November 14, but no decision was made. Howe gave the Americans one last chance to see sense, on November 15. He also gave Magaw the thing longed for by every garrison commander: the opportunity to declare that he would defend his post "to the very last extremity." Greene and General Putnam, who had been in Fort Washington at the time, were making their way across the Hudson when they met their commander-in-chief, mid-river, on his way to inspect the garrison. Assured by Putnam and Greene that the men were in good order and ready for the coming fight, Washington turned back. The following day, the attack began.

Howe was sending men against the same fortifications that he had declared untouchable a matter of weeks ago, but now they were held by a thinly stretched garrison of fewer than 3,000 men. The plan was to drive the Americans from their outer works into Fort Washington itself, and, to prevent them from concentrating their forces to resist, three sections of the defenses would be attacked at the same time. Johann Ewald, who had been asked to reconnoiter the defenses, had declared them to be very formidable, noting that American preparations had been thorough. Trees had been felled to give a clear field of fire, while the naturally difficult terrain had been enhanced with defensive works, including abbatis. Two of the attacking columns moved from the north, von Knyphausen leading a column of Hessian troops, with Cornwallis and Brigadier General Edward Mathew commanding light infantry, the Guards, grenadiers, and the 33rd Regiment. From the south, Percy headed a mixture of British and Hessian regiments. As if to underline the futility of holding the fort in the first place, HMS *Pearl* sat brazenly on the Hudson to provide fire support. Ewald reported that it took more than four hours for von Knyphausen's column to dislodge American defenders from their strong positions (the British grenadier officer John Peebles recorded that they were "slow but Steady troops"), but Cornwallis and Percy made much swifter progress. Cornwallis landed his light infantry in 30 flat-bottomed boats and quickly took possession of a defended hill, forcing the rebels back toward the fort. Percy's advance from the south was so rapid that Howe saw an opportunity to cut off the rebels' retreat. Sending in the 42nd Regiment by boat, they were able to intercept many of the retreating Americans, capturing 170 of them.

Howe would later write with evident pride of the performance of his men, particularly his beloved light infantry, who had advanced "up a very steep uneven mountain with their usual activity." It was Colonel Rall, who had earlier distinguished himself at White Plains, who had the honor of reaching Fort Washington first. Advancing to within 100 yards (90 meters), while retreating Americans crammed into the fort, he demanded their surrender. Forgetting his bold claims of the previous day, Magaw was obliged to accept. Close to 3,000 prisoners were taken, with around 150 killed or wounded. Howe did not mention his own losses in his report to Germain. These were considerable, with 78 men killed and 374 wounded. Howe, in fact, had lost more men in taking an isolated fort than he had lost in the Battle of Long Island.

Washington had a tricky job to do. The loss of the garrison at Fort Washington was the most severe blow yet endured by the American army and required explaining. His letter to Congress on the day of the action came uncomfortably close to an attempt to pin the blame on others. Assuring Congress that he had left the decision to Greene, Washington made it clear that it had been Greene's decision to stand and fight. Washington's account of the battle included the remarkable assertion that he had sent a note to Colonel Magaw after the British and Hessian forces had pushed his men back into the fort itself, ordering the American commander to hold firm. Washington had then planned to withdraw the garrison on the night of November 16. Perhaps Washington believed he could pull off another night-time evacuation, but his assessment of the situation was badly misjudged. The American losses extended to more than just men, since large amounts of supplies and ammunition also fell into the hands of the British. "I am wearied almost to death with the retrograde motion of things," he confided to his brother, "and I solemnly protest, that a pecuniary award of twenty thousand pounds a year would not induce me to undergo what I do." Greene was also deeply disturbed by the loss of Fort Washington and all too aware that the bulk of the blame might fall on him. He declared himself "mad, vexed, sick and sorry" and begged for news of how the defeat was being reported.

Howe's position was obviously more comfortable, but he had his issues to deal with as well. Although the Hessians had gone a long way to recovering the confidence of their commander-in-chief, and the second wave had brought the more aggressive von Knyphausen as well as the mercurial Ewald, there was still the problem of von Heister. He and Howe were barely on speaking terms (not that they could understand each other anyway). The belated appointment of a liaison officer to smooth dealings between the two men came too late to repair their relationship. Von Muenchhausen was an effective aide-de-camp and might have brought Howe and von Heister closer together (von Heister spoke German and French, Howe English only, while von Muenchhausen was fluent in all three) if there had been any will on the part of the two generals.

The situation with Clinton might still have been rescued. Howe certainly attempted to keep their dealings on a professional footing, but Clinton was unreceptive. The second-in-command was becoming consumed by resentment over the southern expedition fasco and Howe's role in it. The two men would not work together again and Howe therefore found himself shorn of the support of his two most important subordinates. There were other men to lean on, notably Cornwallis, and so long as he retained the confidence of the politicians at home he had little to be seriously concerned by. Personal animosities were inevitable under the stress of a campaign, but Howe could afford to be pragmatic. He had every reason to believe that he was moving steadily toward a successful conclusion to the war.

That impression was reinforced four days after the fall of Fort Washington. The Americans had failed to remove stores from the white elephant that was Fort Lee, on the New Jersey side of the Hudson. Ineffective when operating in conjunction with Fort Washington, it was entirely purposeless now, but massive quantities of supplies and ordnance were still there when Cornwallis landed troops 7 miles (11 kilometers) above the fort, on the morning of November 20. It was not an easy matter to drag guns up what Howe described as the "narrow rocky road, for near half a mile, to the top of a precipice," but capturing the fort itself proved more straightforward. The garrison evacuated quickly upon the approach of the British (several inebriated men were left behind) and the fort changed hands without a shot being fired. It could hardly have been a surprise to the Americans that Fort Lee would be the next target in the slow but remorseless advance of the redcoats, but kettles were still warming above fires as the British took possession and Cornwallis spent that night camped outside the fort, "making use of the enemy's tents." More importantly, between Forts Washington and Lee the rebels had lost 146 cannon, close to 3,000 muskets and around 400,000 cartridges.

The invasion of New Jersey had begun, but Germain would not read about it until the end of the year. Howe did not bother to inform the American Secretary of events following the stalemate at the Harlem Heights until November 30 and the letter did not reach London until December 29. It would have made for a pleasant late Christmas present, but Germain would have been justified in wondering why Howe had taken so long to inform him that the campaign was still alive and kicking; it was two months since he had last written. The general was gracious enough to offer an apology ("The service in which I have been employed ... with advice to the reduction of New York, would not allow of an earlier time to send an account to your Lordship of the progress made from that period."), and in any event, the contents of the letter, detailing the landing at Kip's Bay, the capture of New York, the fighting near the Harlem Heights, the Battle of White Plains, and the capturing of Forts Washington and Lee, were so pleasing to Germain that he could afford to overlook Howe's tardiness in writing. The general had obviously been busy and, condensed into a single letter, the events of the campaign took on a rather dashing air. Howe finished by reporting that Cornwallis was in hot pursuit of Washington through New Jersey and that all seemed well with the army. Clinton was singled out for praise, as were the Hessians. "The Hessian troops, under the command of Lieutenant Generals Heister and Knyphausen," Howe wrote, "have also exhibited every good disposition to promote his majesty's interests, and justly merit my acknowledgement of their services."

There was no sign here that Howe believed they had in any way sabotaged his plans at White Plains, or in any way retarded the progress of his campaign. But then, the campaign was not yet over.

NINE

The Pursuit

"My publick letter of the 30ᵗʰ of November relates the
further proceedings of the army, until Lord Cornwallis
arrived at Brunswick in the Jerseys ... I need not
trouble the committee with other particulars in that
period..."

Howe's narrative, April 22, 1779

*T*HE COMMITTEE MIGHT WELL *have welcomed the opportunity
to be troubled with other particulars of that period, because
once more Howe had seemed on the verge of eliminating a corps of
Washington's army and capturing the great man himself, only to let him
slip away. There were big questions to be answered here, but Howe was
determined to sidestep them. Most pressing of all, why had the pursuit of
Washington been called off just as it appeared it might catch him? Howe
had already shown himself unwilling to take advice from an underling,
repeatedly ignoring sound options proposed by Clinton. Following the
fall of the forts guarding the Hudson, his actions suggested that he also
felt uncomfortable leaving subordinates in charge of detached corps
when they might use those corps aggressively. Tasked with pursuing
Washington's men following their hasty withdrawal from Fort Lee,
Cornwallis had surprised everyone with the manner in which he had
tackled the job. The campaign up to that point had been characterized by
the painfully deliberate movements of Howe, which had repeatedly given
Washington time to digest unpalatable truths and take the necessary
decisions to extricate his men from danger. Cornwallis did not show the
same courtesy. Where Howe might have been expected to lead a slow,
plodding pursuit of Washington, Cornwallis had taken off like a bat out*

of hell. Washington, for the first time in the campaign, found himself running for his life.

"On the 24th [of November], the 2nd and 4th brigades of British, and one battalion of the 71st regiment, joined his Lordship [Cornwallis], who, leaving the 2nd brigade at fort Lee, advanced with the main body on the 25th, to the new-bridge. On the enemy retiring from Newark, as his Lordship approached, he took possession of that place on the 28th, and is now following them, retreating toward Brunswick."

Howe's letter of November 30 was a tour de force. It conjured a stirring image for Germain to savor, that of George Washington in full flight from pursuing British soldiers. The possibility of the disintegration of his corps was very real, and although there were other large bodies of rebel troops still in the field elsewhere, the harrying and capture of Washington would have been a severe blow to the revolutionary cause.

Washington, anticipating Howe's move into New Jersey, had split his army after the British had withdrawn from White Plains. It was yet another iteration of his signature error—dividing his force in the presence of a superior enemy—and once more it invited disaster. Joining with Nathanael Greene to bring his corps to around 5,500 men, Washington had left Charles Lee at North Castle Heights with 7,000 and sent William Heath to reinforce the Hudson Highlands with 4,000, in case Howe chose to set the long-anticipated Hudson strategy in motion. In attempting to face up to every possibility, Washington ensured merely that he would be unable to resist the British wherever they chose to strike. Lee was encouraged to hold his ground, and indeed strengthen his defenses, in case the British move on New Jersey should prove to be merely a feint, but Howe had been an obligingly straightforward opponent up to that point and had shown no interest in diversionary actions.

Following the fall of Forts Washington and Lee, Washington had recognized the perilous nature of his position. Not only was his corps too weak to attack the British, it could not even mount serious resistance, and the substantial resources of New Jersey were about to fall into British hands. On November 21, the day after Fort Lee had fallen, he wrote to Lee, ordering him to cross the Hudson and join him with the bulk of his 7,000-strong corps. The American commander's aims were modest. If the residents of New Jersey did not believe that the Continental Army had done all it could to protect them, they might understandably withdraw their support. "It is therefore of the utmost importance," he informed Lee, "that at least an appearance of force should be made, to keep this province in the connexion with the others." Washington foresaw the possibility of the British knocking another colony out of the fight, but doubted whether any effective resistance could be mounted. If New Jersey fell, he believed Pennsylvania might also lose faith in the rebellion; a damaging and potentially fatal domino effect might be set in motion.

Washington was right to suspect that Howe was aiming to knock New Jersey out of the war, but he also had another problem. Lee was maneuvering to take command of the rebel army and was inclined to treat Washington's orders as mere suggestions. He told Heath that he should send 2,000 men to join up with Washington instead, and when Heath pointed out his orders were to secure the Highlands, Lee mocked him for treating the word of the commander-in-chief as unquestionable. "By your mode of reasoning," Lee wrote to Heath, sneeringly, "the General's injunctions are so binding that not a tittle must be broke through for the salvation of the General and the Army." Lee then belittled Heath (referring to him sarcastically as "that great man") in a letter to Washington. Lee's machinations came unstuck when Washington mistakenly opened a letter from him to the Adjutant General Joseph Reed, which hinted at their mutual disrespect of Washington. Rather coolly referring to the contents of this letter, Washington insisted to Lee that it was *his* troops he wanted, and not Heath's. Lee could hardly demur again and started out, though he made sure his progress was as slow as possible—perhaps, if he was slow enough, the British might do the job of removing Washington before he reached him.

Cornwallis had every intention of making Lee's dream come true and the race to catch Washington became hair-raisingly close. His men "cheerfully quitted their tents and heavy baggage as impediments to their march" and hounded the fleeing rebels. On November 28, as the last of Washington's men exited Newark, the first of Cornwallis's entered the town. On December 1, the British corps covered 20 miles (32 kilometers) in a single day, reaching New Brunswick only to find the rebels had left and destroyed the sole bridge across the Raritan. Now, with his men worn out from the pursuit, Cornwallis followed his orders from Howe and halted. Under examination at the Howe inquiry, Cornwallis insisted that his men and horses needed rest and that no immediate advantage could have been gained from pressing on. This was not, however, to be a brief respite. The British remained at New Brunswick until Howe joined them on December 6. The "pursuit" of Washington continued the next day. Rumors were by now circulating that Lee was on his way to reinforce Washington, and that he might look to cut off Cornwallis's communication with New York, but the British were unconcerned. Even so, the pursuit of Washington had undergone a dramatic change of character. "Since General Howe was with the vanguard," von Muenchhausen noted in his diary, "we advanced very slowly." The Americans, grateful for the change of pace, remained tantalizingly close. On December 8 the British reached Trenton and were urged on by the inhabitants, who claimed that Washington's men were even then crossing the Delaware River.

Howe, believing this might be a trap, proceeded cautiously. Gathering some light infantry and jägers, he and Cornwallis (accompanied by three aides, including von Muenchhausen) moved through the town, expecting to find that the Americans had artillery emplacements on the opposite bank of the river. Howe's caution was justified when the anticipated rebel artillery roared out its welcome on the approach of the small British force. The light infantry and jägers retired, having taken several casualties, but

Howe and his staff proceeded to give a perfect demonstration of coolness under fire. Calmly surveying the area, walking their horses up and down while under constant bombardment, the five men, von Muenchhausen reported, remained in range of the rebel guns for an hour. "Wherever we turned the cannonballs hit the ground," he recorded in his diary, presumably after his hands had stopped shaking, "and I can hardly understand, even now, why all five of us were not crushed." Howe was spattered with mud from a near miss, while von Muenchhausen's horse was not so lucky, losing a hind leg. Von Muenchhausen feared he had shared his horse's fate when he felt a sharp pain in his knee at the same time, but it turned out to be only a glancing blow from a stone. Considering the loss of a horse as a sign that their luck was running out, the five men calmly retired, and von Muenchhausen reported that Howe later generously replaced his lost mount with a "superb English horse."

Howe judged a crossing of the Delaware to be too hazardous and the pursuit was called off. There was disgruntlement in the ranks, and Johann Ewald was critical in his journal. Noting how slowly the army had progressed since Howe had joined it, he believed that the only possible reason could have been a desire to allow Washington to get away, and gossip among the soldiers insisted that Cornwallis had orders to that effect. Whatever the real reason behind his latest escape, Washington appeared to be safe for now, but he also appeared to be very much a spent force.

Howe's thoughts on the war had changed. Most historians believe that at this point he altered his strategy, from one of destroying the rebel army to one of fostering support from loyalists by occupying territory. This shift of emphasis certainly occurred, but it was not so much a case of Howe changing his mind about the need to destroy Washington's army, as it was a belief that he could not accomplish it during that campaign. As Howe rode back from the banks of the Delaware the rebel army may have been a small, disorganized rabble, but it was out of his reach. Notions of tackling the army would still be part of his thoughts on the next campaign, but for now he could do no more.

Howe took pains to note, when writing to Germain on the subject of his plans for the following year, that Congress had authorized an army of 50,000 men for the next year. This was a fanciful figure, and the repeated drubbings meted out by the British and Hessian forces over the course of the campaign would make it very difficult to convince so many young men that the cause of liberty was anything other than fatally wounded. Howe would not go so far as to say he needed an army of 50,000 himself (suggesting that a rebel was equal to a redcoat would have been humiliating), but the numbers he did suggest were to prove problematic. In fact, they were to destroy his relationship with Germain.

Just as had been the case with his previous correspondence with Germain, Howe offered the American Secretary a rollercoaster ride. In September, Howe had followed up news of the capture of New York with a declaration that he did not expect to be able to accomplish much else. On November 30, having lifted Germain to dizzying heights with tales of victories and fleeing rebels, he brought him back to earth. Germain would have been musing pleasantly on the image of Cornwallis pursuing the shattered rebel army through New Jersey when he reached for Howe's next letter, received the following day, on December 30. Howe now declared that the troops were about to go into their winter quarters and that it was time to start thinking about the next campaign. Germain may well have scratched his head. The American army was surely beaten, and all that now needed to be done was for Howe to move his men up the Hudson River. Instead, the general detailed his plans for the capture of Rhode Island. This was not an unreasonable target—it had long been desired as a potential winter base for Lord Howe's ships—but it did not advance the Hudson strategy and it seemed to mark a dispersal of effort right at the moment when another concentrated blow might end military resistance altogether.

Cornwallis's presence in New Jersey was now viewed as an occupation rather than a pursuit. Howe had written when

Cornwallis's troops were still in full cry after their quarry, yet he was clearly already seeing it as of secondary importance. "I propose to quarter a large body of troops in that district," Howe wrote, "without which we should be under much difficulty to find covering, forage, and supplies of fresh provisions for the army." Howe then made reference to the failure of the army from Canada to push through to Albany and estimated that it would be almost a full year before it would be able to do so. Howe therefore felt justified in laying out plans for another campaign, and he was not shy about its potential. The war could be finished in one year, "by an extensive and vigorous exertion of his Majesty's arms."

Howe ticked off three elements, encompassing two offensive corps and one acting on the defensive. The first element would see an army of 10,000 move out from the soon-to-be-established base at Rhode Island. This would cut through to Boston and attempt to recapture the city. Rhode Island was to be defended by a further 2,000 men (who could also mount coastal raids in Connecticut), and this theatre was to see Henry Clinton in command. The second element would reinvigorate the Hudson strategy. Another 10,000-strong corps would push up the Hudson, leaving a further 5,000 men in New York to defend the city. Finally, a corps of 8,000 men would sit in New Jersey, "to keep the southern army in check, by giving a jealousy to Philadelphia." Later in the campaign, in the fall, this corps would switch to the offensive and capture Philadelphia. Further operations were mooted in Virginia (in the fall), as well as South Carolina and Georgia (in the winter).

It was in many ways a breathtaking scheme. It was bold and aggressive and it envisioned taking the fight to the rebels. Washington would have to offer resistance if the colonies were not to find themselves choked by men in red coats, but the multiple fronts offered would make it impossible to mount serious resistance to each. Germain would no doubt have been totting up Howe's figures and may have felt a twinge of alarm. Howe's next paragraph would have turned that to outright panic. "... to complete this plan," Howe continued, "not less than ten ships of the line will be absolutely requisite, and a reinforcement of troops, to the amount of 15,000 rank and file…" It was a massive requisition (and Howe wanted an extra battalion of artillery as well), but there was something about Howe's calculations that did not add up. His strategy called for an army of 35,000 men, so why did he need 15,000 reinforcements? His army had been close to 30,000 at the start of the campaign and losses had been modest. There were other elements to question as well. Where had this offensive in New England appeared from? Standard thinking on the subject was that the New England colonies were too strong to tackle head-on; it was the very reason why the Hudson strategy had been embraced in the first place, as it promised to isolate and strangle them indirectly. Now the Hudson strategy was to go ahead at the same time as a major offensive against Boston, which made no sense.

The number of troops to be engaged in defensive duties (2,000 at Rhode Island, 5,000 at New York, and no fewer than 8,000 in New Jersey) was also concerning. Having 15,000 redcoats sitting on their backsides was a luxury that could not be afforded given the difficulties experienced in raising an army for the 1776 campaign. Germain must have wondered why such a large army was needed in the first place. Howe had mentioned rebel plans for an army of 50,000, but he could not have seriously believed this was feasible. Howe acknowledged the fact that military setbacks had disheartened the colonists, but also claimed that rumors of foreign assistance (Benjamin Franklin was known to be in France trying to drum up support for the rebellion) had buoyed spirits. Finally, there was the question of where 15,000 men were to be found. Howe had helpfully suggested the Russians, or another visit to the German states, but the American Secretary knew that the former outlet was closed for business, while the latter was almost out of stock; there was no easy way of finding 15,000 men at such short notice.

Howe's plan had not been formed in isolation. He had consulted with Clinton (as usual) but had discounted his advice (as usual). During a conference, Clinton had admitted to concerns that the rebels might be able to drag the war out and doubted that it would be worth carrying on in that case. Clinton was aware that only through the use of loyalist forces could Britain hope to maintain control of the colonies even if they achieved a military victory. There simply weren't enough regular troops to police the entire country. Howe agreed but, in Clinton's words, he uttered "not a syllable towards effecting it." Clinton was being unfair; the occupation of New Jersey was part of Howe's scheme to encourage loyalist support, and he made this clear during their conference—"We will see what happens in Jersey," he told Clinton, "as we are told there are friends there."

The move to Rhode Island was also a bone of contention. Clinton favored a move southward rather than northward, and believed the capture of Philadelphia would do more harm to the revolutionary cause than finding a winter harbor for the fleet. Just days before heading off to join Cornwallis in New Jersey, Howe scotched any hopes Clinton might have clung to of changing his mind on the matter. The rebels were reported to have evacuated Rhode Island and Clinton was to go there as quickly as possible to take possession. On December 8, the same day that the pursuit of Washington came to an abrupt end at Trenton, Clinton landed his men on Rhode Island without opposition. Howe's second-in-command now wanted to head back to Britain, to fight his corner in the ongoing controversy surrounding the southern expedition, and also to stake his claim to the command of the northern army for the following campaign. Before he left, an aide was dispatched with news of the capture of Rhode Island, and in a private letter to Lord Newcastle, Clinton made his feelings on the affair clear. "The acquisition is thought of so much consequence," he wrote, pointedly, "that Mr. How has directed me to send one of my Aides Camp, Capt. Drummond, to England." The letter suggests his contempt for the move to Rhode Island, as well as including the clearly disrespectful reference to "Mr. How," indicating that Clinton was moving from backbiting and grumbling to open defiance. A private memo, written toward the end of the year, unmasked his true feelings. "I do not esteem the man I serve under," he seethed. "I have born the burden this whole campaign, always command the first attack, always succeed and am never thanked." His absence from Howe's plans at Fort Washington may well have upset Clinton, but one of his suspicions had a ring of truth to it. "Be assured if you ever serve certain men essentially," he noted, "they never forgive it." Clinton may have had a point; his advice to Howe was just too good, which bruised the ego of the commander-in-chief.

Having been rebuffed on so many occasions, Clinton now started to confine his thoughts to personal memos. Perhaps conscious that he might one day be commander-in-chief, or perhaps simply so bursting with ideas that he couldn't restrain himself from making note of them somehow, he started to jot down his ideas. Like Howe, he saw the need for an offensive campaign, but his ideas did not include a defensive corps in New Jersey, or sizable garrisons at New York and Rhode Island. He wanted 10,000 men to operate on the lower Hudson, with a further 6,000 coming south from Canada. A further corps of 10,000 could act on the Connecticut River, with 4,000 engaging in smaller unspecified operations, probably including coastal raids. Clinton's plan called for just 24,000 men (exclusive of the Canadian force) and would not in his opinion require reinforcement. The only alternative, as far as Clinton was concerned, was to "garrison certain points and carry on a war of expedition [raids], if such a war is consistent with the dignity of a great nation." Clinton also showed political awareness when he made a note that more would need to be offered to the rebels in terms of concessions before they might consider a negotiated peace. Removing the precondition of unconditional surrender might not convince Congress to come to the negotiating table, he reasoned, but it might sway public opinion against the armed struggle, an important and subtle consideration. Clinton obviously had very different ideas on the prosecution of the war than Howe, but there was a way out of the awkwardness. Perhaps, if Clinton got his way in London, the two men would not need to serve together in the following campaign.

———

The pursuit of Washington had ended on the banks of the Delaware, but the high point of the campaign had not quite been reached by Howe. He had enjoyed far more than the "tolerable good campaign" grudgingly allowed by Clinton, and he had reason to feel satisfied as he looked forward to a winter of balls, dinners, and other entertainments at New York. Yet there was one element missing—appreciation from home. That changed on December 15, when he received the breathless string of letters from Germain, showering him with lavish compliments and informing him that he had been granted membership of the Order of the Bath. "Sir William Howe" had a nice ring to it, and Germain's praise was so effusive it must have put Howe in the Christmas spirit a few days early. A day later, word had spread to the army, von Muenchhausen noting with satisfaction the honor bestowed upon "our general." Just two days earlier, Charles Lee, making his leisurely progress to join up with Washington, was captured by a party of light dragoons. "The only rebel general whom we had cause to fear," in von Muenchhausen's opinion, was out of the equation.

Uncharacteristically, Howe lost little time in thanking Germain for his generous letters. "The King's most gracious approbation of the behavior of his officers and soldiers, British and Hessian," he wrote on December 18, "is received by them with a sense of gratitude…" Howe went on to make all the right noises, referring self deprecatingly to his "humble endeavours" and his "most grateful feelings for such unmerited goodness" on the part of the King. A more cozy correspondence is hard to imagine. In the highest of spirits, Howe moved himself to write again just two days later, outlining the decision to halt the pursuit of Washington, the occupation of Rhode Island, and the capture of Lee. In hindsight, this letter is remarkable for the number of troublesome elements that Howe unknowingly touched upon.

First, although Clinton had taken Rhode Island, Howe noted that "the season may be found too far advanced for him to proceed to Providence, but, if practical, I am confident the attempt will be made." Second, garrisons had been set up through the western part of New Jersey to protect the loyalist elements of the local population, but Howe admitted, "The chain, I own, is rather too extensive." He had persuaded himself that the risk was acceptable: "... trusting to the almost general submission of the country to the southward of this chain, and to the strength of the corps placed in the advanced posts, I conclude these troops will be in perfect security." Finally, the harrying of Washington's evaporating army had prevented him from destroying supplies as he went, which promised to give Howe all the forage he needed for his horses. In the space of a few pages, Howe had considered three elements that were soon to have serious and entirely unforeseen consequences: the failure to take Providence would finally finish any hope of a reconciliation with Clinton; the "too extensive" chain of posts would prove to be exactly that; and the question of a supply of forage would cost Howe the services of another capable general, Earl Percy. All of these specters danced behind the lines of what, on the face of it, was another letter detailing an unbroken sequence of successes.

Flushed with confidence, Howe took the liberty of tinkering with his plan for the following campaign. The reports of strong loyalist support in New Jersey had already persuaded him to occupy an extensive line of posts to protect the well-disposed among the population and bring the colony back under royal control. Now, he reckoned that neighboring Pennsylvania (home to the rebel capital and the seat of Congress, Philadelphia) was also ready to bend the knee. "The opinion of peoples being much changed in Pennsylvania," Howe wrote to Germain, in a separate letter on December 20, "and their minds, in general, from the late progress of the army, disposed to peace, in which sentiment they would be confirmed, by our getting possession of Philadelphia, I am, from this consideration, fully persuaded, the principal army should act offensively on that side..."

It was a change of direction quite staggering in scale. As if oblivious to the enormity of what he was suggesting, Howe blithely described how the offensive from Rhode Island would need to be postponed until reinforcements arrived. It would now be held by a garrison of just 2,000 men. New York was also getting fewer men under the revised plan, just 4,000 instead of 5,000. Most shocking of all, the 10,000-strong corps to operate on the Hudson was now reduced to a mere 3,000, and it would act defensively, "to cover Jersey, on that side, as well as to facilitate, in some degree, the approach of the army from Canada." If a single church bell had started to ring mournfully when Germain read that line, it would only have been appropriate. Howe was burying the Hudson strategy.

Equally worrying, he was claiming that he had only 19,000 men. What had happened to the rest? Actual deaths in battle had been minimal, perhaps as low as 350. A good proportion of the soldiers injured in battle would have later died, and as a rule of thumb, an 18th-century army might expect to lose eight men off the battlefield for every man lost on it. Camp sicknesses and accidents would take their toll alongside battle wounds, so Howe might have lost a little over 3,000 men in total. To counter this in some measure, loyalist units had been raised. They may not have been as steady as regulars until they got a little experience under their belts, but the so-called provincials were to establish themselves as dependable troops, in much the same way as the American regulars became respectable soldiers as the war progressed.

Howe's revised plan was, of course, only a stopgap, a way of proceeding until the massive reinforcements he had requested could be found, but there was a worrying neglect of the Hudson strategy. Howe spoke of reinstating the offensive on Boston when reinforcements arrived, but made no mention of allocating troops to any offensive actions on the Hudson (he again specified that he was not expecting the northern army to penetrate to Albany before the middle of September). In a disconcerting paragraph, he then asked Germain what he thought should be done: "I request your Lordship to point out any general plans that may be thought most adviseable," he wrote, "both with respect to the present strength of this army, and on the event of reinforcements..." There was an easy answer to this: the Hudson strategy. It was what the entire British war effort to that point had been based upon, and it was the strategy that the army operating from Canada was to follow on the next campaign.

Howe's performance to this point, although steady and not without its triumphs, had not been as rapid as hoped and he had yet to show any commitment to moving troops up the Hudson. He may well have found himself the target for criticism rather than knighthoods, were it not for the fact that the northern army, under Carleton, had made even less progress. Germain had received a poisonous letter from Lieutenant Colonel Gabriel Christie detailing the many failings of Carleton and concluding that "he is totally unfit for such a command, and must ruin his Majesty's affairs and those of England either in a civil or military capacity." The letter, remarkably frank as it was, was no doubt colored by a personal falling-out between Christie and Carleton, but there were indeed faults to be found with the way Carleton had conducted the campaign.

Carleton's position in the north had in some ways mirrored that of Howe in the south. Like Howe, he was a cautious general, and like Howe he had an energetic second-in-command to deal with. Where Howe batted off Clinton's importunate counseling, Carleton had to deal with that of Burgoyne, a flamboyant, colorful figure who favored a more vigorous approach to the campaign. Carleton had done well in first resisting the determined American invasion of Canada, at the end of 1775, and then pushing the rebels back at the start of the 1776 campaign. The proposed move down the Hudson, however, had stalled. Carleton took Crown Point on November 3 but considered an assault on the formidable Fort Ticonderoga, just 15 miles (24 kilometers) further on, to be too risky at so late a time in the year. Ticonderoga would have made a fine staging post for the opening of the 1777 campaign, and Carleton compounded his error by also abandoning Crown Point. "His not proceeding to look at Tycondergoga," Christie ranted to Germain, "... is beyond all human comprehension."

Lord North took a more forgiving view of Carleton's slow progress during the campaign when writing to the King. In words that might have described Howe, Lord North wrote: "In the manner in which he has proceeded, although he has been slow, I dare say he is perfectly sure, & we may be satisfied that no misfortune is likely to happen." Carleton received a knighthood based on his defense of Quebec, but by the end of the year the tide of opinion was turning. (With both Carleton and Howe, it seemed, the ministry had been premature in handing out laurels.) "Perhaps Carleton may be too cold and not so active as might be wished," the King mused on December 13, in a letter to Lord North, "which may make it advisable to have the part of the Canadian Army which must attempt to join Gen. Howe led by a more enterprizing Commander."

Burgoyne, like Clinton, reckoned a return to Britain for the winter would be useful. Clinton had a burning need to defend his part in the southern expedition, but also felt that a detached command from Howe would be preferable to returning to New York in 1777. Burgoyne was also chafing in his role under Carleton and was planning a concerted effort to move a step up the chain of command. As the year drew to its close, both Clinton and Burgoyne headed home, two men in search of the same job.

They were both to find some sympathy from Germain. The American Secretary had reason to mutter about the performance of all his generals in America for one reason or another, but Clinton and Burgoyne were the sort of decisive, aggressive men he was looking for. He had once been convinced that Howe was that sort of commander as well, but events had tended to prove otherwise. Nevertheless, Howe had performed competently and his campaign gained a little luster when contrasted with the dullness of Carleton's. There was some serious thinking to be done on the course of the war, but Howe had done enough to earn a second chance.

Howe had no inkling that the mood back home had started to turn against him. The seeds of his downfall had already been sown, but for now he was at his zenith, aware that his generalship had been rewarded and basking in the generous, even lavish praise heaped upon him by Germain. He was confident that he had the measure of the rebels and, even if they did put a sizable army in the field to oppose him during the following campaign, there was no reason to believe he would not brush them aside as easily as he had done throughout 1776. He wrote to Clinton on December 21, warmly congratulating his second-in-command on his success at Rhode Island, calling it "an acquisition of infinite importance," and noting that Clinton's success would be "highly acceptable at home." Howe's good mood had made him generous even to his difficult subordinate.

The fact was the year was ending in a most pleasant manner and New York promised a season of entertainment to make the winter months palatable. Unlike many other senior officers, Howe was not going home. Although he wrote regularly to his wife, in letters often reaching 18 pages in length, he was enjoying a well-publicized affair with the wife of Joshua Loring, who served as Deputy Commissary of American prisoners-of-war, and had an extravagant pleasure ship at his disposal. A converted East Indiaman, the *Britannia* had been turned into a luxurious floating palace, complete with state rooms, enlarged portholes (for better views), white-lacquered walls, and gold skirting boards. Two decks had been knocked through to make large halls and it was manned by a minimal (and presumably very discreet) crew of 30.

Von Muenchhausen dismissed the dances, concerts, and other pleasant diversions that the British officers threw themselves into at New York as "frivolous," and grumbled about wanting to return to Brunswick "and be a captain." He had little doubt the revolution was all but over. Cornwallis was also sailing home and would only return if there was a campaign the next year. Von Muenchhausen did not expect to see him again.

If Howe was at his zenith, Washington was at his nadir. New Jersey was hostile to the cause, Pennsylvania was proving to be equally resentful of his presence, and his army had dwindled to around 3,000 men by the middle of December. Howe's confidence over the strong loyalist sentiment in New Jersey appeared to be justified; Washington had been unable to raise more than a thousand militia in the colony, which he attributed to either "fear or disaffection." Around 1,500 militia were raised in Philadelphia, but the rest of Pennsylvania "continues in a state of supineness." On December 17, the capture of Charles Lee added another layer to Washington's gloom. His men had so far prevented the British from crossing the Delaware, but as he admitted to his cousin, "how long we shall be able to do it God only knows ... In short, your imagination can scarce extend to a situation more distressing than mine."

TEN

The Affront

"The possession of Trenton was extremely desirable; could we have preserved it we should have covered the greatest part of the country to the eastward of Prince-town, including the whole county of Monmouth, where I had reason to think there were many loyal inhabitants. We should also have been so near Philadelphia that we might possibly have taken possession of it in the course of the winter..."

Howe's narrative, April 22, 1779

*H*OWE WAS ATTEMPTING TO *dig his way out of a hole. He blustered and elaborated on details, but made little headway and his discomfort would have been heightened by the knowledge that he had broken ground on the hole himself, almost three years previously. On December 20, 1776 he had informed Germain of the settling of his army into their winter cantonments, and had been reckless enough to comment that the chain of posts was "rather too extensive." Just six days later he had cause to regret that admission.*

Now, in the House of Commons, he attempted to prove that there should have been no danger to the garrison at Trenton. He had placed it under the command of "a brave officer" (Colonel Rall, who had distinguished himself at White Plains and Fort Washington), and had placed a supporting post just 5 miles (8 kilometers) away under Colonel von Donop. Close to 3,000 men were split between the two posts, supported by 16 pieces of artillery. Posted 12 miles (19 kilometers) away, at Princeton, was the cream of the army—the light infantry battalions, as well as a further brigade of infantry. Howe insisted that it was the Hessians' right to occupy the left-most part of the line of posts. It was their normal position in the line and it would have been humiliating if it had been entrusted to others. The two Hessian commanders were happy with their posts, Howe claimed, and they both had forewarning of the attack that came in the early hours of December 26. The Hessians, Howe continued, curiously oblivious to the fact that he had just moments ago scapegoated them over the White Plains controversy, had been in "very high order" in America.

Finally, he attempted to defend his decision to stretch his cantonments over such an extensive range, citing his desire to protect the local population, "that they might experience the difference between his majesty's government, and that to which they were subject from the rebel leaders." This, he believed, was consistent with his desire to forge a lasting peace with the colonists and in any case, if the government had wanted him to wage a more punitive campaign, it should have said so in clear, unequivocal written orders. "Ambiguous messages," he claimed, "hints, whispers across the Atlantick, to be avowed or disavowed at pleasure, would have been paltry safeguards for the honour and conduct of a commander in chief."

It was one of the finest passages in his entire speech and those listening may have been seduced enough by it to overlook the fact that it was completely dodging the issue. Howe had known the chain of posts was stretched too thinly and he had not been alone in the realization. From the opposite side of the Delaware, the Americans had come to the same conclusion.

Washington understood perfectly what Howe's intentions were in New Jersey: "… to spread themselves over as much country as they possibly can, and thereby strike a damp into the spirits of the people…" New Jersey was being cowed, he reckoned, due to the absence of any credible resistance, and he still feared that the British would find a way across the Delaware as soon as it was frozen and take Philadelphia. He doubted, as so many of his men were nearing the end of their enlistment terms, that he would have an army to oppose such a move. To anyone who would listen,

Washington expounded on the futility of relying on militia. He appeared close to giving up and wallowed in self-pity. "No man, I believe, ever had a greater choice of difficulties, and less means to extricate himself from them," he wrote to his brother on December 18. He maintained a more dignified air in official correspondence, and two days after opening his heart to his brother he was brisk and businesslike in a letter to Congress on the need to establish a corps of engineers, although even here he descended into another rant on the shortcomings of the militia.

Washington's solution to his seemingly hopeless situation was an act of calculated desperation. As he admitted himself, "… necessity, dire necessity, will, nay must, justify *any* attempt." The idea to strike at Trenton appears to have come initially from Colonel Joseph Reed, who reasoned that even a failed attack would be better than inactivity at a time when enlistments were almost expired. A conference had been called and the decision to mount a surprise strike was taken. It was to be the first time Washington had staged a major offensive, and his inexperience was evident in the ambitious plan he put together. Three corps were to cross the Delaware, each at different points, to launch a coordinated attack. Washington himself would lead around 2,400 of his best men, Continentals, landing 10 miles (16 kilometers) above Trenton. Two supporting corps would aim to confuse the Hessian garrison at Trenton and draw potential relief forces away. Brigadier General James Ewing, with 800 Pennsylvania militia, was to land just south of Trenton and seize the only bridge out of town to the south-east, over Assunpink Creek. Further south, a force commanded by Colonel John Cadwalader, combining Continentals and militia and numbering around 1,800, aimed to distract the garrison at Bordentown.

The situation in New Jersey was neither as bleak as Washington painted it, nor as rosy as Howe believed it to be. The population had not universally welcomed the arrival of the British, and not all of those who supported the rebellion had been cowed. Uprisings had flared, concentrating naturally around the British and Hessian posts. Small-scale attacks served to harass the garrisons, and

Joseph Reed not only kept Washington informed of the activity, but saw how it could facilitate a larger action. Rall, commanding at Trenton, recognized the danger as well, knowing that his men were nearing exhaustion. His three regiments slept fully dressed, while artillery horses were kept in harness permanently and frequent patrols were mounted. Rall requested help from multiple sources, and by Christmas Day he had declared that his men were in desperate need of rest and reinforcement.

The Americans' plan was not finalized until late Christmas Eve—and it found its way to the British almost immediately. Rall was alerted that an attack on his post was planned, but the Hessian colonel actually welcomed this as a change from the constant small-scale harrying. A proper battle would be just what his men needed and he had no doubts about putting the rebels in their place. An attack on Trenton by about 50 men duly came on Christmas Day. It wasn't the large-scale affair Rall had been ready to welcome, but it may have convinced him that the strike he had been warned about had come and gone. It had been far from a merry Christmas at Trenton, but the garrison was neither drunk (as legend would have it) nor unprepared when daylight arrived the following morning.

As if Washington's position were not bleak enough as his desperate mission got under way on Christmas Day, he received a letter before crossing the Delaware. General Horatio Gates was addressing Congress, insisting that the rebel army should be withdrawn to the south to regroup. Such a capitulation in the north would almost certainly have resulted in the removal of the commander-in-chief, and Gates clearly had ambitions in that regard. Pushing his concerns over this to the back of his mind, Washington pressed on. To cap the misery for his men, a severe storm blew up, but the underfed, underdressed, underpaid Americans continued doggedly onward, some of them leaving bloody footprints in the snow.

The attack on Trenton was remarkable not only for its audacity, but also for the seemingly insurmountable odds it overcame. Far from enjoying a miraculous run of luck that saw each part of the complex plan fall neatly into place as if guided by a providential hand, the rebels had to endure and overcome multiple failures. Everything went wrong—right up until the moment when they won.

First, neither of the supporting corps managed to cross the Delaware. Washington's men would be advancing on Trenton without the benefit of diversionary actions. Next, Washington was already three hours behind schedule when he arrived at his crossing point. The aim had been to hit Trenton just before dawn on December 26, but that was already looking unlikely. Then there was the small matter of crossing the Delaware, in darkness, with blocks of ice impeding the way and threatening to overturn the Americans' boats. Almost incredibly, not a man was lost in the crossing, and 18 pieces of artillery were also ferried over safely, but the corps was now four hours behind schedule. The attack on Trenton would have to take place in daylight. The march to the town would claim the lives of at least two of Washington's men, who succumbed to the cold and had to be left by the wayside. Halfway to their target, Washington split his command, so as to be able to hit the town from two directions at once. In one of the earliest examples of such precision planning, Washington had his officers synchronize their timepieces to ensure they struck in unison. Almost everything that could have gone wrong had, but the attack was still on. Two parties of roughly 40 men each were sent in advance, to prevent people from entering or leaving the town, and just after 8 a.m. the first Hessian outpost at Trenton was attacked.

The storm, cursed by the plodding rebels, had been welcomed by the Hessians, who believed they were safe under its cover. The regular morning patrol had even been canceled and the strung-out garrison felt able to relax a little for the first time in days. Despite this, they reacted like a wasps' nest at the first sign of the rebel attack. The entire garrison mustered quickly as Rall was apprised of the situation. The 24 men at the outpost had staged a fighting withdrawal, but now their commanding officer made a critical error. Lieutenant Wiederholdt informed Rall that the Americans had already encircled the town, cutting off the route across the Assunpink. It was probably too early to be thinking of a withdrawal, but Rall's decision to counter-attack may have been influenced by the belief that he had no means of retreat.

The most fierce fighting of the day centered on two Hessian guns, which Rall quickly advanced to tackle American forces above the town. The guns exchanged hands several times, finally resting with the Americans, who turned them on the Hessian troops and loaded them with canister. At this moment, Rall himself was struck by two musket balls. The bulk of the Hessians withdrew from the town, taking refuge in an orchard before surrendering. One regiment attempted to escape over the Assunpink, but the bridge was by now in American hands and this regiment also surrendered. Only 22 of the garrison had been killed, but 896 had been captured, and 83 of these were badly wounded. Scattered parties of men had been able to escape, including the small number of 16th Light Dragoons in the town, a number of jägers and around 50 desperate men who actually swam the Assunpink and made their way to the British garrison at Princeton.

Washington's losses were remarkably light. He reported just two officers and either one or two privates wounded. The winter storm had turned out to be a more lethal enemy than the Hessians, and more men would die in the subsequent withdrawal back over the Delaware. In his report to Congress, Washington noted: "In justice to the officers and men, I must add, that their behavior on this occasion reflects the highest honor upon them." It was something of an understatement.

Prior to Trenton, the Americans had to look hard for positives in the campaign. The sacrificial stand of the Marylanders on Long Island and the creditable action on the Harlem Heights a month later stood out amid a catalogue of disasters. Now they could enjoy a clear-cut victory, one that had an impact out of all proportion to its size. As far as it affected the British, it all but rendered the work of an entire campaign moot. Yes, the Americans had been winkled out of every nook they had wedged themselves into and sent scurrying for their very existence. They had been outgeneraled, outmaneuvered, and outfought at every turn, but now they had a victory. The British had laid more cards upon the table, but Trenton trumped Long Island, New York, White Plains, and Fort Washington combined.

"Thus had the times changed!" declared Johann Ewald. "The Americans had constantly run before us. Four weeks ago we expected to end the war with the capture of Philadelphia, and now we had to render Washington the honor of thinking about our defense ... Since we had thus far underestimated our enemy, from this unhappy day onward we saw everything through a magnifying glass." Ewald was especially pained that it was his fellow countrymen who had been surprised and defeated. He noted that the chain of posts was too extended, but was also highly critical of Colonel von Donop, commanding at Bordentown, who had not supported Rall despite repeated requests for help in the build-up to the attack, and of the regimental commanders who had lost their nerve when Rall had fallen (the Hessian commander had died of his wounds on the night following the battle). Finally, he wondered why the entire garrison hadn't simply swum across the Assunpink like the small numbers who had escaped in that manner. "Thus," he concluded, "the fate of entire kingdoms often depends upon a few blockheads and irresolute men."

The seismic news traveled across the colonies swiftly. By early January, Clinton, at Rhode Island, was hearing rumors of what he later referred to as "that cursed Hessian affront." In a letter to General Harvey he lost no time in suggesting that the cantonments had been too thinly spread, adding pointedly: "I dare say there were good reasons for this extending the chain." Howe had already written to Germain with news of the setback. He was careful to point out that Rall had received prior warning and attributed the defeat to his going on the offensive rather than staying in a defensive position inside the town, but at the same time Howe must have been remembering his letter of the previous month; his admission that the chain of posts was too extensive now loomed large. Howe's embarrassment was not at an end, however, because Washington had not yet finished.

The rebel army, exhausted by its efforts, was resting on December 27 when Washington received the remarkable news that Cadwalader's force, which had failed to cross the Delaware to support the attack on Trenton, had belatedly done so that very morning. Cadwalader was now to the south of Trenton with his 1,800 men, who were apparently refusing to re-cross the river. Cadwalader believed that the British, in a state of confusion, could be driven entirely from the western part of New Jersey. There was considerable doubt over the wisdom, and even the possibility, of further operations on the other side of the Delaware, but Washington carefully steered his officers toward acceptance of lengthening the campaign by a few more days and a new plan was adopted, on an even bigger scale than that against Trenton. The start date would be December 29.

Howe's first reaction to the news of Trenton had been to dispatch Cornwallis to take command of the garrison at Princeton and drive the rebels from Trenton, if they were still there. Cornwallis had been about to set sail for home, but he accepted his new orders and set off, with even more alacrity than usual, on January 1, 1777. He would have found an empty town when he arrived at Trenton, were it not for the fact that the Americans had by then returned in considerable force. The Delaware, which had frozen over in places, proved more difficult to cross than in the previous operation, and it took several days for American forces, including up to 40 cannon, to cross. Washington was now also facing an enemy more dangerous than the redcoats. The terms of enlistment for large numbers of his Continentals were due to expire on December 31. Only by offering them the extraordinary sum of $10 for a six-week extension to their enlistments could the men be persuaded to stay, but most of them did.

Their situation was not hopeful. Just two days after routing the Hessian garrison at Trenton, Washington's men found themselves back in the town, but this time as defenders. The importance of the bridge across Assunpink Creek was borne out in the events that followed. After being forced from the town when Cornwallis arrived on the afternoon of January 2, Washington drew up his men on high ground on the opposite bank of the creek, forcing the British to attempt a crossing under fire.

The force with Cornwallis included some of the best troops in the army—light infantry, Highlanders, grenadiers (both British and Hessian), jägers, Guards, and the 16th Light Dragoons, as well as a train of artillery—but thanks to his defensible position, Washington was able to fend off determined attempts by the British to ford the creek. Johann Ewald was caught in the maelstrom as light infantry and jägers attempted to find a route over the river. The German captain had been determined to "give the enemy a beating" in retaliation for the Hessian disgrace at Trenton, and now found himself engaged in serious fighting, his men manning the houses on one side of the creek, the rebels those on the other. Ewald's men could make no progress, but held their ground despite Washington bringing up howitzers to dislodge them. Severe casualties were inflicted on Cornwallis's corps, estimated at more than 350, while the rebels suffered only 50 or so. With daylight fading rapidly, Cornwallis withdrew his men to ponder his options, confident of forcing a crossing and destroying the rebel position the next day.

Washington's next move was a stroke of genius. Recognizing that Cornwallis could not fail to break through the following day, considering his substantial advantage in numbers, the rebels quietly abandoned their positions, leaving their fires burning to deceive Cornwallis, and marched toward Princeton under cover of darkness. En route, just after sunrise, they met a column of about 700 redcoats, commanded by Lieutenant Colonel Charles Mawhood, marching toward Trenton on orders from Cornwallis. A fierce fight ensued, but with the Americans able to steadily feed more men into the battle, Mawhood's command was eventually overwhelmed. His delaying action, however, gave the remainder of the Princeton garrison time to escape, with most of the British baggage, and it sapped the remaining energy from Washington's army. He had intended to proceed to Brunswick, where he would have captured a huge amount of supplies, but his men were spent. The withdrawal from Trenton and advance on Princeton had been an audacious, almost cavalier move, which spoke volumes of the Americans' ability to move fast and hit hard where least expected. Ewald was furious, noting that had Cornwallis advanced on Trenton in two columns rather than one, as von Donop had recommended, Washington would not have been able to escape. "But the enemy was despised," he grumbled, "and as usual we had to pay for it."

More audacious even than the first victory at Trenton, Washington's latest success caused fingers to point in many directions on the British side. Clinton chose to single out not Howe, but rather Cornwallis, claiming that he had been bamboozled by Washington in his march to Princeton and had lost a golden opportunity to punish "the rebel general's temerity ... when his little army was hemmed in by Lord Cornwallis at Trenton." Howe underplayed the episode in his report to Germain, and also underplayed the cost, admitting to just over 200 casualties. In fact the number was more than 800 and followed hard on the heels of the loss of 918 Hessians at the First Battle of Trenton. Howe was reeling from the most severe blows he would absorb in the entire war, but his suffering in New Jersey was far from over.

The operations at Trenton and Princeton acted like a rallying cry for the revolution and it was suddenly open season for hunting redcoats. New Jersey was now swarming with motivated militia and a rash of small-scale actions erupted. Patrols were ambushed, garrisons harassed, foraging parties set upon. Howe was forced to withdraw men from some of his cantonments, abandoning territory only recently occupied. It was a bitter lesson for loyalists, who had to watch their protectors skulk away almost as soon as they had arrived. The British may have been close to untouchable when faced on the field of battle, but swatting off a swarm of mosquitoes was a different matter, and it made for a miserable few weeks. The so-called forage war was to have a seriously debilitating effect on Howe's army. The experience of the Hessian garrison at Trenton, worn out with constant alarms and under constant threat of a more serious attack, became the common experience for the 10,000 or so men who occupied the colony. Even reinforcement only added to the misery of the men, forcing them into ever-more crowded billets. John Peebles and his men, arriving from Rhode Island, were forced to remain on board transport ships on the Raritan River.

Howe remained in New York and could not even be dislodged when a rebel force was bold enough to threaten Fort Independence, just north of Manhattan itself. Washington had spotted an opportunity to force the British to abandon New Jersey (along with its supply of forage) by threatening New York, and General Heath had been instructed to advance on the fort. On January 18, Heath demanded its surrender and Howe was forced to act, but rather than going personally to Fort Knyphausen (the renamed Fort Washington), he sent his aide, von Muenchhausen, to give instructions. A lavish party was scheduled in New York to celebrate the Queen's birthday, and Howe was also due to be awarded his Order of the Bath; the inconvenience of the war could be handled by someone else. Von Muenchhausen did as ordered, the rebels were driven from Fort Independence, and he returned to New York in time to witness a fireworks display and attend a ball. "A crazy life it is," he noted, drily, in his diary. Howe seemed unable to comprehend the fact that the war had not stopped for the winter. He had applied the brakes on his campaign, but Washington was still willing to move when possible. By robbing the British campaign of its momentum, Howe had turned his army into a stationary target. Time and again Washington had been unable to tempt Howe to attack strong defensive positions—now he had discovered a new way of fighting the war.

Howe was not blind to the dangers. On January 20 he informed Germain that "the design of the enemy seems to be to harass the troops, by keeping them assembled where there is not sufficient accommodation for their numbers, hoping, by that means, to force us to relinquish our posts in Jersey." Three days later, the mood of the commander-in-chief had darkened still further. "The unfortunate and untimely defeat at Trenton has thrown us further back than was first apprehended," he informed Germain. Howe did not see any hope of ending the war except by drawing Washington into a major battle. This would be difficult, he claimed (conveniently forgetting the way Cornwallis had pursued Washington), because the Americans were able to move so much more quickly than the British. Having already asked for 15,000 men back in November, he now declared that 20,000 would "by no means exceed our wants." He would probably be able to manage with just 15,000, he admitted, but the larger number would allow him to send a corps to Philadelphia by sea, catching the rebel capital in a pincer movement. Philadelphia was now Howe's primary target for the 1777 campaign, but the larger number of reinforcements would also allow him to reinstate the offensive from Rhode Island. No mention was made of the Hudson River, and he finished with an ominous word on the consequences of a smaller number of reinforcements than requested: "... if the reinforcements are small," he warned, "the operations will be much curtailed; or if none should arrive, we shall be confined to act in one body in Jersey, leaving only a small corps at Rhode Island, and another of sufficient force for the defense of this island and its dependencies." Howe's horizons were constricting. It appeared that the only hope for a vigorous campaign in 1777 lay with Germain and his ability to find the large number of reinforcements requested.

The loss of territory in New Jersey was also impacting on British supplies. Forage was essential for the horses of the army and Howe felt the need to call in supplies from elsewhere. Rhode Island, a fine source of hay, and safely in British hands, was the obvious place to turn.

———

Hugh, Earl Percy, was very pleased with life. An ambitious, optimistic soul, he was relishing his chance to distinguish himself in the war and was convinced that he was doing well. He regularly updated his father on his exploits, including the successful contribution he had made to the assault on Fort Washington ("... it required coolness in conducting my attack," he wrote with evident satisfaction, "or else I should not have carried so many of the rebel entrenchments with so little a loss.") Even before that, he had informed Germain of a minor action while in command of the garrison at New York. Though the action itself was inconsequential, Percy's letter went into great detail and painted a picture of a young officer of great diligence—a serious soldier who knew his business. He may have gone further than was necessary to keep Germain apprised of events, but his pride in his work shone through, especially concerning an orderly withdrawal from a position of some danger near the enemy's works on the Harlem Heights. "I do assure you I am almost a little vain on this retreat," Percy informed Germain, who would have worked that out for himself by that point of the letter, "and all agree in calling the manoeuvre a masterly one."

Two months after his creditable performance at Fort Washington, Percy was given another chance to distinguish himself when he took over the garrison at Rhode Island on Clinton's departure for England. "I live in some hopes of being able to bring about the submission of this whole province," he wrote to his father. He was not to get the chance to act on those hopes. On January 7, Howe had written to Clinton, informing him of the setback at Trenton. The letter was not received until January 17, by which time Percy was in command. Percy and Howe had never been on the best of terms; Howe had routinely left Percy out of consultations and had recently confided in Germain that he did not feel he was up to the job of a separate command, "not having had much experience." Unsurprisingly, the young officer was happy to find himself removed from Howe on Rhode Island. In contrast, his reverence for Clinton approached hero worship, gushing praise and protestations of brotherly love often ending his letters. With Clinton sailing back to England, Percy may have felt a little exposed as he read Howe's letter. The forage situation was serious, Howe had written, and Percy was to send as much as he could spare from his stock on Rhode Island.

This was the starting pistol for an unseemly falling-out, because Percy never did send Howe the hay he had requested. On January 11, Howe asked for men from the Rhode Island garrison to be sent to beef up his presence in New Jersey and by January 26 he was repeating his request for hay, explaining that the outbreak of hostilities in New Jersey had cut off his supply from that province. Howe was becoming insistent, but remained on the right side of politeness: "I must therefore beg of you," he wrote, "to give every necessary assistance to your commissary to send me a supply of hay from Rhode Island."

Howe's letters continued, and became increasingly irate. He thanked Percy for sending the reinforcements requested, but returned quickly to the request for hay, pointing out that he had been informed Rhode Island produced 15,000 tons of hay per year; "I entreat your lordship will attend to this necessity." On the same day a further letter arrived, having been written two days later, in which Howe's patience had clearly snapped. "Permit me to express my concern that you have not allowed your commissary to send to this place a quantity of hay required by the commissary general," Howe wrote in icy tones. Particularly infuriating to the commander-in-chief was the fact that Percy had not replied personally, but left correspondence to the deputy commissary at Rhode Island, John Morrison, and the commissary general at New York, Daniel Chamier. Howe had seen communications between the two men that did not do any credit to Percy. "I mentioned your request to Lord Percy," Morrison had written in response to Chamier, "and gave his lordship a return without making any comment upon it, he told me he had received a letter from General Sir William Howe on the same subject, but did not think it prudent to send any." In a later letter, Morrison had presented an even less flattering account. "I have made the strongest representations to Lord Percy respecting your situation," Morrison insisted, "but his Lordship cannot consent that any kind of forage should be sent from this island ... he is of opinion there is not more than a sufficiency for the army here."

Enclosing extracts of this correspondence in his letter to Percy of February 4, Howe proceeded to humiliate the man with minute advice on how to respond to activities on the part of the rebels, as if he were incapable of acting independently. As a final broadside, Howe even hinted that Providence ought to have been taken as part of the initial descent upon Rhode Island. It was a bizarre accusation—Percy had not even been in command at the time— and suggests that Howe was feeling intense pressure following the rebel successes at Trenton and Princeton and the deteriorating situation in New Jersey. Clinton later commented that he believed Howe's temper had got the better of him, but whatever the reasons behind his actions, it would have made for excruciating reading for Percy. On the same day he received the inflammatory letter, Percy also heard from Captain Robert Mackenzie in New York. Mackenzie had worrying news of the situation in New Jersey. Cornwallis was losing a steady stream of men on foraging missions and more supplies were desperately needed. There was a fear that the next campaign might be delayed if a supply of forage could not be found. What may have seemed like a petty affair to Percy had suddenly become one of the utmost importance. The failure to send hay was being viewed as detrimental to the entire war effort. Suddenly aware of the gravity of the situation he was in, Percy considered his position for two days and then resigned.

Howe continued to send aggressive letters, unaware that the matter was already closed. Percy's response, when it finally came, was dignified and may have caused Howe to regret his behavior, but the damage was irreparable. Percy, protesting that Howe's accusations had "hurt me more than I can express," told a very different story to that proposed by Howe. Percy insisted that he had made every effort to obtain an accurate return of the amount of forage on Rhode Island, but that he had been frustrated by the incompetence or deliberate obstruction of Morrison. Percy left no doubt that what upset him most was the fact that the word of a deputy commissary had been valued above his own. A day after asking permission to resign his commission and return to London, Percy wrote once more to his father. "Sir William Howe has thought proper to charge me by insinuation with inattention and disobedience to his orders," he complained, "founded on a letter from a deputy commisary."

Howe attempted to backpedal, but it was a half-hearted attempt. "You are now going home from discontent," he wrote, "and even under an apprehension that your character may be liable to injury by serving longer under my command. Not being conscious of any act which could give rise to such an opinion, I have thought it my duty to send home the correspondence that has passed between us." Neither man had covered himself in glory. Howe had allowed a difficult situation to wear down his patience. Percy had not acted decisively enough on the matter, and his failure to keep Howe personally informed of his progress had invited the sort of complicated entanglement that had arisen. As well as his temper, Howe had lost the services of a capable and popular general. As events played out, it would become clear that the falling-out with Percy would cause collateral damage on an even bigger scale.

ELEVEN

The Strategy

"And here I must beg leave to call the attention of the committee to my separate letter of the 30th of November 1776, wherein is set forth my first plan for the next campaign, with the force requisite, in order, if possible, to finish the war in one year."

Howe's narrative, April 22, 1779

*E*ARLIER IN HIS NARRATIVE, *Howe had set out his intentions, listing the points he would address in his speech. Among them was the fact that he had "never flattered the minister [Germain] with improper hopes of seeing the war terminated in any one campaign, with the force at any one time under my command." He had ignored the matter of his letter from June 1775, in which he had declared that he could do the job in one campaign with just 19,000 men, and now he was walking a tightrope. He would need to convince his audience that the request for 15,000 men had been reasonable and, moreover, that he had no hope of ending the rebellion in 1777 with any fewer men.*

He would also need to provide a convincing argument for the metamorphosis of his original plans for 1777. He had sketched out an ambitious, wide-ranging campaign that still had the Hudson strategy at its heart, yet the operations he eventually undertook bore no resemblance whatsoever to his original plan.

By February 1776, less than three months since he had first committed his thoughts on the next campaign to paper, Howe's world was collapsing around him. His relationship with von Heister had been fatally undermined by events at White Plains, leaving him barely on speaking terms with the commanding officer of the Hessian corps. He had alienated Percy and convinced the young general that he could no longer serve under him. The Hessians had let him down badly at Trenton and then Cornwallis had failed to clean up the mess. The rebellion had been reinvigorated and his men were now involved in a nasty partisan war in New Jersey, having to risk their lives every time they ventured out to find forage.

Johann Ewald described the miseries endured by both British and German soldiers in the dispiriting forage war of early 1777. The whole area, he pointed out, had been "completely sacked" during the pursuit of Washington's army at the end of 1776. Supplies for the men themselves flowed in from New York— it was the horses that needed to be fed from the surrounding countryside, and "since the Americans were close on our necks, we could not procure any forage without shedding blood." Foraging parties had to proceed with caution, but even then casualties were inevitable. At daybreak on January 27, one such party set off, comprising 200 British light infantry, 50 Hessian jägers, 400 regular British infantry, a battalion of Hessian grenadiers, and 50 mounted troops. Even this substantial party was not immune to harassment. Although it was too substantial to be attacked head-on, the Americans nevertheless mounted several smaller attacks, and men were lost on both sides.

On February 8 an even bigger column marched into the countryside, with close to 2,000 men, supported by light artillery. The foraging went on until 3 p.m., at which point the tricky matter of withdrawal had to be negotiated. "I had hardly begun the movement," Ewald noted, "when I was so heavily attacked from all sides by a vast swarm of riflemen that only a miracle of bravery by my men could save me." The Americans snapped at the heels of the retreating column until it reached its outposts, and Ewald reported that "many brave men were lost." Ewald, a thoroughly professional soldier, saw these small actions as valuable for his men, giving them experience of war and effectively seasoning them for the campaign to come, but he also recognized that the army would be whittled away to nothing if they continued indefinitely.

The forage war cost Howe close to a thousand casualties, a severe blow to his hopes for the 1777 campaign, especially when added to those men lost in the fighting at Trenton and Princeton. Although it served a valuable purpose merely by making the redcoats' stay in New Jersey a thoroughly miserable one, Washington had a bigger scheme in mind. By preventing British horses from being properly fed through the winter months, they would lose condition, which would in turn delay the opening of the next campaign. The plan appears to have been effective; by the end of March, Ewald was reporting that the snows had gone and the land was green, but Howe's army was not to move for months.

Howe was able to brush off his personal differences with von Heister and Percy, unwelcome as they were. He had taken steps to remove the Hessian commander, while Percy had removed himself. On the last day of 1776 Howe had written to Germain to insist upon von Heister's recall. Having laid a little groundwork by freely criticizing both Rall and von Donop for their parts in the Trenton affair, he stuck the knife into von Heister, claming that both he and von Knyphausen were too old for the job. He conceded that at least von Knyphausen seemed energetic, "but I tremble when I think the former may remain with us another campaign. He is exceedingly unsteady and so entirely averse to carry the Hessians into action, I must be very anxious for his removal." This letter included a hopeful note that if Clinton were granted command of the army in Canada, Burgoyne might be shifted to New York to act as Howe's second-in-command. The deteriorating relationship with Clinton was clearly very much on Howe's mind.

One relationship he did not have any concerns over was that with the American Secretary. He had only recently basked in the glow of Germain's praise following the victory on Long Island, and even though troubling clouds had appeared on his horizon since the heady days just prior to Trenton, Howe would be able to shrug everything off if he was given his requested reinforcements and allowed to embark upon his devastating plan for 1777. All he needed now was another agreeable letter from Germain, and Clinton, von Heister, Percy, Trenton, and the cursed forage war could all be forgotten. The eagerly anticipated letter finally arrived on March 9.

Germain had clearly been caught off guard by Howe's request for 15,000 reinforcements. Not receiving the request until the end of the year, he might have reasonably wondered where Howe expected so many fresh soldiers to be found at such short notice. When he came to reply, two weeks after receiving Howe's request, he took care to first offer praise for the decision to send a sizable force to occupy Rhode Island. There was flattery here, as Germain expressed his utmost confidence in troops "whom you have accustomed to success in all their undertakings." When turning to the actions of Cornwallis, still pursuing Washington through New Jersey as far as Germain was aware, he flattered again ("... the men have been brought into such a state of perfection while under your eye...") and Howe might well have been anticipating with pleasure the inevitable rubber-stamping of his plans that was surely about to follow. But Germain was not yet ready to tackle the most important subject of his letter. He continued to dance around the matter, even throwing in a little criticism of Carleton's struggles in Canada, perhaps to help his praise of Howe stand out more strikingly. Finally, though, the subject could not be avoided. "Your well digested plan for the operations of the next campaign has been laid before his Majesty," Germain started, and it is easy to imagine Howe leaning forward in his chair as the letter finally reached its point, "but I must decline, at present, to trouble you with any remarks upon it." If he had leaned forward in his chair, Howe must have slumped back at this disheartening passage. Germain then attempted to explain: "... as your next letter (of which I am in daily expectation,) will probably throw new lights upon the subject, his Majesty thinks proper to with-hold his royal sentiments thereupon..." Conditioned to a steady diet of praise from his political and royal masters, Howe must have been puzzled by this lukewarm reception for such a bold plan. What could Germain be hinting at? Was he hoping Howe would come up with a different plan? Had his scheme for 1777 been found wanting in some way?

Germain was clearly buying time, and he had done so, perhaps a little awkwardly, but effectively nonetheless. He could have finished his letter there, confident that circumstances across the Atlantic might quickly change and force Howe to suggest a different plan. That Germain did not end his letter at this point is nothing short of baffling. Having declared that he would not pass any comment upon Howe's proposed strategy (other than including the ambiguous description of it as "well digested"), he proceeded to comment upon the number of reinforcements Howe had requested. Germain admitted to having been "really alarmed" at the figure of 15,000, claiming that he could see no way of matching that figure. This news would have been disappointing enough, but Germain went on to suggest that Howe's math was faulty. "As soon, however, as I found from your returns that your army, if reinforced with 4,000 more Germans (which I trust will be procured for you), 800 additional Hessian chasseurs, and about 1800 recruits for the British, and about 1200 for the Hessian troops under your command, will consist of very nearly 35,000 rank and file, I was satisfied that you would have an army equal to your wishes..." Germain was claiming that Howe really only needed 7,800 reinforcements to bring his army to the desired strength.

The returns Howe had submitted at the same time as his proposed plan for 1777 had been used against him. Germain, in a separate letter, made pointed reference to the fact that Howe had navigated his way through the 1776 campaign without heavy losses. It was dressed up as more praise ("I cannot sufficiently admire the greatness and rapidity of your success ... inasmuch as they have been obtained with so inconsiderable a loss"), but the words were intended to back up Germain's insistence that Howe did not actually need 15,000 men. Germain's reasoning continued: the rebels were "greatly weakened and depressed"; Howe would no doubt be able to recruit many loyalist troops to augment his forces, and help for the rebels from foreign powers was unlikely to materialize quickly enough to impact on the oncoming campaign. Germain would not be able to provide Howe with the requested battalion of artillery (but he would get as many guns as could be found), nor could he oblige Howe in his desire for 300 horses. Germain would instead send 100, which was more than enough, judging by Howe's own returns. If more were needed, they would have to be found in America, not an unreasonable suggestion given the difficulty of shipping the fragile animals across 3,000 miles (4,800 kilometers) of ocean. As for the extra 10 ships of the line, Germain had passed that on to Lord Sandwich at the Admiralty, who would inform Lord Howe of his decision as soon as it had been looked into. Safe in the knowledge that this would not be his responsibility, Germain was bold enough to confide that he thought the 10 ships would be found.

What had started as a dispiriting letter had deteriorated into something far more bleak; the campaign was now hanging in the balance. Howe had not exactly been rebuffed (Germain had promised to write more fully when the matter had been given more consideration), but a lot would now depend on how he chose to view Germain's words regarding his reinforcements. Unfortunately for the British war effort, Howe chose to view them as a personal insult.

As Howe pondered the contents of Germain's disappointing letter, Clinton was in London, arguing his case on multiple fronts. There was the fallout from the southern expedition, about which he was still in communication with the hapless naval commander Sir Peter Parker. Clinton also wanted to be relieved of his position as second-in-command to Howe and, as a means of achieving this as well as advancing his own career, he was interested in the command of the army to act from Canada. Clinton was therefore juggling with many different elements at once. He was steadily wearing Parker down (in January, the admiral had commented that the southern expedition "had best be confined to oblivion"), and there was a desire in the North administration for Clinton to be appeased on the matter. Membership of the Order of the Bath, the same laurels granted to Howe for the defeat of Washington's army on Long Island, was dangled before Clinton for his part in the humiliating failure at Charleston. The fact that Clinton was unable to see the absurdity of the situation speaks volumes for his blinkered approach to the affair. He had threatened to publish his own account of the operation, and the award of the knighthood was principally made to shut him up. Oblivious, Clinton was able to note, in a private memo, that he was to receive the knighthood "as a mark of his [Germain's] highest approbation of my conduct throughout, but in particular on the expedition to the southward."

That little matter dealt with, Clinton moved on to his unwillingness to serve under Howe for the following campaign. There was an easy solution. Carleton was in disgrace for failing to take Ticonderoga and then abandoning Crown Point, but he would remain as commander-in-chief in Canada. The army to move down the Hudson, however, would have a new commander. The problem for Clinton was that in the race to gain command of that army, he was already a lap behind his chief rival. Having come back to England in December of the previous year, Burgoyne been able to push his case for weeks before Clinton showed up. A lengthy memorandum, rather grandly entitled "Thoughts for Conducting the War on the Side of Canada," had helped to solidify his position as front-runner for the post, and within days of Clinton arriving home, Burgoyne was selected as the new commander for the Canadian army. Clinton, as Burgoyne's superior, could have protested and the job would have probably been his for the asking, but he felt that was beneath his dignity: "I had a delicacy upon those matters," he noted in a memo, "that would not permit me to do anything of the kind."

Clinton was therefore doomed to serve again under Howe. He made sure to explain to Germain his own thoughts on how the previous campaign ought to have been run, including his plans for landing behind the rebels when their forces were divided between Manhattan and Long Island, and his preference for going to Philadelphia rather than Rhode Island at the end of the year. Germain, according to Clinton, was impressed by these ideas, but he mostly wanted Clinton out of his hair. "Lord Germain expressed his anxiety for me to be gone," Clinton noted, with a disarming lack of awareness, "and wished me to name a time."

His mission had been only partly successful. He had got himself a knighthood, but he was also heading back to New York to work once more with Howe, while Burgoyne, a junior officer, was being given the chance to find glory in a separate command. Clinton was far from happy with his situation, and warned that he was accepting the Order of the Bath as redress for past injustices, but would not consider it as advance payment for any more. Seeing enemies everywhere, he was suspicious that once he was safely out of the way in America, Germain would undermine him. Surprisingly, however, his jealousy over the northern army and his growing paranoia did not impact on what was a solid relationship between himself and Burgoyne. Nobody would try harder than Clinton, in the months to come, to help extricate "Gentleman Johnny" from the situation he was walking into.

Clinton had perhaps dissipated his energies by fighting on several fronts when a more focused approach might have delivered all he wanted. His returning to New York was already hard to swallow, and then he received word from Percy in Rhode Island of the falling-out with Howe. The insinuation, that Providence ought to have been taken during the initial invasion, had been intended by Howe as a slur on Percy's performance. It had been badly judged, as Clinton had been in command at the time, and he now had a genuine grievance against his commander-in-chief. Clinton returned to America in a simmering rage. While at sea, on July 1, he wrote a memo outlining his thoughts on the coming campaign. Philadelphia ought to be left for the end of the year, he believed, while the main army concentrated on moving up the Hudson in support of Burgoyne. In relation to this, Clinton had made an earlier note, back in January, while still entertaining the idea that he himself might command the army from Canada. "With respect to any army from Canada penetrating as far as Albany," he had written, "it is a great doubt to me whether 'tis practical or expedient. As to the first, certainly not so without a co-operation in great force up the Hudson's river." His words would prove prophetic.

At the same time that Clinton's plans were unraveling in London, Howe's were unraveling in New York. On April 2 he finally replied to Germain's letter, having brooded on it for almost a month. His response was truculent. Despite the fact that Germain had deferred comment on the actual operations for the year, Howe chose to view his remarks on the impossibility of finding the requested number of reinforcements as the death knell for his campaign. Despite having waited so long to reply, he was clearly still angry when he committed his response to paper. He started with deceptive calm, accepting the various disappointments in Germain's letter and even proposing ways to proceed—on the failure to provide the requested artillery battalion, for instance, Howe reckoned he might be able to form a unit from provincial troops, and he touched on the need to abandon the offensive from Rhode Island. As this had never been part of official thinking on the war until Howe himself had raised it, completely out of the blue, its loss was not a serious blow, and its shelving seemed to suggest that here was a general who was prepared to cut his coat according to his cloth. This reasonable consideration of his circumstances, however, was not to last.

"From the difficulties and delay that would attend the passage of the river Delaware, by a march through Jersey," he continued, "I propose to invade Pennsylvania by sea; and from this arrangement we must probably abandon the Jersies, which by the former plan would not have been the case." This was nothing other than deliberately destructive. Howe was perhaps forgetting that he had already outlined the consequences of receiving a smaller number of reinforcements than requested in an earlier letter. He had remarked, quite reasonably, that it would result in a curtailment of operations, but even in the event that no reinforcements at all were forthcoming, there had been no talk of abandoning New Jersey. There was more; the corps to operate on the Hudson would be made up of provincial troops, not regulars, and his army as a whole would be "too weak for rapid success." When reinforcements did arrive, he suggested that his invasion of Pennsylvania would have first claim upon them, although he did mention strengthening the other corps. He also declared that the campaign would open later than planned due to the difficulties he envisaged in evacuating New Jersey.

Howe's letter veered once more to the reasonable. He hoped to be able to find a large number of loyalists in Pennsylvania who could form both militia and provincial units that would be able to defend the province and free up the regulars for offensive operations. After this brief, hopeful passage, he delivered his bombshell: "Restricted as I am from entering upon more extensive operations by want of forces, my hopes of terminating the war this year are vanished."

There had been only the most cursory mention of the Hudson strategy, in the vague reference to strengthening the "other corps" mentioned in his original plan. Germain would have clung to that like a security blanket—he had, after all, promised to deliver close to 8,000 men and that might yet be enough to see the Hudson strategy resurrected. Such hopes would have been thoroughly dampened by Howe's enclosure of a copy of a letter he had sent to Carleton in Canada, which left no room whatsoever for optimism.

"Having but little expectation that I shall be able, from the want of sufficient strength in this army, to detach a corps in the beginning of the campaign to act up Hudson's River, consistent with the operations already determined upon," Howe had informed Carleton, "the force your Excellency may deem expedient to advance beyond your frontiers after taking Ticonderoga, will, I fear, have little assistance from hence to facilitate their approach." This was bad enough, but Howe added that, since he would be in Pennsylvania when Carleton's army was ready to cross into northern New York, he would not even be able to communicate with the commander of that corps: "… he must therefore pursue such measures as may from circumstances be judged most conducive to the advancement of his Majesty's service…" The northern army, in other words, was on its own. Howe did propose opening the Hudson for shipping by taking control of the rebel-held forts in the Hudson Highlands above New York City, but he would not be sending any ships up the Hudson himself. Howe signed off, "With my most earnest wishes for your health and success." He was unwilling to offer anything more.

Howe was attempting to portray this as the inevitable result of Germain's refusal to provide enough reinforcements, and he made much the same case during his speech in the House of Commons. "For is it not self evident," he declared on April 22, 1779, "that the power of an army must diminish in proportion to the decrease of their numbers? And must not their numbers for the field necessarily decrease, in proportion to the towns, posts, or forts, which we take and are obliged to preserve?" Howe's logic was unassailable, of course, but he was forgetting (or at least ignoring) an important fact: he had not been expected to take towns, forts, and posts, he had been sent to play his part in the Hudson strategy. He also seemed blind to the fact that his new plan for 1777, the capture of Philadelphia, would inevitably weaken his army still further, through casualties and the necessity to garrison the town once it had been taken.

In a separate letter to Germain, Howe detailed his strength in April 1777 and his proposed distributions. The Pennsylvania corps would be his strongest, numbering 11,000. A corps of 3,200 would be left to defend New York, with 2,400 at Rhode Island, 1,200 at Staten Island, and 300 at Paulus Hook. This totaled 18,100 but did not include 3,000 provincials, cavalry, artillery, the sick, and soldiers currently held as prisoners by the rebels. It was an interesting note, putting his strength at something around 22,000 men, excluding the sick and prisoners. Considering that most of the casualities and taking of prisoners (a total of close to 3,000 men) occurred in the New Jersey campaign, *after* his initial request for 15,000 reinforcements, it seems he had underestimated his strength. Germain had some justification, therefore, for challenging the numbers needed to bring the army to 35,000 men fit for duty. Howe could not see this, and instead viewed Germain's offer of 7,800 men to be insulting, suggesting as it did that he, 3,000 miles (4,800 kilometers) away, had a better grip on the strength of the army in America than its commanding officer. Howe would later claim that at this point he began to worry "that my opinions were no longer of weight; and that of course the confidence so necessary to the support, satisfaction, and indeed, security, of every man in a responsible situation, was withdrawn."

There is more to consider in Howe's tearing up of the strategy for 1777. In his letter to Carleton he had gone so far as to admit that the move up the Hudson was "consistent with the operations already determined upon." With a strength of around 22,000 he would have been perfectly capable of modifying his original plan, shelving the offensive from Rhode Island and moving up the Hudson with 10,000 men, leaving a 5,000-strong garrison at New York and a further corps to hold New Jersey. Not only was this still possible, it was blindingly obvious, as it gave Howe the added security of sticking with the original plan; if it failed to deliver the anticipated results, at least he could claim that almost everybody had believed in it.

Changing the goal at this stage left him vulnerable to censure if anything went wrong, either with his campaign or with that of the northern army, and it made no sense to take such a dramatic gamble when the potential gain (nothing more than the capture of Philadelphia) was so inferior to the potential failings (defeat at Philadelphia and/or the possible failure of the northern army to reach Albany). A desire to prove he had been correct in anticipating strong loyalist support in America has often been advanced as an explanation for Howe's switch of focus for 1777. The argument runs that if Howe could have demonstrated that a large proportion of the population in Pennsylvania had indeed been loyal, and order had been restored in that colony, it would have proved that he had not been reckless in extending his chain of posts in New Jersey. It is an unconvincing argument, and dreams of loyalist support had already proved to be little more than that in the south and in New Jersey, where patriots had been far more ready to mobilize. Howe's actions at this point look more like those of a man who had lost faith in his ability to end the war and had no idea how to proceed. The decision to go to Philadelphia by sea reinforces this impression. By putting his army aboard his brother's ships, Howe was removing himself from any responsibility regarding the progress of the campaign. His men would reach Philadelphia when wind and weather allowed.

Howe's reaction to his disappointment may have been excessive, but the situation was to get worse with Germain's next correspondence, received on May 8. In the interim period, the American Secretary had received news of the setbacks at Trenton, which he described as "extremely mortifying," as well as hinting that some of the "brilliance" of Howe's campaign had been tarnished. There was a suggestion that it should be impressed upon detached corps not to let down their guard, or underestimate the enemy (Percy had found this sort of unsolicited "advice" humiliating when received from Howe, and the result here was much the same). Germain also suggested that the Howe brothers might need to start treating the rebels more harshly, the clear implication being that their treatment so far had been too lenient; "... through a lively experience of losses and sufferings," Germain suggested, "they may be brought as soon as possible to a proper sense of their duty..."

Germain was also ready by now to deliver the official verdict on Howe's proposed campaign. Curiously, however, he completely ignored the original plan and instead referred to the revised ideas submitted in December, declaring Howe's reasons for deviating from his original plan to be "solid and decisive." There was more prodding on the need to be firmer with the rebels, pointing out the need for "a warm diversion upon the coasts of the Massachusett's Bay, and New Hampshire," both to tie up men who could otherwise join the Continental Army and to lessen the impact being made by

American privateers. The Howe brothers were given discretion to decide for themselves whether or not this was feasible, but the hint was strong. There was disappointing news on the reinforcements. Germain tried to confuse the issue by suggesting he had promised a corps of 3,000 Germans as part of the total number of reinforcements when he had actually promised 4,000. Now he would be able to find just 1,280, together with some jägers and four companies of Highlanders. The total number to be expected had dropped to 2,900.

The reduced reinforcements would make it impossible to reinstate either of the original two offensives, from Rhode Island or New York, if Howe persisted with targeting Philadelphia, yet Germain had given his blessing to Howe's revised plan. There would be no supporting operations on the lower Hudson, apart from the defensive corps of provincial troops. Remarkably, Germain wrote to Carleton three weeks after green-lighting Howe's revised plan, as if the Hudson strategy were still very much alive. The army to move down the Hudson would take its orders from Burgoyne, while Carleton was to remain at Quebec with a 3,000-strong defensive force. Burgoyne's orders were clear: he was to "proceed with all possible expedition to join General Howe." In case there was any doubt about this, Germain elaborated. "With a view of quelling the rebellion as soon as possible," he wrote, "it is become highly necessary that the most speedy junction of the two armies should be effected." Burgoyne was to "force his way to Albany," while a smaller supporting column under Lieutenant Colonel Barry St Leger moved down the Mohawk River.

Germain appears to have lost control of the campaign at this point, and to have effectively authorized two operations that were entirely incompatible, but it must be remembered that he was agreeing to Howe's original revised plan, to invade Pennsylvania by land—he was as yet unaware of Howe's sudden desire to take the scenic route to Philadelphia, on board his brother's ships. There was a chance (perhaps a remote one, given how slowly Howe tended to move) that the job of capturing Philadelphia could be accomplished early in the campaign, allowing Howe to then march his men to the Hudson and move them up to Albany. Germain had no way of knowing that Howe now proposed to invade Pennsylvania by sea, nor of foretelling that it would take him so long to get started. That Germain still believed the Hudson strategy could be implemented is revealed in his decision to send an envoy, Major Nisbet Balfour, to deliver this latest letter to Howe and to personally impress upon him the need to take a firmer hand with the rebels. Balfour was not sent to America to insist on Howe moving up the Hudson, because Germain still thought that was possible after the capture of Philadelphia. He was sent to get the Howes to start treating the Americans like enemies. His entreaties had no effect anyway; Howe simply declined to comment on any discussions he might have had with Balfour.

Hopes for a quick opening to the campaign were fading. Howe was proving as reluctant to open operations as he had been the previous year. In 1776 he had been awaiting substantial reinforcements, which at least gave him a solid excuse for delaying his offensive against New York. In 1777 his reinforcements were to be minimal, yet he still found reasons to stall. The clear impression is that he was unsure of how to proceed. Charles Lee, the captured rebel general, had his own ideas on why Howe was struggling to make headway in the war. As a prisoner of the British he had been able to spend time with Howe and was rumored to have submitted a plan for defeating the rebels. The opinion he formed of the British general was revealing: "I thought him friendly, candid, good natured, brave, and rather sensible than the reverse," Lee wrote to a friend, before adding that he was also "illiterate, and indolent to the last degree." He was "totally confounded and stupefied by the immensity of the task imposed upon him. He shut his eyes, fought his battles, drank his bottle, had his little whore, advised with his counselors … shut his eyes, fought again…" Although Lee allowed that, as a soldier, Howe was "brave and cool as Julius Caesar," he insisted that he now recognized that the task he had been given was morally wrong, that he had been used, in fact, as "an instrument of wickedness and folly."

There is no evidence that Howe thought the war against the colonists was unjustified, but following his disappointment regarding plans for the 1777 campaign it is clear that he had no clear idea of how to win the war. Howe had once more mentioned the need for fresh camp equipage ("being articles greatly wanted for the opening of the campaign"), but that arrived on May 24, at which point he declared the campaign would open immediately, "in Jersey, where the enemy's principal strength still remains." Almost three weeks later, Howe had still not moved on Pennsylvania, and was instead trying to prize Washington out of his base near Quibbletown. On June 14, the army moved out from Brunswick in two columns, but was unable to tempt Washington into an action. Howe gave up on the effort and resolved to move on Pennsylvania, stating his intention of embarking his men at Staten Island before the end of the month.

During the withdrawal, however, Washington had nipped at the British army's heels and also shifted his base, tempting Howe to once more turn and offer battle. The fringes of the armies tussled with each other to no great effect and Howe had to again give up the hope of bringing Washington to battle. It had been a curious interlude, which clearly showed Howe's confusion over whether to target the Continental Army directly, or to stick to his plan of going to Philadelphia on the assumption that Washington would follow him and give battle there. The dithering cost Howe weeks of the campaigning season, weeks that Germain had not taken into account when assessing the chances of taking Philadelphia quickly.

As the campaign sputtered uncertainly into life, Clinton arrived in New York and met with Howe, for the first time in more than six months, on July 6. Absence had not made hearts grow fonder. A long, fractious conversation marked the final breakdown of their relationship, one that had struggled from the start, but which now had deteriorated into open disdain on Clinton's side. It was to be just the first of several painful conversations between the two men, which would follow a repeating pattern: they would meet, argue, attempt to patch things up, and apparently part on acceptably good terms, only for the argument to flare up again. At the heart of it was Howe's "insinuation" regarding the failure to take Providence. Clinton at first seemed willing to take a charitable view of this, believing that Howe had written to Percy in the heat of the moment following the setback at Trenton. It was a reasonable assumption, and Howe had admitted before to Clinton that he had trouble controlling his temper and "sometimes made use of sharp expressions." This understanding on the part of Clinton did not last long.

Howe was ready for the argument, revealing that he had heard of Clinton's outburst during the retreat from White Plains, but he also regretted their inability to work together. He commented that they had never been able to agree on anything, to which Clinton replied that it was not surprising, considering their different military educations. Clinton insisted that he had always given his opinion with due deference, but Howe despised formality and found the very word "deference" distasteful. "We argued a little bit," Clinton noted, "and both thought it right to drop the subject." They agreed that they had high opinions of each other (Clinton at least was obviously lying at this point) but "by some cursed fatality we could never draw together." Talk turned to the upcoming campaign and Clinton raised the hopeful prospect of Howe making quick progress in Pennsylvania. In that scenario, might he then be able to send as many as half of his corps to join Clinton, who could then use them either from Rhode Island or on the Hudson? Howe declared himself uncertain that the rebels would bother defending Philadelphia, so perhaps both Clinton and Germain would have their prayers answered.

Immediately after his conference with Howe, Clinton dashed off a letter to Duncan Drummond (the aide-de-camp dispatched to London with news of the capture of Rhode Island at the end of 1776), expressing his amazement at the plan of campaign that had been authorized. "By God these people can not mean what they give out," he spluttered, "they must intend to go up Hudson's river and deceive us all." It was a hopeful thought, but Howe was unlikely to have deceived his own second-in-command, however fractious their relationship had become, and it had become very fractious indeed. Two days later the pair met again and Clinton noted that the conversation was "very warm at first, but on his [Howe's] declaring he had not insinuated, I was composed." On July 11 the issue was raised again, with Howe professing that "he had but one wish left, that was that we should draw together." It was a forlorn wish; Clinton lost his temper again on July 13, with Howe once more insisting he had meant no insinuation against him. For Howe, it must have been a trying period. He was aware that he had overstepped the mark in his criticism of Percy, but he also repeatedly assured Clinton that he had not meant to imply he had been remiss in not taking Providence immediately. The fact that Clinton repeatedly appeared to be mollified, only to return to the attack mere days later, must have been disconcerting. The day when he could set sail for Philadelphia and leave Clinton in command in New York would be a happy one for Howe.

Conversations between the two men managed to touch on serious matters; Clinton was still waging a campaign to convince Howe to reinstate the Hudson strategy. Perhaps realizing the importance of his task, he made a better attempt at diplomacy than usual, conceding that Philadelphia was a worthwhile target for operations, and that the motive behind it (the supposedly strong loyalist element in Pennsylvania) was sound, but suggesting that the long-proposed move up the Hudson would effectively crush colonial resistance. Infuriatingly, Howe expressed sympathy for this idea, but insisted that, since he had approval for his operation against Philadelphia, he was not at liberty to alter his plans. Clinton tried another tack, pointing out the very fact that Howe would later use in his own defense—"that if he conquered ... he must afterwards keep." In other words, any conquests Howe made would require garrisoning, which would weaken his army for future offensive action. Howe insisted that if Pennsylvania (which he believed was tired of the war) fell, then so would New Jersey, and he also professed to be unclear about what Burgoyne's orders actually were. Clinton, no doubt alarmed at this, told Howe as much as he could.

Clinton's hopes that the move to Philadelphia was just a cover proved vain. On July 9 he received his written orders from Howe on how to manage his defensive corps at New York. Any offensive actions Clinton contemplated were only to be risked after the security of New York had been given priority, "which is always to be regarded as a primary object." Clinton's bitterness erupted once more in a series of letters to friends and confidants. In one to General Harvey he declared, "...'tis mortifying thus to serve." The long hiatus in operations would have given the rebels time to recover and gather their strength, while he had no confidence whatsoever that Howe could end the war either in the 1777 campaign or the next. The rebels, he declared, "are in hopes of holding their breath longer than we can." He felt trapped in New York, vulnerable to attack, and robbed of any chance of personal glory, while Burgoyne, a junior officer, had an independent command to play with. On Burgoyne, Clinton had more to say. Everyone seemed convinced that he would make steady progress down the Hudson River, with or without assistance from Howe, but Clinton was not so sure. "As it is," he commented to Harvey, "I almost doubt whether the Northern army will penetrate as far as Albany."

TWELVE

The Capital

"It was not one province, but three, that I conceived we had reason to take possession of at the end of the year 1777. The first object was Philadelphia, a city from whence, by means of the River Delaware, the rebels drew the greatest part of their supplies—the capital of Pennsylvania—the capital, as it were, and residence of the Congress in North-America, situated in one of the most fertile provinces of that Continent... I concluded that the arrival of the northern army at Albany, would have given us the province of New-York and the Jerseys; all of which events I was confident would lead to a prosperous conclusion of the war."

Howe's narrative, April 22, 1779

*H*OWE WAS SINGING A *different tune to that he had entertained Germain with prior to the opening of the 1777 campaign. Then, he had been full of gloom and had insisted there was no chance of ending the war that year. With the need to present his campaign in the best possible light, it was understandable that he would attempt to rewrite history, but any of his audience who had taken the time to look through the letters gathered for the inquiry would have been able to piece together a very different story.*

Howe was in an almost impossible situation. He needed to convince the House that he had mounted a vigorous campaign with very specific aims. After that, he needed to demonstrate that he had achieved those aims, and counter suggestions that he had wasted the year and ought to have cooperated with Burgoyne in the Hudson strategy. His argument would have to be good, because his audience knew how the story had ended. It had ended at Saratoga, with the loss of an army.

As late as June, it had still been assumed by most officers in the British army that Philadelphia would be approached by land, via a crossing of the Delaware River. On June 12, Johann Ewald reported the arrival of Howe at Brunswick, with ten infantry regiments, the 17th Light Dragoons, heavy artillery, and some pontoon bridges. Limited numbers of reinforcements had by then arrived, including a number of jägers from both Hesse and Ansbach. Ewald dismissed them as "bad rubbish," but despite being inexperienced and rough around the edges, they quickly proved themselves to be effective soldiers. The anticipated crossing of the Delaware, however, never materialized and instead the army had withdrawn slowly, aiming for embarkation points on Staten Island.

The weather, which had been uncharacteristically mild for the preceding campaign, had become unbearably hot. Howe's Hessian aide, von Muenchhausen, noted succinctly on May 25 that "it was killing hot today," and he was not exaggerating. On the withdrawal from New Jersey as many as 20 men died of heatstroke, including seven of the newly arrived jägers, intended to act as mounted troops after receiving horses in America and struggling along with hussar boots and sabers until mounts were found for them. On the morning of June 30, the bulk of the army had made it safely across to Staten Island. Loftus Cliffe anticipated a victorious campaign, and reckoned that Washington was running out of time. "If he does not do something he may as well submit," Cliffe wrote home. "He has now assembled a large banditti ... we are told with a good train of artillery, this flatters us that an effort to his cost may terminate this disagreeable business..."

Howe had regained his composure, keeping Germain informed in civil terms of the progress of the army during its withdrawal from New Jersey and taking care to praise the officers and men for their attention to duty during trying circumstances, with enemy troops

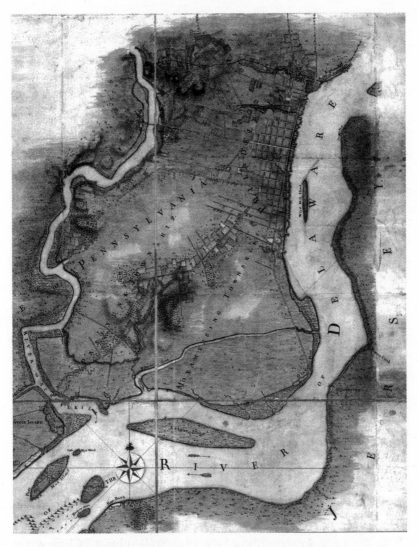

'A Survey of the City of Philadelphia and its Environs.' Nicole, P. & Montrésor,
J. (1777). Place of publication uncertain. (Geography and Map Division,
Library of Congress.)

looking for any opportunity to attack and the weather causing
its own problems. Another disappointment from Germain was to
change that. Back in February, Howe had requested permission
to elevate lieutenant colonels in his army to the temporary

rank of brigadier general, to make good a shortfall in general officers he expected to encounter with his command becoming so splintered over the course of the ensuing campaign. Expecting to thus promote six lieutenant colonels from the Guards, he had asked that the same number of junior captains could be sent out to replace them. Germain refused this request (in a letter Howe received on July 5), reporting that the King considered it would be "very inconvenient to send out junior Captains of the Guards." It was a small matter, but Howe was in a sensitive frame of mind and any further rejection on the part of Germain was likely to sting. When he next wrote, on July 7, all his pessimism had returned.

The war, Howe insisted, was now on a different scale. The enemy was much stronger than it had been in the previous campaign and was benefiting from an influx of French officers. The Americans were building a respectable train of artillery, with reports coming in of 50 brass cannon being landed at Boston. Howe was determined to get down on paper once more a request for more men, and suggested that a 10,000-strong corps of Russians would "ensure the success of the war to Great-Britain in another campaign," but he did not make it clear whether he meant another campaign *after* the present one. It was not helpful to revisit the question of Russian troops, nor was it helpful to point out that he would need a great many reinforcements for the next campaign, in 1778, if he were to hold on to the provinces already taken (which would by then include Philadelphia if the current campaign was successful) and also mount an offensive. He talked blithely of needing three armies to subdue the "northern provinces" (New England), but that had always been considered too difficult—it was why the Hudson strategy had been so tempting in the first place.

As his army sweltered aboard its transports, waiting for sufficient wind to set off for the South, Howe received disturbing news. Washington was moving men toward King's Ferry, on the Hudson, with the apparent intention of placing himself firmly between Howe and Burgoyne, to prevent the junction of the two armies. Howe's reaction was no less disturbing. The news, he informed Germain, "... will no further affect my proceeding to

Pennsylvania than to make a small change in the distribution of the troops." He would leave Clinton some extra regiments, but only so that he could act defensively against Washington if attacked in New York. If Washington subsequently followed Howe to Pennsylvania, he would recall those regiments; they were not to be left with Clinton to open a possibility of offensive operations on the Hudson. He anticipated no problems for Burgoyne "otherwise than the difficulties he must encounter in transporting stores and provisions for the supply of his army," but even if Washington took his army north, Howe had no concerns over Burgoyne's safety. There was, finally, a hint at supporting action. If Washington did not attack Burgoyne, but intended only to slow his progress southward, Howe claimed the rebel general "may soon find himself exposed to an attack from this quarter." This hint may have given Germain some comfort when he contemplated his two armies setting off in their different directions.

Washington, meanwhile, had found himself in a familiar position: puzzling over the intentions of the British army. He had been confused by Howe's maneuvers in June, wondering if he was looking to attack the rebel army or maybe cross the Delaware. He apologized on June 20 for not keeping Congress better informed and insisted he would have done so "had their designs been clear." Washington believed a crossing of the Delaware would have been difficult, because the local population was hostile to the British and the militia had turned out with a will when needed. In fact, Washington had been both surprised and impressed by the militia's spirit, but he was unaware that Howe had no plans of crossing the Delaware. Howe's intentions had remained unclear as the withdrawal from New Jersey began, the British leaving burning buildings in their wake as they headed toward their embarkation points. Washington was delighted at the realization that the British appeared to be heading toward Staten Island and relished the idea of clearing New Jersey, but he also had no idea where Howe's army would proceed after taking ship. To his brother he confided: "By means of their shipping ... they have it much in their power to lead us a very disagreeable dance."

By July 2, Washington was clearer on British intentions. News was coming in of an offensive getting under way from Canada, under Burgoyne. This, Washington believed (if it turned out to be a serious offensive and not just a feint), was proof that Howe's army was intended to move up the Hudson, to clear the rebel forts in the Hudson Highlands and open up the possibility of a juncture with Burgoyne. Washington sent two brigades to reinforce the forts and ordered four Massachusetts regiments to march for Albany. A "respectable body" of the New York militia was also to be called out. Washington had still not got the measure of the man he was opposing, however; to Israel Putnam he wrote that Howe "will make a rapid and vigorous push to gain the Highland passes." Washington had a better appreciation of Burgoyne's temperament. Pondering on the fact that his offensive could be a feint, he discounted the possibility, reasoning that a man like Burgoyne would not have returned from Britain just to stage a feint. He would want glory and was likely to be pushing hard down the Hudson. Keeping the two British armies from taking control of the entire length of the river was of paramount importance. "If we can keep General Howe below the Highlands," Washington wrote to Philip Schuyler, "I think their schemes will be entirely baffled."

By July 7, intelligence was suggesting that Howe had no intention of moving northward. British deserters were informing Washington of the amount of provisions and the number of horses being embarked at Staten Island. The preparations seemed excessive for a move up the Hudson, but the final destination was still uncertain and Washington even feared a move to tackle the New England colonies. The news made Washington wonder again whether Burgoyne's offensive might be a diversion after all, but he could not imagine that a serious push down the Hudson would be attempted without a supporting operation from Howe. Washington was not alone in feeling confused; von Muenchhausen, Howe's Hessian aide, was also puzzled about the delay in setting sail. He wondered if Howe was waiting for definitive news from Burgoyne and believed the job of taking the capital could already have been accomplished if the army had set out four weeks earlier, and men could now be on their way to assist Burgoyne.

The uncertainty was to continue for some time. Loftus Cliffe wryly noted in correspondence that "I shall in the concisest manner lead you on from my taking shipping at Staten Island the 9th July, or rather from the 23rd July that we sailed, for the interim was taken up only in consuming our fresh stock, very scantily laid in indeed." John Peebles' diary noted frequent delays due to unfavorable winds and, as Cliffe had reported, it was July 23 before the huge fleet (Peebles reckoned on 260 ships, together with ten Men of War) put to sea.

Howe had originally planned to travel to Pennsylvania via the Chesapeake. He had reconsidered, recognizing the need to stay as close to Washington's army as possible, and had come to favor the shorter route via the Delaware River by the time the fleet got under way. The amount of provisions loaded on the ships for the voyage suggests that a long stay at sea had not been anticipated. "Our sincerest wish was for a short passage," wrote Cliffe. "Three weeks we were told to lay in for ... we steered to the southward and expected to go up the Delaware..."

According to notes taken by von Muenchhausen at this time, the number of men embarked for Philadelphia was 16,498, far more than Howe had anticipated needing in the plans he submitted to Germain. The failure to leave more men for Clinton, which would have opened up the possibility of a move up the Hudson, is puzzling in this light. The only step Howe took to help Burgoyne was the writing of a letter (which he allowed to fall into rebel hands), filled with inaccurate reports of his intention to attack Boston and ironically describing news of the move to Pennsylvania as just a ruse. It was a paper-thin deception and an insignificant attempt to support Burgoyne, but Howe at one time felt the need to wave it, rather pathetically, in his defense during his narrative, planning to say, "I mention it merely to show that I was not inattentive to the advancement of the northern army." Perhaps realizing how flimsy this was, he omitted any reference to the letter in the final version of his speech. Howe's true intentions had, in any case, already been made clear in a genuine letter to Burgoyne. Showing a complete lack of awareness, Howe informed Burgoyne that Washington was detaching men to oppose his move down the Hudson at the same time that he informed him of his own decision to go to Philadelphia. His efforts to assure Burgoyne that he was not being forgotten fell flat: "... if he [Washington] goes to the northward ... and you can keep him at bay, be assured I shall soon be after him to relieve you." That Howe felt able to promise this at the same time that he was preparing to take his army to Pennsylvania by sea is little short of stunning.

Feeling that one last effort needed to be made before Howe disappeared over the horizon, Clinton had penned a letter on July 21, in which he suggested a diversion to assist Burgoyne. He feared that time had already run out to move up the Hudson quickly enough, but he dreaded the move to Philadelphia, feeling that Howe should, "nay must," realize that going south would be a mistake. Supporting Burgoyne was critical: "such things may be at this instant done there as will decide the war." The message was never sent; Clinton heard of Howe's fake letter and felt that to suggest a diversion after one had been attempted, however weak, would be humiliating. Clinton later regretted not sending his letter, but Howe was never going to change his mind. On July 23 he informed Clinton that he was now tempted to sail via the Chesapeake, due to favorable winds, but that correspondence should be sent to the Delaware until his final destination was known for certain. With that, Howe and his army were gone.

The men had already been on ship for two weeks, but their suffering had just begun. A week after sailing from New York, the fleet reached the mouth of the Delaware, where it was joined by a frigate. The captain of the *Roebuck*, Andrew Snape Hamond (who had been patrolling the river for some time), came aboard the *Eagle*, Lord Howe's flagship, for a conference with the brothers. Hamond, a protégé of Lord Howe's, had been called to give his opinion on whether it was safe to proceed up the Delaware. He presumably thought not, because, to everyone's disappointment, the fleet turned away after the conference. Loftus Cliffe reported that "... the *Roebuck*, who had been some time stationed in the river, came out and gave us, we suppose, such an account of it, as to our very great disappointment, made the *Eagle* give the signal for the other tack."

It was a decision that had serious ramifications. A week later, John Peebles noted in his diary: "This Voyage proving longer than we expected sea stores run short." The same day, the horses packed into the transports began to die. By the time the fleet finally reached its destination, a scarcely credible 33 days after leaving New York, more than 400 horses had died, many having been tipped over the sides of their transports, drowning being considered a kinder fate than starvation. The horses that remained were in a pitiful state, described by John Montresor (now chief engineer) as "mere carrion."

It had been a miserable voyage for all concerned. Von Muenchhausen noted the tedium of the journey. "Today, no less than yesterday," he wrote on August 2, "the Admiral changed our course several times, and it was difficult to tell where we were heading." Violent storms had also plagued the fleet, scattering them at one point and almost putting an end to von Muenchhausen's war, as well as to Howe's personal ship, the *Britannia*, when a lightning strike set fire to the ship. Only the force of a falling mast, which pushed the prow of the ship underwater, extinguished the flames. Eleven days later another storm had killed seven horses, while Montresor noted on August 11 that the stores of fresh water on his ship had become "very offensive." Being able to smell the land, most notably the fresh scent of pine trees, only added to the torture and the men had the surreal experience of being serenaded by crickets in the evenings, the insects having been blown aboard during the violent storms. Mosquitoes, having arrived in the same manner, were less welcome. Although the weather had been cool at the start of the voyage, it had become unbearably hot by the fourth week, Montresor reporting that pitch in the seams of the ship was melting.

The mood of the army after disembarkation started on August 25 was mixed. There was relief at the nightmare voyage being over, and recognition of the skill of Lord Howe in taking the fleet so far up the Chesapeake. Cliffe reported that the rebels had not anticipated this and had been unable to remove all livestock from the surrounding countryside; on August 31 a Hessian party gathered 261 head of cattle, 568 sheep, and 100 horses. Disgruntlement and signs of faulty preparation were evident. There was not enough salt to preserve meat from the cattle found by the river ("We have thrown away many a good piece of beef for want of that," Cliffe wrote) and there was no rum to make grog for the men. The capture of a rebel officer gave Howe the chance to gain valuable intelligence of Washington's intentions. The man, a German, was interviewed by von Muenchhausen, who found that the American general was coming under intense pressure from the European officers in his army to attack the British. It looked like Howe might soon get another chance to secure a decisive victory.

Lord Germain, much like Clinton, had made a last effort to get the two elements of the 1777 campaign back in step. On May 18 he had received notice that Howe intended to travel to Pennsylvania by sea—hopes of a rapid conquest of Philadelphia now seemed fanciful and he wrote to Howe the same day, obviously in a state of alarm. Still, however, he held back from directly ordering Howe to follow the Hudson strategy. He passed on the King's confidence in Howe's latest plan, "… trusting, however, that whatever you may meditate, it will be executed in time for you to co-operate with the army ordered to proceed from Canada…" Howe had made it perfectly clear that the army proceeding from Canada was not in his plans at all, but the vagaries of 18th-century communication had left Germain with just enough optimism until it was too late to effectively intervene. His letter also carried more than a suggestion of his desire to get something on paper to use as evidence if everything came unstuck.

Although he was at a distance of 3,000 miles (4,800 kilometers), when it came to influencing Howe's decisions Germain had greater hope of success than Clinton, for he had the power to give positive orders. He had shown himself willing to do this with Carleton, going into great detail on how he should allocate forces from Canada, right down to the division of regiments between the various corps, and the force of his orders would later be used by Burgoyne to defend his own conduct, just as Howe would hide behind his lack of positive direction. But Germain was contemptuous of Carleton by this point and unconcerned about insulting the man. With Howe, he was still trying to hold things together for the good of the war effort, but he was becoming increasingly frustrated. Howe had shown himself unwilling to be nudged or persuaded to prosecute the war more vigorously, but Germain had never tried a direct order, always deferring to Howe's judgment. This had not been an issue when it appeared that Howe was following the desired path, or at least not straying too far from it, but as he had struck off on his own course, deaf to the cries of those attempting to bring him to heel, Germain had become seriously concerned. He must have known, as he wrote to Howe on May 18, that it was probably already too late to change the momentum of the campaign—Howe and Burgoyne were like two great oil tankers, heading in different directions when Germain would have dearly loved to see them on a collision course—but fate was especially unkind. The letter took ten weeks to reach New York and another two to find Howe, on August 16, during his voyage southward.

Perversely, as Howe made painfully slow progress, Burgoyne was blazing a trail. Part of Howe's reasoning, weak though it was, concerning the lack of need for early operations on the Hudson had been that Burgoyne was unlikely to penetrate as far as Albany until September, but that was starting to look like a hopelessly conservative estimate. He reached Crown Point, the position abandoned by Carleton at the end of his 1776 campaign, on June 25, and five days later, following the reading of an order that "this army must not retreat," the real work had begun. Ticonderoga was taken on July 6, and after that signal triumph, Burgoyne's men continued to make steady progress. However, problems were already beginning to become manifest. As well as heat and humidity there were swarms of biting insects, and retreating rebel forces made Burgoyne's job even harder, felling trees and damming waterways to impede his march. To move from Skeensborough to Fort Edward, a distance of just 23 miles (37 kilometers), Burgoyne had to construct 40 bridges and the short hop took 20 days. At Fort Edward, Burgoyne received Howe's letter of July 17, informing him that there would be no operations on the lower Hudson. Uncertain of how to proceed, Burgoyne now waited for two weeks. He had never considered cooperation from Howe as essential—his own plans had even gone so far as to suggest that his army might act as a diversion to allow Howe to enact his own plans in the south—but reality was starting to bite. His line of communication was long and vulnerable and he had not been given the number of horses and wagons he had requested for hauling supplies.

He hoped to counter this difficulty with a raid on a rebel magazine at Bennington on August 16, but troops under Lieutenant Colonel Baum ran into a swarm of militia and a relief column was also badly mauled. Burgoyne had lost around 500 men and was sensing danger. There would probably have been time to withdraw to Ticonderoga and rethink, but that would have been humiliating given his towering confidence about the certainty of his success. On July 11 he had, in a letter to Germain, lamented the fact that he was not authorized to proceed directly to the New England colonies, which he was sure he could subdue before the end of the year; he hoped he might be able to put this plan into operation after reaching Albany. Such boundless optimism suddenly seemed misplaced, but he could hardly retreat a month after such an exhibition of bombast. He took the fateful decision to press on.

Burgoyne's best hope now lay with the only man (Burgoyne himself included) who had displayed the slightest doubts over the ability of the northern army to make easy progress: Henry Clinton. Fuming in New York, in what he called a "starved defensive," he was nevertheless sympathetic to Burgoyne's situation and fearful of his fate. In a masked letter (it appeared innocuous until a cut-out piece of paper was placed over it, covering extraneous content and revealing the letter's true message) from early August, he informed Burgoyne that Howe had gone and that he had been left "with too small a force to make any effectual diversion in your favour..." Later that month the precarious nature of his own position was brought home by a three-pronged assault on New York and its surroundings. Clinton was impressed with the organization of the attacks and believed they might have proved effective if Washington had committed more men.

By September 11, Clinton was becoming concerned. News had reached him of the defeat at Bennington and, perhaps more than any other British general in North America at the time, he recognized the potential consequences of blood in the water. The last he had heard from Burgoyne, the commander of the northern army had been at Fort Edward, on August 6, at which time he had confidently predicted he would be at Albany by August 23. More than two weeks past that date, all Clinton had was news of a defeat many miles from Burgoyne's interim goal. Feeling the need to offer some sort of help, but unwilling to go beyond Howe's orders to view the safety of New York as his primary responsibility, Clinton wrote to Burgoyne to ask if a diversionary raid on the Hudson Highlands might be useful. By the time Clinton was in a position to do anything about the offer, following the arrival of 1,700 British and Hessian reinforcements, it was already too late. Burgoyne had fought the Americans at Freeman's Farm, on September 19, and had again lost around 500 of his men, while the rebels had stood firm in the face of several bayonet charges.

Rebel militia units were by now drawing in, attracted to the news of an army in mortal danger. Clinton's move to clear the forts in the Hudson Highlands was effective and well managed, but he recognized that it was not enough to save Burgoyne. Four days before taking the forts he had received more news from Burgoyne, delivered by Captain Alexander Campbell. Gentleman Johnny was no longer feeling confident, his army reduced to 5,000 men, with 12,000 rebels in front and more behind, running short of provisions, and communications with Canada cut off. It was a dire situation and, perhaps most worryingly, Burgoyne was requesting explicit orders from Clinton on how to proceed, a sure sign that he was seriously worried. Clinton immediately sent word to Howe and jotted down a formal reply for Burgoyne ("Sir H Clinton cannot presume to give any Orders to General Burgoyne"), before taking the Hudson Highlands forts. He could only hope it might ease the pressure on the northern army.

After taking his roundabout route to Pennsylvania, Howe found himself approximately 15 miles (24 kilometers) further away from Philadelphia than he had been nearly nine months ago, while being saluted by the rebel artillery on the opposite side of the Delaware at Trenton. One of his first jobs was to write to Germain regarding his troubling letter, which Howe had received at sea on August 16. Germain was clearly holding out hope that Howe might be able to cooperate with Burgoyne's army in its push southward, and this hope needed to be firmly scotched. Howe's reply was as definitive as possible: "It is with much concern I am to answer," he wrote, "that I cannot flatter myself I shall be able to act upon the King's expectations in this particular."

It would make for disappointing reading when Germain received the letter, but even more disappointing would be Howe's comments on the local population: "… my progress, independent of opposition from the enemy's principal army, must be greatly impeded by the prevailing disposition of the inhabitants," he wrote, "who, I am sorry to observe, seem to be, excepting a few individuals, strongly in enmity against us, many having taken up arms…" Howe's entire reason for going to Pennsylvania, the fact that the population seemed ready to submit, had proved illusory. Far from being ready to flock to loyalist units, the locals had either joined the rebel army or abandoned their homes. Just five days after landing, the campaign had proved itself to be wasted. He reiterated his belief that he did not have enough troops to accomplish much in the current campaign, but assured Germain that he would still do his best.

The only thing that could redeem the campaign now was the smashing of Washington's army, and there was every sign that this might be possible, because he had obligingly followed Howe's move to Pennsylvania. On August 10, the American commander had been convinced that Howe was heading eastward to tackle the New England colonies, and was actually marching to meet him when intelligence arrived that the British fleet had been sighted off the Delaware Capes. Thrown once more into a state of confusion, he pondered the possibilities inherent in the developing British position. Clinton, he reasoned, could not have been left at New York with no other orders than to hold the place ("an officer of his rank and military estimation would scarcely be left to keep garrison only"). Surely, he must have been instructed to attack from New York at the same time as Burgoyne descended from the north? The reality of the pitifully limited objectives of Howe's campaign simply never occurred to him.

Eleven days later, it appeared that Howe must be going far to the southward, perhaps targeting Charleston, because otherwise he would have already arrived in the Chesapeake. This presented Washington with an onerous choice: leave Charleston undefended, or potentially ruin his army on a lengthy march in the unhealthy summer climate of the southern colonies. The choice never had to be made; the next day the British fleet was reported as entering the Cheasapeake and Washington could finally march his army to Philadelphia, confident that it was Howe's target after all. He decided to parade his men through the city itself, in order to make an impressive show of strength to reassure patriots and depress loyalists. On August 24, the Continental Army put on a good show of discipline and martial prowess for the population of the city, just two days after starting its march. Howe's army had by this time been on board its transports for almost seven weeks.

While Howe's men and horses recovered from their grueling voyage, the Howes issued a "declaration," assuring the local population that British and Hessian troops had been warned to be on their best behavior and that nobody would come to any harm if they stayed peacefully in their homes. Even former patriots could gain amnesty if they swore allegiance to the Crown and surrendered themselves to British forces. It was an unimpressive, unconvincing document, which had been pre-emptively undermined by the conduct of occupying troops in New York and New Jersey. The abandonment of loyalists in New Jersey also did little to inspire faith in the power of the British army to protect anyone and rebel soldiers had little reason to give up their fight when retreat and escape had always been an option left open by Howe's brand of generalship. Charles Lee, the captured rebel general, would later claim that Howe had not even seen the declaration until several days after it had been published.

Howe, unable to offer anything tempting to the rebellious colonists, aware that Germain had expected him to still cooperate in the Hudson strategy, and awakened to the reality of minimal loyalist support in the region, could only rescue his campaign with a decisive victory. Had he known the situation that Burgoyne was being dragged into in northern New York, he would have realized that it was not only his campaign, but possibly his career that was on the line. As it was, newspaper reports of a rebel success at Bennington were troubling, but dismissed as exaggerated.

Howe, so indecisive and dilatory in his conduct of the campaign thus far, recognized the importance of grasping this chance. Simply occupying Philadelphia (effectively giving himself another mouth to feed, alongside New York and Rhode Island, when it came to making plans for the next year) was not going to be enough. Howe may have been puzzled that his conquests were not having more of an effect on the rebels. He had cut his teeth, after all, in a war where the fall of Quebec had effectively given Britain control of Canada. Now, belatedly, he seemed to appreciate that only by destroying the main rebel army could he rescue his campaign. He stripped his army of much of its baggage (including the tents he had used as a reason for delaying the opening of operations) and sent them with his brother's ships via the Delaware, with the aim of reuniting with the fleet after taking Philadelphia. The British and Hessians were now able to move more quickly than usual and Howe outflanked an initial rebel position at Wilmington, forcing the Americans to fall back and cross the Brandywine Creek. Chadd's Ford was now the focal point of the rebel defenses, and hasty entrenchments were thrown up to contest a British crossing. Washington was ready to make a stand; John Peebles reported news that the rebel general had impressed upon his men the importance of their defense holding, claiming that all was lost if Philadelphia fell. Parallels with the position at New York were clear. On Long Island, it was the passes through the Gowanus Heights that had needed defending. At the Battle of the Brandywine, it was the multiple crossing points over the creek. Two divisions guarded Chadd's Ford and Chadd's Ferry, supported by a North Carolina brigade. Further potential crossing points at Gibson's Ford and Pyle's Ford were the responsibility of Pennsylvania militia units, while Brinton's Ford was watched by another division. Smaller units were detailed to guard less important crossing points, but, as on Long Island, the Americans failed to cover all possible routes of advance. Believing Buffenton Ford to be the most remote crossing available to the British, it was the last one defended, but a further option was on hand, with two branches of the creek passable at Trimble's Ford and Jeffery's Ford. A long flanking march would be required to get there, but it promised to unhinge the entire rebel position, exactly as the unguarded Jamaica Pass had on Long Island.

Howe was not afraid of a long march, especially if it might bring him the sort of victory he now badly needed. At 5 a.m. on the morning of September 11, he set out with the elite of his army. Jägers, both mounted and infantry, the British light infantry, British and Hessian grenadiers, Guards, the bulk of the 16th Light Dragoons, and both the 3rd and 4th brigades of infantry embarked on a nine-hour march. Cornwallis commanded the division, with Howe in attendance, exactly as he had accompanied Clinton more than a year earlier during the night march on Long Island. Von Heister having been recalled, von Knyphausen now commanded the Hessian troops and headed a smaller division, incorporating four Hessian battalions, the 1st and 2nd brigades of British infantry, the 71st Regiment, a squadron of the 16th Light Dragoons, and the provincial unit known as the Queen's American Rangers. Shortly after the flanking column set off, von Knyphausen marched directly to Chadd's Ford with the intention of diverting the rebels' attention from their right flank. They had driven American screening troops back across the creek by 10 a.m.

Four hours later, the flanking column crossed the Brandywine and marched on the Americans' right flank. The column had been aided by the knowledge of a guide (possibly the famous loyalist John Galloway, who would later write scathing critiques of Howe's leadership), of whom Johann Ewald commented: "His description was so good that I was often amazed at the knowledge this man possessed of the country." Despite this local insight, however, progress had not been easy; many men had been left by the roadside in the heat, and a break of an hour was taken for the remainder to recover before the attack commenced.

The march had been a surprise, but not a complete one—Washington had received word of the danger at midday and had managed to hastily arrange a defensive line above Birmingham Church, which Howe was forced to assault around 4 p.m. A determined charge put the rebels to flight, but the chasing British were in for a nasty surprise. "Our troops pursued the fugitives thro' the woods & over fences for about three miles," Peebles reported, "when they came upon a second & more extensive line of the Enemys best Troops drawn up & posted to great advantage…" Another charge dislodged this second defensive line, but as light began to fail and the troops felt the effects of their long march and the fierce fighting, the pursuit could not be sustained. "Night fell over this story," Ewald noted, "and the hot day came to an end."

Von Knyphausen, on hearing the attack of the flanking column, had turned his diversionary action into a serious assault and had also crossed the Brandywine, but his position had been tenuous. Washington, when made aware of the flanking column around midday, realized that a divided army might be vulnerable and had tried to take the battle to von Knyphausen. American units had pushed across the Brandywine to destroy the Hessian general's command, but faulty intelligence caused Washington to lose his nerve, believing that the flanking march was actually the diversion and that the bulk of the British army was lying in wait across Chadd's Ford. It was a missed opportunity, but more costly was that missed by the British. Ewald bemoaned the fact that Howe had not set out on his march earlier (as he had done, with great success, on Long Island), or moved more quickly. Sniffing a conspiracy, Ewald suspected that the march had been deliberately slow in order to allow the rebels to escape and strike a blow against the Tories in government back home, but he also declared that the battle proved that Howe was "not a middling man but indeed a good general." Like all conspiracy theories, Ewald's was entertaining but could not survive contact with the facts.

Washington had been beaten again, but his losses, estimated at around 1,300 in killed, wounded, and captured, were trivial compared with the possibility of total annihilation. Howe himself lamented the absence of "an hour's more daylight," which may have allowed his pursuit to have become a rout. Perhaps recognizing that his victory, though significant and well constructed, was not the sort of total success required from him, Howe waited until October 10, effectively a month after the battle, to write to Germain. Von Muenchhausen was defensive of Howe, detailing the appalling conditions encountered in the days following the Battle of the Brandywine, which made any effective pursuit impossible, and declaring: "I am convinced that everyone in Europe would admire General Howe if they were as familiar with all the obstacles he faces, as we are." The failure to quickly follow up the victory of September 11 was more to do with a shortage of wagons than with any lackadaisical attitude on the part of the general, von Muenchhausen argued. There weren't enough to both bear the wounded back for treatment and carry provisions for the army.

There were other efforts to bring Washington to action (notably the "Battle of the Clouds," when the Americans were saved by a timely cloudburst), and Philadelphia was duly occupied on September 26, Cornwallis entering the city with 3,000 redcoats. But the parade of successes did not have the luster of those Howe had been able to write of the previous year. Washington, unaware that he needed to do nothing more, attempted to replicate his success at the tail end of 1776 by launching an ambitious attack on the bulk of the British army, based at Germantown. Washington enjoyed local superiority in terms of numbers during the battle, but his four columns failed to coordinate their night marches and the battle became a disordered affair. With the fiercest fighting focused on a house to which British units were driven for refuge, Washington's attack foundered, with a heavy fog adding to the confusion. Running low on ammunition, the Americans began to disengage around 8 a.m., having suffered substantially more casualties than the British. Washington had failed to replicate his success at Trenton and turn the tide of the campaign, but his aggressiveness and willingness to take the fight to the British had impressed many observers, and there would soon be another victory to celebrate.

As in 1776, Howe had taken his time to move, but had attained his goal in the end, with the defeat of the main rebel army in a major battle and the occupation of an important city. Unlike those in 1776, however, his successes in 1777 had become nothing more than a side note to the far more significant events taking place to the north.

At the Hudson Highlands, Clinton had been weighing his options for offering further assistance to Burgoyne. His successful assault on the rebel-held forts had left him flushed with confidence; in fact that was an element of his giddiness in his report to Burgoyne on his success: "*Nous y voici*," he exulted, "and nothing now between us but Gates." Had Gates not been commanding an army significantly bigger than the remnants of Burgoyne's, this message might have offered more comfort, but when Clinton heard from Rhode Island that Robert Pigot (commanding after Percy had flounced home) could spare 1,000 men, Clinton recognized a genuine opportunity. Grasping it, he organized a small force of 2,000 to head upriver to Albany, carrying six months' provisions for 5,000 men. By October 15, this force was roughly halfway to Albany.

Clinton was stretching his orders to the limit, but under the circumstances he felt the risk was worth it. Two letters from Howe would change his mind. On October 8 Howe requested reinforcements from New York—he had warned Clinton that this would happen if Washington did not either stay around New York to threaten the city, or move toward Burgoyne. The 7th, 26th, and 63rd regiments, along with two battalions of Anspach troops, were ordered immediately to Philadelphia, with the 17th Light Dragoons (except a detachment based at Kingsbridge) following as soon as suitable transport for their horses arrived. These reinforcements would significantly weaken Clinton's force and make any move to Albany highly questionable, if not impossible. Clinton, having been on the receiving end of Howe's inflexibility before, saw little possibility of ignoring this order, and in any case, Howe took paper in hand again the following day. This second letter repeated the request for reinforcements, but insisted they should be sent without delay. Clinton could hold on to them only if he was involved in a "very material and essential stroke," which would only require his retaining the troops for a few days. The move to Albany would take far longer than this.

Howe's letters were most remarkable for their timing. Before they were written, he had received news of Burgoyne's plight in upstate New York. Knowing that a British army was in dire straits, and that Clinton was the only person in any position to do anything about it, Howe nevertheless informed his second-in-command that he should send reinforcements to the main body of the army. Howe was apologetic, insisting that he would not be asking for the men "were we not much in need of them at this crisis." Crestfallen, Clinton had no option but to cancel his Albany venture. He simply could not take the chance of ignoring such an unequivocal and insistent order. By October 25, Howe was commanding Clinton to return to New York and the next day he ordered the 1,000 men sent by Pigot back to Rhode Island.

Burgoyne surrendered his army on October 17. Clinton's push up the Hudson (the first such movement, supposedly the cornerstone of the entire British strategy in the war, in two full campaigns) had come too late and the ramifications of the loss of an entire army would be huge. Burgoyne lost little time in starting the case for his defense, writing to Howe on the matter on October 20 and referring to his orders to "proceed by the most vigorous exertions to Albany." On October 25 he wrote to Clinton. "Had Sir Wm Howe enabled you to make the same movement you lately made one month sooner," he argued, "or perhaps half that time, I believe our junction would have been effected." Burgoyne also took the ever-popular option of denigrating his German troops, whom he accused of being just bad enough to "undo you," but not so bad as to deserve open censure.

Burgoyne's downfall would create an abundance of blame, enough for everyone to have a share, and Howe was most concerned about the size of the portion that he would have to swallow. His actions throughout the campaign appeared at best indifferent to, and at worst willfully negligent of, Burgoyne's operations. In the full knowledge that Burgoyne was sinking, he had called for more than 2,000 men from Clinton's already meager force and ordered another 1,000 back to Rhode Island.

Explaining such conduct is not easy. It is possible that Howe could not accept that Burgoyne's position was really as bad as he was making out. Howe's experience of the rebel soldiers had perhaps conditioned him to believe that determined action on the part of British regulars would always win the day. The message from Burgoyne, however, was clear and it seems likely that, far from being oblivious, Howe recognized the disastrous nature of Burgoyne's situation all too clearly. At the moment when he heard of the plight of the northern army, he must have remembered Clinton's warnings about the difficulties Burgoyne might experience in moving south. He must have thought back to Germain's last letter, in which he had expressed his hope that Howe would be able to cooperate with Burgoyne after taking Philadelphia. He must have recalled his own championing of the Hudson strategy, more than two years previously. He must, therefore, have realized that at least some of the blame for Saratoga was headed in his direction. All he could do at that moment was create an impression that he had done everything within his power, that he had left more troops with Clinton than he would ideally have liked, and that he now desperately needed reinforcements himself. It would also serve the purpose of once more underlining his assertion that Germain had let him down, and suggest that the lion's share of the blame for the catastrophe unfolding at Saratoga ought to be piled on another man's plate.

THIRTEEN

The Resignation

"From the remainder of my correspondence, gentlemen must have seen, that I continued my remonstrance for more troops. Perhaps it was impossible for the minister to send more. Such an acknowledgement would have been no reflection upon himself, and would have relieved my mind from the uneasiness it labored under, in conceiving, that my opinions of the necessity of reinforcements were deemed nugatory: and that, of course, I had lost the confidence of those, who were in the first instance to judge of my conduct. It cannot be surprising, that finding myself in this situation, I desired his Majesty's permission to withdraw from the command."

Howe's narrative, April 22, 1779

*H*OWE WAS NOW STAKING *everything on an assertion that a withdrawal of confidence by the American Secretary was justification for his resignation. Personal honor was a delicate subject in the 18th century, and he had reason to hope that his assertion might be accepted. Percy had used the belittling correspondence he had received from Howe as justification for turning his back on the war and had received no criticism; his loss had been lamented, by Germain and the King. If Howe could convince the House that he had equal cause to feel slighted, he might be able to persuade its members that his resignation was a matter of personal honor, rather than one having been forced upon him by his own failure to end the war. He was correct in pointing out that he had continued his remonstrance for more troops, but having received a disappointing reply in April 1777, he was unlikely to garner a more pleasing one months later. He never reframed the question, never suggested methods of getting* *more men, except for repeated and facile suggestions that Russians might be hired. In short, he never appeared to be working with Germain on the problem.*

He also clumsily offered the American Secretary a get-out clause, noting that a mere acknowledgment that the number of reinforcements requested could not be found would have been acceptable. Germain's initial response on the matter, saying that he had been "really alarmed" and "could not see the least chance of my being able to supply you with the Hanoverians, or even with the Russians in time," would seem to fit such a description perfectly. Howe therefore concentrated on Germain's attempts to blur the issue by suggesting that Howe needed far fewer men to bring his fighting strength to 35,000. Here, Howe was on more solid ground. His speech referred to Germain's "misconceived calculation" and he made political capital by interpreting Germain's response as insulting, but had he done enough to convince his audience that Germain had withdrawn his confidence from the commander-in-chief? And was that reason enough to abandon a war that had not yet been won, but was also not yet lost?

While Howe was pondering his position, having learned of Burgoyne's situation, he received further communications from Germain. Already obsolescent when written, they had become obsolete in their two-month transit across the Atlantic, yet they touched on matters that could only have lowered Howe's spirits still further. Written on August 6, they talked of hopes that the rumors surrounding Burgoyne's progress toward Albany had been confirmed and that Howe had been able to strike a decisive blow against Washington. By the time they were received on October 19, the stories surrounding Burgoyne had taken on a very different complexion, and although the victory at the Brandywine had been solid, it had not delivered any "decisive consequences." There was also a dispiriting mention of the King's disappointment at Howe's inability to mount the suggested raids on the coast of Massachusetts. Germain declared that he had always done his best to get Howe as many men as possible, but this reassurance was followed by a pointed reference to the fact that he was receiving news of the movements of Howe's army from private letters and would welcome an official update.

While Germain was still attempting to be civil with Howe, the same could not be said of his correspondence with Howe's brother, the admiral. He was bitingly sarcastic in "praising" Lord Howe for his policy of leniency regarding American shipping. The decision to allow American ships to leave port for fishing had resulted in "so many privateers upon our coasts and such encouragement given to them by the French, that I was apprehensive a few weeks ago that we should have been obliged to have declared war." The brothers would not be able to compare notes on their treatment by Germain for some time because the fleet had not yet been able to link up with the army, a rebel fort on Mud Island preventing the fleet from opening the Delaware. The stubbornness of the defense of Mud Island would have been viewed wryly by Montresor, tasked with destroying it—he had designed and constructed the fort in 1771, never receiving payment. (Joseph Galloway, the prominent loyalist, may also have pondered on the turn of events. He had sold the island to the authorities to allow the fort to be built in the first place.)

Howe, uncharacteristically, was prompted to offer a quick reply to Germain's letters. Just two days after receiving them he wrote a polite response in which he commended Clinton for his successes in command at New York and requested 5,000 uniforms for provincial soldiers, whom he anticipated being raised in Pennsylvania and other provinces. He had already despaired at getting any meaningful number of loyalist recruits from the region, so this comment was an unsubtle attempt to give support to his earlier confidence over Pennsylvania's willingness to submit. A day later, Howe had much more to say. He opened with a protestation that he had never had any doubt of Germain's good intentions toward him, but it closed with a request to resign. His request was couched in extraordinary terms: "From the little attention, my Lord, given to my recommendations since the commencement of my command, I am led to hope that I may be relieved from this very painful service, wherein I have not had the good fortune to enjoy the necessary confidence and support of my superiors..."

It had been a stomach-churning fall from the heights enjoyed at the end of the previous campaign. From a seemingly untouchable position, newly knighted and with his enemies scattered before him, Howe found himself ten months later in the role of a sideshow to the main event in North America. Two defeats, at Trenton and now at Saratoga, had completely undermined the British position in the colonies and Howe must have felt bitter that these had both been suffered by soldiers away from his personal command. In each case, however, at least some of the blame could be traced back to him. He would later rail against the lack of clear orders from Germain (while Burgoyne would rail against the exact opposite), but it was not "whispers across the Atlantick" that had undone him, but rather the lack of a firm guiding hand and his own paucity of ideas on how to proceed when the first blows against the rebellion had failed to subdue it.

Having delivered his request to resign, Howe continued to keep Germain informed of progress at Philadelphia, including the final capture of Mud Island on November 16, which finally opened the river for the fleet. The army at Philadelphia could now be supplied and Howe spoke of "a forward movement against the enemy," which he hoped might yet bring decisive results. He did make an effort to bring on such an engagement, marching out of Philadelphia on December 4 to confront the rebel army at Whitemarsh. A stand-off ensued the next day as Howe assessed the strength of the rebel position, and he relocated on the evening of December 6, before launching a tentative assault (little more than an extended skirmish) the next afternoon. After the armies disengaged, Howe again reconsidered and, in a fitting way to mark the end of his active duties in America, he once more turned away from American defenses.

Howe was now contemplating a third winter in America. His first had been spent under siege at Boston. His second had started well at New York, but had been spoiled by events at Trenton and

Princeton. His third promised to be the most uncomfortable yet, as recriminations swirled following the loss of an entire army.

The men who had surrendered at Saratoga expected to be back in England before too long. Under the terms of the "convention" entered into by Burgoyne, they were to be allowed to go home on the assurance that they would not return to America to serve against the colonists again. They were generous terms, and completely unrealistic. Even if adhered to, their presence in Britain would free up troops to come out to America, so the loss of men would prove illusory. Howe had just such thoughts in mind and planned to contravene the spirit of the agreement, but the Americans wisely got their contravention in first. Burgoyne's men, the so-called convention army, were never returned home, but were marched up and down the country, evaporating through desertion and disease, inflicting the maximum impact of the loss on the British.

Von Muenchhausen was gloomy about the prospects for Britain. "Many of us here hope that England will give in," he wrote on October 31 after definitive news of Burgoyne's surrender had been received, "or else send 20,000 men early next spring. The first would be the most desirable, because I fear that England cannot accomplish the latter." Henry Strachey wrote to his wife of his wish for more troops ("many more") in the new year, which might bring "victory and peace." Johann Ewald was beginning to despair of ever defeating the rebels and noted with approval their willingness to learn. Captured knapsacks of American officers would often contain books on military theory, which Ewald would beg his English counterparts to read, only to be rebuffed by men who "consider it sinful to read a book or think of learning anything during the war." Spirits were low in the army, but at least Ewald was ending the year on a personal high. As Cornwallis prepared to leave for Britain, he left a note for the Hessian captain, expressing his admiration and esteem. "If the war should continue," he wrote,

"I hope we shall serve again together. If we should be separated, I shall ever remember the distinguished merit and Ability's of Captain Ewald."

"If the war should continue" was the thought on many minds. By the end of the year the rumor mill was whirring again, with reports of 20,000 Russians about to depart from Britain, but who would command the men? News did not leak to the army of Howe's resignation request until the following year, but Germain was wrestling with the question from December, when he received Howe's letter. His initial response was calm, declaring that, as it was possible that Howe's campaign had not yet closed, a full appreciation of it could not yet be made. Germain, however, had been gradually losing faith in his commander-in-chief and his developing disaffection had crept into his correspondence with the King. As early as June he had been commenting with frustration on Howe's inability to keep up a steady stream of communication. "It is surprising," he wrote with irony, "that the General should be so fond of concealing his operations." His frustrations had grown by the time he informed the King of Howe's request to resign, on the evening of December 1. He admitted the request was not a surprise, but believed Howe's claim of a lack of support was unfair. There was still a hope that news of Burgoyne's surrender might have been exaggerated, but that was snuffed out the very next day, when Lord Sandwich at the Admiralty passed on firm news of the defeat.

The King was measured in his response, believing the situation to be "very serious but not without remedy," but the report of the defeat made the decision on Howe's resignation a formality. The manner in which Germain conveyed the conclusion to Howe was to become another bone of contention. Once possessed of the full details of Burgoyne's defeat, and also of all information on the closure of Howe's 1777 campaign, Germain informed Howe that the King was "graciously pleased to order me to signify to you, his royal acquiescence in your request of leave to resign the command..." The wording could not be anything other than deeply insulting to Howe and this would create a problem, because although Howe had been given permission to come home, there was still a big question to be answered: who would succeed him? Clinton, the obvious choice given his experience in America and his position as second-in-command, was agitating for his own return to England, heartily sick of his treatment during the war. He was also unpopular and promised nothing but trouble if elevated to overall command; the man had extricated a knighthood from the King for failing to capture a fort. Sir Guy Carleton had been so insulted by his removal from command of the northern army that he was unable to enter into civil communication with Germain, let alone accept a job from him. The most energetic general in North America, the sort of man who might have waged the vigorous campaign Germain had long envisioned, had just surrendered an army at Saratoga, removing himself from the running. Many other senior generals, including Sir Jeffrey Amherst, were unwilling to serve in America at all.

When the scant menu was perused it had to be accepted that an unappetizing option might have to be selected; in early 1778, the leading candidate to command the British army for the following campaign in America was ... Sir William Howe. The King wondered if the damage done by Germain's insulting letter might be undone by sending a second letter. This, if sent on the copper-bottomed *Andromeda*, might reach the general first and persuade him to reconsider his decision. It was a desperate and muddle-headed dream. Howe had proven himself incapable of waging an active war and his thoughts on the following campaign had already proved he was barren of ideas. On January 7, Germain had received Howe's ideas, which had talked gloomily of the need to hold Philadelphia, New York, and Rhode Island. A single offensive corps might be scraped together if one of the principal holdings was relinquished, but there was also the possibility of remaining on the defensive for the entire year while planning for a return to vigorous operations (with the significant reinforcements required for such an effort) in 1779. Howe was effectively smothered under bonds of his own making, tied down by the possessions he had laboriously amassed over two campaigns. A man with such limited ideas could not remain in charge of the army, and the inevitable decision was finally taken. Every effort would be made to persuade Henry Clinton to accept overall command, and on March 8 Germain wrote to Clinton to inform him of his good fortune.

Serious consideration had been given to the form the next campaign should take. Germain had learned his lesson from the loose rein he had kept on Howe. The general had not so much run amuck without a firm guiding hand as strayed from his intended course and repeatedly stopped to graze for extended periods. A firmer hand, with a taste of the whip, would be offered to the new commander, while both Amherst and Lord Sandwich were invited to submit their appraisals. Sandwich noted that through two campaigns in America, the fleet had been subservient to the army, Lord Howe's ships often acting as little more than a taxi service for his brother's troops. He wanted the roles to be reversed, with the army taking and holding bases along the east coast, enabling the navy to impose a blockade on the colonies that would strangle them into submission. Unsurprisingly, as First Lord of the Admiralty, he recommended the building of new ships.

Amherst broadly agreed with Sandwich. If the war were to be won on land, he reckoned, no fewer than 40,000 reinforcements would be needed, which probably caused Germain to reminisce about the good old days when Howe was only demanding 15,000. Amherst's intention, however, was simply to demonstrate how futile it was to prosecute the war on land. He too favored a strict naval blockade.

Satisfied with the input, Germain formulated his plan and sent it to Clinton. To start with, the new commander-in-chief was given permission to evacuate Philadelphia if he deemed it necessary to concentrate force elsewhere. The city Howe had spent an entire campaign in taking was considered expendable. Clinton was also to receive substantial reinforcements. A loan of £6,000,000 had been secured (albeit on what Lord North called "exorbitant terms") and new troops had been authorized by Parliament. Gentlemen of means and even cities had come forward to offer to raise new regiments, and in all, Clinton was promised 12,000 new

British soldiers, along with (hopefully) one or two more regiments of Germans. It is impossible not to note that this came very close to matching Howe's request for 15,000 men, made at the end of 1776. Why was it possible now when it had been dismissed out of hand then? The loss of an army can concentrate the mind, and perhaps the establishment suddenly became aware that the war might actually be lost if strenuous efforts were not made.

Clinton's newly enlarged army was ordered to cooperate with the navy on a string of raids, from Nova Scotia to New York, which ought to be completed by October. Focus would then switch to the South, to Georgia and South Carolina, where the hopeful vision of teeming loyalists was again conjured up. The use of the loyalists, however, was to shift. Rather than being embodied in provincial corps, they were to act as holding forces to maintain order in the region, allowing the regular army to proceed to pacify more areas before repeating the process in them. Diversionary raids would be mounted in Virginia and Maryland to prevent the rebels from concentrating their forces against the army acting in the South. Clinton was given latitude to engage Washington if the chance for a decisive victory presented itself, but that was to be of secondary importance. Howe had wasted two campaigns chasing Washington and Germain was determined not to repeat the mistake.

The new strategy could be viewed as a different method of reaching the same goal—the isolation of the New England colonies. The Hudson strategy had intended to physically cut them off, while the new plan would pacify the South, just as effectively cutting off the New Englanders from their supply base. It was a sensible plan, one born of careful contemplation, and it recognized the lessons to be learned from the war up to that point. Before Clinton received his orders, however, they had already been countermanded.

The prospect of French involvement in the war had been a concern from the opening of hostilities. Support in the form of weapons had been provided from the start, and officers had soon appeared, to add experience to the Continental Army. More worrying, however, was the prospect of more tangible backing, in the form of soldiers and ships, and Saratoga offered encouragement to the French to take a more active role. The Royal Navy had enjoyed superiority at sea throughout the war, notwithstanding the rebels' ability to launch privateers and take their toll on British transports. The arrival of a sizable French squadron would completely change the situation, and could threaten an isolated British garrison, such as that at Rhode Island, with capture. French involvement would also shift the emphasis of the war, with Britain's territories in the West Indies considered to be more important than the American colonies.

The reassessment of the war effort in 1778 had always considered French involvement to be likely, but had curiously fixed on a plan that made no provision for it. Just days after Germain had outlined the new strategy for Clinton to follow, the French ambassador informed the British that a treaty had been signed with the Americans on February 6. The effect was so spectacular it was as if the British had never even considered its possibility before. The King now declared it was "a joke to think of keeping Pensilvania," and Clinton's orders were hastily revised. He was ordered to evacuate Philadelphia and told that he could also abandon New York if he saw fit. His reinforcements disappeared like a morning mist, and instead he was now ordered to find 5,000 men for an attack on French-held St. Lucia in the Caribbean. The Americans, having succeeded in their aim to land a major European ally, were becoming an afterthought in a war that had suddenly and dramatically expanded. In July, the French finally declared war on Britain and there were also fears that Spain would take its chance to get involved. The thought of bribing the Spaniards with the return of Gibraltar was considered, but eventually shelved as too outrageous for the British public to swallow.

Still, there was genuine concern in Britain, not only for the position in the colonies and the West Indies, but also regarding an invasion of home soil by the French. A peace commission, headed by the 5th Earl of Carlisle, Frederick Howard, was dispatched to try to end the American conflict by diplomacy and Germain showed a ridiculous level of optimism when assuring Clinton that further military operations would almost without doubt be unnecessary, given the Carlisle Commission's near certainty of success. Whether the commission might have had a chance earlier in the war is an interesting debating point; it effectively promised the Americans everything they wanted short of independence, including negotiation (and presumably repeal) of all acts passed since 1763. After capturing a British army, however, the Americans were interested in negotiating on nothing except a timetable for Britain's withdrawal from her former colonies. The French were nevertheless spooked by news of the terms about to be offered by Carlisle and moved more quickly on their treaty with the Americans than originally planned; a last-minute reconciliation between Britain and her colonies would have been a terrible disappointment for the French.

Amid the turmoil, and in the middle of fears of a war with France and Spain, a possible invasion of Britain, and the loss of colonies and territories in North America and the West Indies, Howe had just one thought: clearing his name. Germain was well aware of the possibility of inquiries regarding the generalship of both Howe and Burgoyne. By the time Howe's resignation had been accepted, the American Secretary was putting together notes for such an eventuality. Regarding Howe, his notes raised some pertinent questions. Why had Howe not followed up his victory at White Plains with a determined pursuit of Washington? Why did he stop at the Delaware instead of taking Philadelphia? Why were his posts so thinly spread in New Jersey? Why were Hessians entrusted with such an important post as Trenton? Why did he not cross the Delaware in 1777, having built pontoons and carriages for flat-bottomed boats for the purpose? Why did he not engage Washington's army in New Jersey? Why did he go to Philadelphia by sea at such an unhealthy time of the year? Why did he spurn the opportunity to land at the Delaware? Why did he not pursue Washington more vigorously after the Battle of the Brandywine? Why did he take two weeks to occupy Philadelphia after that battle? Why was Washington left undisturbed in his winter quarters at Valley Forge? They were interesting questions, but notable by its absence was the obvious one: why, in two years of campaigning, did he never think to send a body of men up the Hudson River in accordance with the agreed-upon strategy for the war? Even without this, however, Germain had a formidable armory at his fingertips, but there was still hope that a full inquiry might be avoided.

As usual, winter had been a difficult period for the British and Hessian troops in America. Johann Ewald noted a brief, blissful period after going into winter quarters at Philadelphia when the Americans behaved themselves, but the war soon flickered back into life. As guerrilla operations resumed, the local population became unwilling to make the risky journey to town and the price of provisions rocketed. By January 26, Ewald was engaging in the same sort of partisan warfare that had marked out the preceding winter in New Jersey.

News of Howe's departure had filtered through to the army by April, von Muenchhausen noting that it had "seriously depressed everyone's spirits." It had been a trying appointment for the Hessian aide, who vowed never to serve with English officers again, although he expressed affection for Howe personally and respected his overriding concern for the safety of his troops. But even Howe had kept himself at arm's length from the Hessian officers; von Muenchhausen reported on a dinner in a tavern in New York, that 55 English officers had attended just prior to the army setting sail for Philadelphia, with not a single Hessian representative.

Howe habitually viewed the winter as closed season for campaigning and could see no reason to change his habits with his return to England imminent. The Americans, shivering at Valley Forge, were left unmolested through the entire winter ("Do not let anyone ask me why we tolerate this!" von Muenchhausen noted in his diary). Howe defended himself during his narrative by insisting that any action at this time might have weakened the army that he was to leave for his successor, but the truth was he was fundamentally opposed to winter operations and heartily sick of the war. There was a hint that some officers were heartily sick of him as well. On February 21 a British officer was arrested, along with all rebel officers then on parole, on suspicion of collusion in a plan to murder Howe. There were rumors of a secret correspondence with Washington, and when the British officer was released on March 12, owing to a lack of "proof and evidence to convict him," von Muenchhausen noted that such a phrasing would lead many to suspect he was guilty. A young American woman, Mary Figis, was later tried and convicted of perjury in the trial and sentenced to be "turned out of the lines," with a sentence of half an hour in the pillory and six months' imprisonment if she returned.

Most British soldiers, however, were sorry to see their commander-in-chief depart and an elaborate going-away party, known as a "Mischianza," was staged in his honor. The festivities, which lasted well into the following morning, included mock jousts, fireworks, and a ball and were badly out of kilter with the realities of the situation, with the rebels undefeated, a British army lost, and the likelihood of French involvement turning a domestic quarrel into a world war. Tickets for the event were designed by Captain John André (who would be captured and executed as a spy in 1780) and bore the triumphal motto *"Luceo discendens aucto splendore resurgam,"* which translates as "Descending I shine; with added splendor I rise again." Whether or not Howe would rise again remained to be seen. Mauduit Israel would later pen an acerbic comment on the affair in a pamphlet, "Strictures on the Philadelphia Mischianza or Triumph upon leaving America Unconquered," a salvo in the pamphlet war that erupted after Howe's return from America. Mauduit's pamphlet was typical of the breed, piling savage criticism upon the general. Had Sir William withdrawn from his command quietly, it argued, he may have been left to a peaceful retirement. Instead, he chose to "suffer himself to be crowned with laurels, and to have triumphal arches erected to his honour," having been "out-generaled even by a man that was none."

Howe left America in May 1778 and received a cordial welcome from the King. The general soon became aware, however, of murmurings about his performance in America and came to believe that, if not actively encouraged by the North administration and Germain in particular, the murmurings were not being repudiated with enough vigor. With North's administration in difficulties over the unpopular war, and with an energetic opposition looking for chinks in its armor, Howe needed to be handled carefully. The opposition, by supporting Howe, could undermine the government, and much thought was given by the administration on how to keep the general quiet. North suggested a sinecure might appease Howe, and the King hopefully suggested the Lieutenant Governorship of Minorca. Worryingly, Howe had started to agitate for an inquiry, trying to force Germain into a rash outburst in the House of Commons that might make an inquiry unavoidable. Attempts to light Germain's touchpaper were crude. On December 4, Howe rose to speak out on the whispering campaign that was undermining his reputation and bluntly stated that he was convinced the war would never go well if Germain was running it. The American Secretary kept a tight grip on his famous temper and defended himself with dignity, so Howe was forced to become more explicit in his demands for an inquiry. His brother, who had by this point also resigned his position and returned to England, joined in the campaign. By February 1779, Howe was insisting that an inquiry was needed to determine if it was the commanders of his Majesty's fleets and armies or the ministers of state who were to blame for the failure to end the rebellion. He moved that copies of his correspondence with Germain be laid before the House. Lord Howe insisted he wanted merely to retire in peace, and was content with the reception he had received from the King, but not so with that received from the King's ministers.

Lord North attempted to smooth ruffled feathers, pointing out that he had never criticized the brothers and had great respect for them, but opposition members were sensing their chance. Charles

Fox commented that he could not accept that the Howes (he spoke of "the noble lord and his gallant brother") had been given sufficient men to win the war, for the simple reason that the war had not been won. The battle lines were drawn, and by April Cornwallis was writing gloomily to Clinton: "Sir William Howe, in spite of all that can be said to him, will have a parliamentary inquiry into his conduct. He is himself prosecutor and defendant." Cornwallis's opinion on the matter was clear: "People of all parties seem to think it is an ill judged business, and can answer no purpose for Sir William." Cornwallis had his reasons for dreading an inquiry. His wife had recently died, making it unbearable for him to remain in England, and he longed to return to active duty. He was even willing to build bridges with Clinton, who still mistrusted him over his reporting of his outburst after White Plains. "If you should think that you can have any material employment for me," he wrote to the new commander-in-chief, "send for me and I will most readily come to you. I really shall come with pleasure."

Cornwallis had another reason for suspecting that the inquiry would be "a serious misfortune for me." He was to be Howe's star witness.

FOURTEEN

The Inquiry

"And now, Sir, having endeavoured to bring before you, by the most impartial quotations, all the evidence that I thought necessary to collect upon the papers on your table, I shall only remind you, that the House has ordered the attendance of several of the most respectable officers who served in America during my command. Their testimony may confirm the truth of the facts I have advanced, and will undoubtedly explain and prove any other material circumstances, which you may think necessary for your investigation.

"And, Sir, if the House of Commons, or any other individual member, shall have any charge or accusation to make against me, I declare myself ready and willing to meet it. The Committee is open for the reception of any other papers, and for the examination of any other witnesses. My only wish is, that every possible light may be thrown upon every part of my conduct.

"I move that Earl Cornwallis be called in."

Howe's narrative, April 22, 1779

*I*T HAD BEEN A *long speech, and not nearly as entertaining as the House might have hoped. Howe had progressed at much the same rate he had in America, and in much the same manner as well, his route bypassing most of the serious issues, while making long and irrelevant detours. As a stand-alone speech, it could not possibly hope to clear his name, but against a backdrop of bitter factionalism, the merits of the speech itself became insignificant in relation to its ability to hurt the North administration. Members of the opposition would* *applaud the speech and hail it as proof of the ministry's abject failure to support its commanders in America. Supporters of Lord North would dismiss it as weak and ineffectual. The speech, to all intents and purposes, need not have been made for all the impact it had upon those listening.*

The calling of witnesses, however, promised something more. If eyewitnesses to events in America could be examined, then genuinely new information might be turned up. And in any case, the prospect of a good courtroom drama was too good to resist. North and Germain, dreading close scrutiny of their running of the war, were determined that the inquiry should end immediately, but it would take great political skill to ensure that happened.

There is no way of knowing Howe's mood as he sat down after delivering his speech. It is most likely that he felt satisfaction. In his opinion, the speech had been crafted and tuned for maximum impact, and he had never had any real understanding of the power of words so the frequent flat notes may well have sounded like stirring music to his ears.

Only the existence of a draft of the narrative proves that it had been revised in an attempt to find the strongest arguments. In many instances, the draft revealed more than Howe would have liked. On the subject of the Hudson strategy, which he himself had championed shortly after reaching Boston four years earlier, Howe had struggled. His speech considered two possible alternatives to his expedition to Philadelphia: an attack on the New England colonies, and a move up the Hudson River. The first consideration was nothing more than a red herring. Nobody had seriously proposed attacking the rebellion in its heartland. The second was more relevant. Howe asked what might have happened had he moved up the Hudson. First of all, he claimed, the rebel-held forts on the Hudson Highlands would have needed to be cleared, which would have been costly (Howe was conveniently forgetting the relative ease with which Clinton accomplished the task toward the end of the 1777 campaign). Then he believed that Washington's army would have prevented him from moving quickly up the river, wasting time and making it impossible to take Philadelphia that year. This ignored the fact that the introduction of Philadelphia into the equation had been entirely his own doing. It was not a target that had been imposed upon him from home.

Still weaker was his assertion that the movement of his army to Albany would have been of no more assistance to Burgoyne than his attack on Philadelphia, which had removed the main American army from Burgoyne's path. In reality, had Howe been at Albany in force, the rebel concentration that doomed Burgoyne would have been threatened from the south as well as from Burgoyne's army. Finally, Howe reached for a quite stunning argument: had he pushed up the river, he might have been accused of trying to steal Burgoyne's thunder, that he "had enviously grasped a share of that merit, which would otherwise have been all his own." Howe, graciously, had left all the merit for Burgoyne, and doubtless wanted him to accept much of the blame as well.

Clumsy as this defense was, it served Howe better than his original ideas on the matter. The draft of his narrative is far more revealing of his ambivalence toward the entire Hudson strategy. Such ambivalence, strongly implied in his actions, was made explicit in his draft, but it also suggested more: that Howe had never understood the strategy in the first place. Why, he asked, could Burgoyne not have shipped his army to New York and then marched up to Albany? This, he reasoned, would have effectively given control over the province of New York, which he saw as the entire point of the strategy, so why not accomplish it "by a more ready route"? The Hudson strategy had actually required British control over the entire length of the river. Albany was merely a convenient point of juncture for the two armies, and the fact that Howe saw the strategy as requiring nothing more than the occupation of Albany suggests he did not understand it at all. Howe went on to explain why he had not thought to mention this brilliant plan to Germain. "I answer," he said, "because I did not consider myself in any degree called upon to do it." In Howe's view, Sir Guy Carleton, in Canada, was far more qualified than he to decide on the operations of the northern army. Moreover, Howe continued, "ever considering the Northern Expedition as a measure determined by Government, to have obtruded my objections might not only have been deemed an officious impertinence, but would have carried the appearance of my seeking to have the whole American army placed immediately under my command."

Had this passage been left in the final version of his speech, even opposition members would have struggled to support him. It demonstrated clearly that he considered the Hudson strategy to be none of his business, and he did not understand it in any case. His apparently inexplicable indifference to the progress of Burgoyne is suddenly explicable.

On the subject of his perceived gentle treatment of the rebels, Howe was again more revealing in his draft than in his final speech. By referring to his attempts to curb the depredations of his troops on the civilian population, his speech touched on the matter lightly, and mentioned the absence of any explicit orders to "turn the plan of the war into an indiscriminate devastation of that country." In his draft, however, he strongly hinted that had such explicit orders arrived, he would not have been willing to carry them out. The suggestion that he would have ignored direct orders was too risky and was understandably left out of the final speech, but Howe had already shown his willingness to defy Germain when ignoring his exhortations, via Major Balfour, to wage a more punitive war.

Howe's muddled thinking on the war was also revealed in a revised section on the strength of the New England colonies. He accurately pointed out that the colonies at the heart of the rebellion were the most populous and boasted the most effective militia. In his draft he then went on to make the following claim about those colonies: "and being the most powerful in every respect, [they] were therefore to be the last to be regularly attacked. This opinion will, I trust, be assented to, at least by every military man." The opinion probably would be assented to by every military man, but it had clearly not been assented to by the military man in command of the army in America, because Howe had suggested a major offensive against Boston in his initial plan for the 1777 campaign. Again, a judicious revision prevented Howe from embarrassing himself before the House.

A less judicious revision saw Howe actually remove a strong argument from his final speech. Referring to a letter received from Burgoyne following his capture of Ticonderoga, Howe had originally intended to say, "Here, Sir, was no symptom of the distress which afterward befell that unfortunate general—no apprehension of future difficulties—no insinuation that he either expected or wished assistance from me." It was a telling point, and a fair one, but Howe struck it from the final version of his speech.

Overall, Howe's speech was undermined by the need to make every one of his decisions appear to have been driven by a clear strategic goal. This he could never hope to do, because he had had no strategic vision at all. The result was a narrative that could have been savaged in the House, had the opposition chosen to view Howe as the chief culprit in the failure to end the war, or had Germain not been more concerned with avoiding any investigation of his part in the affair. Howe had not enjoyed much luck in America. Bad weather had repeatedly arrived to frustrate his plans, other officers had made bad decisions at critical moments, and such loyalist support as existed had been reluctant to show itself. But he enjoyed an extraordinary stroke of fortune in finding nobody willing to take issue with the highly dubious contents of his speech.

Now, mercifully, that speech was over, and while it was one that only committed enemies of the North administration could love, it had at least avoided the worst of the pitfalls present in the draft. Howe had survived its delivery and could now look forward to pressing his case through the examination of witnesses. With another display of his remarkable ability to be utterly oblivious to the thoughts or wishes of others, Howe now called upon a man who had no wish to be there. The question now was, would Cornwallis ever be brought before the House?

North and Germain were determined that the Howe inquiry should end right there. The examination of witnesses could only serve to cast more light on the running of the war, and there were some dark corners they would prefer to remain unlit. There was only one possible way of heading off the examination of witnesses—they would need to present a convincing argument that they had no criticisms whatsoever of the command of the Howe brothers and that their reputations were therefore unsullied. It would be tricky, especially considering the fact that Burgoyne was on hand, pressing for his own inquiry and full of invective against the administration. The critical factor would be Germain's ability to control his temper. Howe had failed to bait him effectively in his calls for an inquiry, but as the debate over whether or not to hear witnesses proceeded, he would come under increasing pressure. The King had dreaded the day when the question of Burgoyne's defeat came to be examined in an inquiry, believing that Germain would attract vicious criticism from the opposition. Now there was the prospect of both Burgoyne and Howe attacking Germain at the same time. At some point, he was likely to blow.

A week-long adjournment gave everyone a chance to digest the finer points of Howe's narrative, and on April 29 he rose again to repeat his request that Cornwallis be called to the bar. Earl Nugent, a staunch supporter of the North administration, opened the debate on whether or not witnesses should be called. He started by asking Howe about his planned questions for Cornwallis, receiving the reply that Howe would quiz the Earl on military matters. Nugent then spoke at length, and well, insisting that neither of the Howe brothers had any cause to feel slighted, as they had repeatedly received praise for their zeal and activity. Only "runners and whisperers and coffee-house politicians" had made any accusations against them, and if everyone so mistreated were granted an inquiry, the House would have no time for anything else. Nugent continued, declaring the House unqualified to pass judgment on military matters, nor was a court-martial an appropriate undertaking, because there was no accuser. And in any case, had not Howe been given his opportunity to clear his name? Had he not been "furnished with a full opportunity, in a very long and able speech, of proving that every idle or loose discourse concerning his military conduct, was false and ill-founded?"

Nugent then touched upon the delicate matter of Burgoyne, present only under the terms of the Convention of Saratoga and therefore not liable to judgment or punishment from any body other than the American Congress. Was it fair to give Howe an inquiry or a court-martial when one could not be offered to Burgoyne, whom Nugent referred to as "that gallant but unfortunate officer," causing some rumblings in the House. Nugent then attempted to shift the focus of the Commons, insisting that there was more important work to be done and little enough time to do it. The French were probably preparing an invasion force, and Nugent managed to provoke uproar by referring to the present pitiful state of Ireland. After rambling on for a while longer, he moved "that the chairman doth quit the chair." In other words, the inquiry should be wound up.

North expressed agreement with Nugent, stressing that there was no accuser and no charge to answer, and that he was happy to declare that Howe had done his duty "in every particular." He commented on the delicate matter of examining inferior officers regarding the actions of their superiors and insisted that if Howe intended to make any direct accusations against a member of his ministry, then he needed to do so before witnesses were examined, in order that a defense might be prepared. The general, however, had made it clear that he only intended to examine Cornwallis on military matters, and North shared Nugent's opinion that the House was not the place for military judgments to be passed. He then touched on the real nub of the matter, the fact that nobody's mind was going to be changed whatever happened in the inquiry, so it would be better to move on to other matters. North expressed his suspicion that the intention of pressing on with the inquiry was actually to examine the conduct of ministers rather than generals, "to try and determine upon the conduct of administration by a side wind, in an oblique indirect manner."

Burgoyne, eager to bring his own case before the House, insisted that military men deserved the right to defend themselves from accusers and proceeded to protest that he had not been granted an audience with the King on his return from America. When Germain stood to respond, members of the North administration must have held their breath, but he retained his composure, although he did make clear that he thought Burgoyne's place was with his men, in America, rather than in London.

The opposition heavyweight Charles Fox was the first to support Howe in his call to prolong the inquiry. Surely, he asserted, any attempt by the ministry to avoid the examining of witnesses was due to their fear of having their own conduct examined. He spoke of the "scandalous pretence that the House was not competent to receive or decide upon evidence respecting the conduct of military commanders," noting that many of its members had already been passing such judgments freely. He also insisted that the praise offered to Howe by Germain in the correspondence that had been laid before the House was being disingenuously used as evidence that the minister had no criticism to make of the general. Germain, Fox asserted, had been undermining Howe in secret.

The debate continued for the rest of the day, often becoming confused (two motions had been put on the table, one to examine Cornwallis and the other to abandon the inquiry altogether), and the two sides were so firmly entrenched that it seemed an impasse had been reached. Germain, although showing a flash of displeasure at Burgoyne, had managed to keep his temper in check and there was hope that it might all now blow over. The King wrote with satisfaction to North the morning after the debate, stating that "it is probable this business will not be further agitated." He admitted fearing that Germain would have been unable to restrain himself from countering some of the assertions in Howe's speech, and he was happy to have been proved wrong. Three days later, he was proved right.

On May 3, the debate had picked up again, at first seeming doomed to consume itself on trivial matters: it became intensely interested in the technical differences between the House of Commons and a committee made up of the entire House of Commons. Things took a nasty turn when Fox, attempting to stir things up, asserted that, as their running of the war had been so catastrophic, it would have been better had North and Germain never been born, but the critical moment arrived when Burgoyne accused Germain of denying him discretionary powers in his advance down the Hudson. He had been ordered to press on to Albany and had been honor-bound to make the attempt. He did not mean to accuse anyone, he insisted while doing exactly that, but rather to defend his own actions. Ministers could then see if any explanation on their part was required for the loss of his army.

Germain, quietly seething as Burgoyne spoke, rose. North may have closed his eyes while waiting to hear how the American Secretary would respond. At first, it seemed as if Germain might retain his composure. He had never accused Burgoyne of anything, he insisted, either inside the House or outside, but if the general wanted an inquiry, he would not object. There were signs, however, that Germain was about to explode. He always spoke cautiously, he insisted, but felt compelled to defend himself on this occasion. Like a rogue firework, however, he was about to go off not in Burgoyne's face, but in Howe's. He chose this moment to counter many of the assertions made in Howe's narrative, insisting that he could have pursued Washington after White Plains and taken Philadelphia at the end of 1776. As far as 1777, it had been impossible to provide the requested reinforcements because he, Germain, had not been expecting such a large request and was unable to find the men at such short notice. Howe's army may therefore have been too small for all of the plans he had initially submitted, but it was not so small that nothing could be achieved at all. The decision to waste time trying to bring Washington to action in New Jersey, the decision to go to Philadelphia by sea, and the choice of the Chesapeake rather than the Delaware were all criticized. He did not understand the decision to go to the southward at the time, he asserted, nor did he understand it now.

Too late, Germain attempted to disengage. He insisted that he saw no need for the inquiry to continue, that the House seemed satisfied with the general's conduct, and that he "cheerfully acquiesced in the opinion," but the damage had been done. Having directly criticized Howe in the House, the examining of witnesses could not be avoided.

On May 6, Cornwallis was finally invited into the House of Commons and prepared to answer whatever questions might be put to him. He had served Howe loyally for the time they had been together in America and proved himself a capable and energetic officer. Howe also had reason to think of him as an ally, and clearly expected great things from him as his first and most important witness—the opinion of Charles, Earl Cornwallis would count for a lot in the case to clear his name. Given these facts, it seems remarkable that the two men had not spoken about the questions Howe was about to pose, but there can be no other explanation for the answers Cornwallis gave.

Howe chose to open his questioning with an obscure point. "Was not the knowledge of the state of the country of America, for military purposes," he asked, "extremely difficult to be obtained from the inhabitants?" Cornwallis, rising and removing his hat, gave a prepared answer, in which he stated he was happy to have the chance to declare his great respect for Sir William and that he believed the general had served his country faithfully. He then offered a disconcerting statement: "I beg this house will understand that I do not come here to answer to questions of opinion, but merely to questions of fact; the private opinions of a subordinate officer can give very little satisfaction to this house." Howe repeated his question regarding the difficulty of acquiring knowledge of the country in America, and Cornwallis agreed.

More inconsequential questions followed until Howe chose to tackle weightier matters. "Did your Lordship see the enemy's lines at Brooklyn during the action of 27th of August 1776?" he asked. Cornwallis's response was disappointing: "I did not see them on that day with any accuracy; I was on the left with the second battalion of grenadiers, and could form no judgment."

Howe pressed on. "From the knowledge you had of those lines after the action," he asked, "would it have been a prudent measure to have assaulted those works on that day?" Cornwallis again disappointed. "I apprehend the latter part of that question is matter of opinion," he replied, adding that he had never heard anyone suggest the lines could have been carried by assault. Howe persisted: would an assault on the lines have been worthwhile, given the number of men that would have been lost in the attempt? Cornwallis, having given Howe ample warning, now felt the need to be firm. "I apprehend this to be entirely a question of opinion," he replied, and refused to give one. In the space of just seven questions, Howe's star witness had shown himself unwilling to cooperate.

On six further occasions he refused to answer questions of opinion. On other occasions he noted that it was not his conduct that was under scrutiny and therefore he felt no need to explain any of his own actions, and he refused to give any details of private conversations with Howe. Sir William, presumably dispirited by the feeble display, gave up his witness for other questions, but Cornwallis was at least as reluctant to answer to them as he had been with Howe. Responses on any of the critical matters under debate included "I cannot answer that question," "I don't know," "I can't tell," "I really do not know," "I cannot recollect," and "I do not think it would be prudent or proper for me at this time to answer that question." Attempts to coax more from the general proved ineffective. When asked, "Does your Lordship know of any advantage in fact gained by landing at the head of the Elk, that would not have been gained by landing on the Delaware?," Cornwallis stubbornly replied, "The honourable gentleman, by ushering in the question, by asking if I know in fact, does not alter the nature of the question; I think it matter of opinion, and therefore shall not answer it."

Cornwallis departed the scene having disappointed everyone, but further witnesses did not bring much more to the affair. Only calling well-disposed witnesses, Howe received the answers he wanted from everyone else, while they batted away any criticisms from other interrogators. Major General Charles Grey proved far more of a tame witness than Cornwallis, offering fulsome support for Howe's decisions, while countering any insinuations made in the questions of others. Grey showed a quick wit at times. When asked "How far did the movement to Philadelphia carry the British army from Hudson's River?," he replied, "The same distance as General Washington's army." He also had no qualms about offering his opinion. When asked if the war might still be won with the force currently there, under Henry Clinton, he replied, "I think the House has the right to the opinion of every general officer that has served in America ... I think that with the present force in America, there can be no expectation of ending the war by force of arms."

The following day, questioning continued, with Andrew Snape Hamond, captain of the *Roebuck*, called to the bar. Hamond's presence underlined the futility, touched upon by Lord North in his objections to the hearing of witnesses, of examining subordinates; Hamond owed his entire career to Lord Howe. In 1765 Lord Howe had been instrumental in getting Hamond command of a sloop of war, and six years later he was informing the young officer that Lord Sandwich was "looking for a frigate" for him to command. Hamond was never going to say anything prejudicial to the admiral or his brother, and this was borne out when private documents were found following his death. Although he declared at the inquiry that there had been many cogent reasons for the decision to go to Philadelphia via the Chesapeake rather than the Delaware, an unpublished personal account of the affair told a very different story. Hamond claimed that having joined the admiral and general on board the *Eagle* on July 30, 1777, he had been amazed to discover that the Chesapeake was being considered as a route and had tried strenuously to change the minds of the brothers. The questioning of Hamond was symptomatic of the way the inquiry had become bogged down in meaningless detail. One question went, "What way do you conceive a fleet of men of war and transports could make against a tide of three knots and a half an hour, with an unfavourable wind, but such as would permit them to lie in their course, supposing moderate weather?"

The engineer John Montresor was examined next and delivered concise and convincing testimony regarding the strength of the rebel lines at Brooklyn, which he had been able to examine personally. He declared the lines had been fully completed (contrary to evidence from the Americans themselves that they had been incomplete on the morning of the battle and only hastily patched up at the last moment as the British approached) and then fended off incompetent questioning from other members of the House. "What was the number of effective men that the King's army consisted of on the attack of the 27th August?" he was asked, replying, "I humbly conceive it is a properer question to ask of the adjutant-general than the engineer."

The questioning sometimes descended to comical levels:

"Q: Was you not chief engineer at any time during the campaign?
"A: Yes, in 1777.
"Q: In what situation was you when General Howe sailed for the Chesapeak?
"A: Chief Engineer.
"Q. Supposing General Howe had gained possession of the Highlands, and General Washington had crossed the North River, could we, having possession of the navigation of the river, not have cut off General Washington from all support from the southward?
"A: I apprehend this is rather excentric from my line."

With constant repetition of the same facile questions, which Montresor repeatedly declared himself unfit to answer given his profession as an engineer, his evidence brought proceedings to a close for the day. It was interesting not only for his wit, but also because he had no great esteem for Howe. The commander-in-chief had failed to credit Montresor for his work in subduing the fort on Mud Island (Howe believed it should have been accomplished far more quickly), and in Montresor's eyes this had ended his career. He had left the army in 1778 and was still trying to get personal expenses paid at the time of the inquiry, in which quest he needed Howe's support.

When the inquiry continued, on May 13, the North administration made an effort to call witnesses of its own. A passionate debate followed, in which it was denounced on the one side as a sneak attack on the Howes, and supported on the other as only fair, considering the Howes had been allowed to call their witnesses. Fox, delighting in the chaos, invited evidence from anyone who had something to say, while both the Howes and Germain insisted they were acting merely in self-defense and were not accusing the other party of any wrongdoing. It was a fight in which neither combatant would throw a punch.

Howe examined two more witnesses, his personal secretary, Robert Mackenzie, and Sir George Osborn, muster master general of the foreign troops serving with the British army in America, but the inquiry was running out of steam and the testimony was far briefer than with previous witnesses. Lord Howe declared their case closed, but warned that if the ministry insisted on calling its own witnesses, and if they contradicted any points made by the Howes or their witnesses, then they reserved the right to continue the inquiry. Here, then, was both hope that the affair might finally be over, and a warning that it might yet continue, zombie-like, to lurch forward. The latter course appeared most likely, as the North administration seemed set on examining its own witnesses, but that was put off to another day.

Burgoyne, seeing a chance to interject but having been taken by surprise by the sudden ending of the Howes' testimony, objected that he wasn't ready to give his own narrative yet, which no doubt delighted a House becoming bored with interminable speeches and aimless questions. Still, he insisted it was only fair that he should be heard. Nugent testily condemned the inquiry and moved again that it should be wound up, but Burgoyne was determined to have his say. The date for the hearing of his evidence was set for May 20, meaning that Burgoyne had managed to insert an inquiry into an inquiry.

Burgoyne's narrative and witnesses devoured the rest of the month. He had originally intended to blame Howe for his defeat, but on his arrival in Britain he had been informed that the opposition was supporting Howe and could not support Burgoyne if he attacked the general. This robbed Burgoyne's case of its strongest argument and he declared it closed on June 3, having made less of an impact even than Howe. When Germain rose on June 8, when the committee next sat, he was therefore defending himself on two fronts. His case, as he laid it out, rested on an assertion that loyalist support in America was strong and that he had sent out an adequate force for Howe to achieve his stated goals. Germain was careful not to suggest that the army had been big enough to conquer a united America, but merely argued that it had been sufficient to end the rebellion. He made the telling point that Howe had intended to invade Pennsylvania with 11,000 men, and had actually, by his own admission, taken 14,000 (von Muenchhausen's notes suggested that even more had been taken). Surely, Germain argued, those extra 3,000 men could have been better employed on a diversionary action in New England? Still, bafflingly, he declined to tackle the abandonment of the Hudson strategy.

As witnesses, he called Major General James Robertson and the prominent loyalist Joseph Galloway, but the Howes did a better job of questioning them than Germain, and the inquiry was threatening to drag on forever before it came to an unexpectedly sudden end. It was adjourned until June 29, when the Howes were expected to renew their demands to hear more witnesses and continue with their defense, but the brothers simply did not turn up at the House and the committee was hastily dissolved in their absence. The motivation behind their actions is unclear, but it is possible the Howes realized there was little point in continuing with endless debate when nobody's mind, on either side, was about to be changed. There was also the risk that Germain might decide he had nothing left to lose and embark upon a more robust challenging of Howe's narrative and witnesses. Sir William, having retired in the face of formidable defenses on so many occasions as a general, did so one more time. On June 30, he expressed mock surprise at the inquiry being wound up, but when he insisted one last time on asking Germain why his confidence had been withdrawn, the American Secretary took his chance to finally draw a line under the whole affair; he bit his tongue and declined to respond. The inquiry was over and no judgment on the Howes' conduct was ever passed.

EPILOGUE

The controversy over Howe's period in command did not end with the inquiry. A pamphlet war erupted, in which both sides published accusations and ripostes, to no great effect. The pamphlets accusing Howe of mismanaging the war made some effective points, but too often strayed into the realm of fancy. In "Letters to a Nobleman," written by Joseph Galloway, it was stated that Howe had an army in excess of 40,000, which was so patently false it undermined all other arguments in the pamphlet (the accusations of "want of wisdom in the plans, and of vigour and exertion in the execution," for example, were fair debating points).

His reputation defended at the inquiry, if not exactly cleared, Howe nevertheless descended into obscurity. For joining the ranks of the opposition, and for threatening the administration of Lord North with collapse (North believed a vote of thanks to Howe might be made in the House of Commons, which he feared would "be understood by the bulk of mankind not unreasonably as a censure upon the administration"), he fell out of favor with the King. Others were more fortunate. Cornwallis, who would continue to serve in America and who would "pull a Burgoyne" by surrendering an army at Yorktown in 1781, was nevertheless able to resurrect his career in India, while Lord Howe won glory at the Third Battle of Ushant in 1794, immortalized as the Glorious First of June.

Contradicting the Latin motto from his Mischianza, Howe did not rise again with added splendor, nor did Clinton (still commander-in-chief when Yorktown signaled the final loss of the colonies), and nor did Burgoyne. The three ambitious major generals who had sailed together on the *Cerberus* in 1775 had all seen their careers end in America, although Clinton did have the satisfaction of overseeing the greatest British triumph of the war, the capture of Charleston in 1780, which set the record straight for his failure there four years earlier. Lord Germain never lost his appetite for the war, pushing for a continuation of hostilities even after Yorktown, but he had become a lonely voice and was by then an impediment to the North administration, as it desperately tried to cling on to power. Pushing Germain out bought North a little time—several weeks in fact—before a motion of no confidence in the House of Commons forced him to step down.

Howe was nominated to command a force under the threat of a Spanish invasion in 1789, but it was not considered a likely event and he never commanded an army in battle again, although he made the rank of full general in 1793 and became the Fifth Viscount Howe on the death of his brother in 1799, the same year his wartime sparring partner, George Washington, died. The old soldier was fading away, and no active duty could be found for him during the long crisis of the French Revolutionary and Napoleonic Wars. By 1812 he was unable to attend a meeting of the Order of the Bath due to a "long and severe illness" and his signature on the letter declining the kind invitation to attend was extremely shaky. He died two years later and was buried in Twickenham.

Henry Clinton left us a detailed account of his adventures during the War of Independence, as well as holding on to seemingly every scrap of paper that crossed his desk. Howe was not so motivated to explain his actions, but although there is (as far as we know) no chest of personal letters and documents, the official correspondence relating to the War of Independence and the private letters of other officers bring Howe briefly to life. They also raise as many questions as they answer. Howe did not seem to be a particularly ambitious man, yet he clearly manipulated the situation in 1775 to gain command of the British army in North America. Having been given the army, he seemed nonplussed over what to do with it and showed a total lack of understanding over the distinction between tactical and strategic success. He was undoubtedly the wrong man for the job, but then there were so few men to choose from when hostilities broke out with the Thirteen Colonies. Many senior generals were not interested in serving against fellow members of the British Empire.

The insights into Howe show clearly the dangers of viewing historical figures as cardboard cutouts who act predictably and always display the same character traits, repeatedly responding to the same stimuli in the same manner. He was indolent, yet had a fiery temper. He was capable of making quick judgments on a person, and once they were in his good books he took pains to keep them there—he overlooked quite startling insubordination from Clinton and repeatedly attempted to repair their relationship, which had started so well on the *Cerberus*. On the other hand, he disliked the Hessian general von Heister on sight and made no effort to get on with him, even going out of his way to prod the German (such as when he commended Johan Ewald after the jäger commander had been rebuked by von Heister). There seemed to be no limit to the length of time Howe could nurse such a grudge. In 1777, Loftus Cliffe reported that his regiment, the 46th, "stands but ill with our chief, ever since a damned private quarrel between Vaughn and him in Ireland." Howe had been colonel of the 46th more than ten years earlier.

An emotional and passionate man, Howe's personal relationships were of great importance to him, but he was doomed to see his most important ones disintegrate under the stress of war, with the notable exception of that with his brother, Richard. Clinton had little good to say about his commanding officer, but did concede that he worked well with the admiral. "Separate the two brothers," Clinton commented, "their equals are to be found in either profession; but together they are irresistible and to be equaled only by two such brothers."

It was a similarly mixed story when considering Howe's relationships with officers further down the chain of command. Cornwallis was professional, capable, and willing to follow Howe's orders to the letter. He remained in favor to the end of Howe's period in command and even afterward. Howe could also be indulgent to his favorites, willing to overlook impetuosity in Ewald because he reminded Howe so much of himself as a younger man, when he too led light infantry in the field. Where someone got off to a poor start, however, there was no improving the situation. It is not possible to know exactly why Howe did not rate Percy highly, but he eventually drove him from the service.

Given that Howe commanded the British army in America during the first two campaigns of the War of Independence, when the American cause was on its most unsteady ground, historians have been unable to simply ignore the man, but it has proven difficult to conjure a coherent image. Legend has often been used to fill in the many gaps, with "Mrs. Murray's strategy" (the idea that progress across the island of Manhattan, after the landing at Kip's Bay, was deliberately impeded by a local widow, who served Howe and his officers cake and wine and made such an entertaining host that they simply forgot their duty) a prime example. Howe's depiction has sometimes descended to the level of caricature and there are also conspiracy theories suggesting that he was actually a patriot sympathizer, a traitor, or merely spinning out the war for financial gain.

The draft of Howe's narrative added subtle new elements to our understanding of the man. His willingness to make a scapegoat of the Hessians for the failure to attack at White Plains, his distaste for punitive warfare (greater even than suspected before), and his clumsiness in framing an argument were all revealed. Most noteworthy, however, was his thinking on the Hudson strategy. By clearly demonstrating that he did not understand how this was meant to work (by suggesting an army moving from New York to Albany would have fulfilled its aims even without a corresponding force moving down from Canada), he shed the strongest light yet on the reasons behind his failure. Because if Howe did not understand the theory behind the Hudson strategy, then his championing of that strategy in his critical letter of June 1775, written to his brother but intended to catch the attention of Germain, was merely a parroting of other people's views.

Howe was clearly willing to say whatever was necessary to get the job of commander-in-chief in America, but had no comprehension of, or sense of obligation to, the strategy he was presenting. This, more than anything else, explains how the British could enjoy such military superiority in the early years of the war, how they could win one tactical victory after another, and yet find strategic triumph elusive. It explains why Howe, on learning that he would not have the massive reinforcements he had requested for his second campaign, fell into apathy and expended the year on a listless and pointless expedition to take Philadelphia. It explains why his letters, full of assurances that he was following the main strategy, stood in such stark contrast to the reality of what was actually happening in America. It explains why he chose at various times to capture cities, to target Washington's army, and, when he was most bereft of ideas, to merely occupy territory.

Howe took not a single step up the Hudson because that was never the strategy that he was following. The real problem, and what undid the British war effort in the first two campaigns of the conflict, was that he never thought to tell that to anyone else.

BIBLIOGRAPHY

UNPRINTED/MANUSCRIPT SOURCES

British Library, London, England
Collections of the Duke of Northumberland Papers: DNP MS 52,
Letters and Papers American War.
Egerton Manuscripts, 2135, original letters and papers relating to
military and naval operations in North America and the West Indies;
1762-1795.

Maine Historical Society, Portland, USA
Dispatch from Lt. Henry Mowat to Vice Admiral Graves about the
destruction of Falmouth (Portland)

The National Archives, Kew, England
Military Dispatches:
(TNA): PRO CO 5/92   1774-1775
(TNA): PRO CO 5/93   1775-1776
(TNA): PRO CO 5/94   1776-1777
(TNA): PRO CO 5/95   1777-1778

National Army Museum, London, England
"Discipline established by Major General Howe for Light Infantry in
Battalion, Sarum September 1774," 6807/157/6

Staffordshire Record Office, Stafford, England
Dartmouth Manuscripts

*William L. Clements Library, University of Michigan, Ann Arbor,
Michigan, USA*
Henry Clinton Papers
Henry Strachey Papers
Loftus Cliffe Papers

Richard and William Howe Collection
Thomas Gage Papers
William Howe Orderly Book

PUBLISHED PRIMARY SOURCES

Baldwin, T. W., *The Revolutionary Journal of Col. Jeduthan Baldwin,
1775–1778* (Bangor: De Burians, 1906).

Barker, J., *The British in Boston, being the Diary of Lieutenant John Barker
of the King's Own Regiment from November 15, 1774 to May 31, 1776;
with Notes by Elizabeth Ellery Dana* (Cambridge, Massachusetts:
Harvard University Press, 1924).

Bolton, C. K., ed., *Letters of Hugh Earl Percy from Boston and New York
1774–1776* (Boston: Charles E. Godspeed, 1902).

Burgoyne, B. E., ed., *A Hessian Diary of the American Revolution, by
Johann Conrad Döhla* (Norman, Oklahoma: University of Oklahoma
Press, 1990).

Burgoyne, Lt-Gen. J., *A State of the Expedition from Canada, as Laid
Before the House of Commons* (London, J. Almon, 1780).

Clarke, J., *An Impartial and Authentic Narrative of the Battle Fought on
the 17th of June, 1775, Between His Britannic Majesty's Troops and the
American Provincial Army, on Bunker's Hill* (London: J. Millan, 1775).

Clinton, H. C., *Observations on Mr. Stedman's History of the American War*
(London: Printed for J. Debrett, 1794).

Cobbet, W., ed., *The Parliamentary History of England*, Vol. XVIII
(29 Nov. 1774 to 13 Dec. 1776) (London: T. C. Hansard, 1813).

Cobbet, W., ed., *The Parliamentary History of England*, Vol. XX
(7 Dec. 1778 to 10 Feb. 1780) (London: T. C. Hansard, 1814).

Cumming, W. P. and Rankin, H., eds., *The Fate of a Nation: The American
Revolution Through Contemporary Eyes* (London: Phaidon Press,
1975).

Force, P., *Peter Force's American Archives*, Fifth Series, Vols. I & II
(Washington, D.C.: M. St. Clair Clarke and Peter Force, 1848).

Ford, W. C., ed., *The Writings of George Washington*, Vol. III (1775–
1776), Vol. IV (1776), Vol. V (1776–1777) & Vol. VI (1777–1778)
(New York and London: G. P. Putnam's Sons, 1889–1890).

Fortescue, Sir J., ed., *Correspondence of King George III*, Vol. III, July
1773–December 1777 & Vol. IV, 1778–1779 (London: MacMillan
and Co., 1928).

French, A., ed., *A British Fusilier in Revolutionary Boston: Being the Diary of Lieutenant Frederick Mackenzie, Adjutant of the Royal Welch Fusiliers, January 5–April 30, 1775* (Cambridge: Harvard University Press, 1926).

Galloway, J., *Letters to a Nobleman on Conduct of the War in the Middle Colonies* (London: Printed for J. Wilkie, 1779).

Galloway, J., *A Reply to the Observations of Lieut. Gen. Sir William Howe on a Pamphlet Entitled Letters to a Nobleman* (London: Printed for G. Wilkie, 1780).

Gibbon, E., *The Miscellaneous Works of Edward Gibbon Esq.* (London: B. Blake, 1837).

Graham, J., *Extracts from the Journal of the Reverend John Graham, Chaplain of the First Connecticut Regiment at the Siege of Havana* (New York: Society of Colonial Wars, 1896).

Gruber, I. D., ed., *John Peebles' American War, 1776–1782* (Stroud: Army Records Society, 1998).

Hersey, C., ed., *Reminiscences of the Military Life and Sufferings of Col. Timothy Bigelow* (Worcester: Henry J. Howland, 1860).

Historical Manuscripts Commission, *Report on the Manuscripts of the Marquess of Lothian, Preserved at Blickling Hall, Norfolk* (London: His Majesty's Stationery Office, 1905).

Howe, W., *The Narrative of Lieut. Gen. Sir William Howe, in a Committee of the House of Commons, on the 29th of April, 1779, Relative to his Conduct, During his Late Command of the King's Troops in North America* (London: H. Baldwin, 1780, Second Edition).

Huntington, E., *Letters Written by Ebenezer Huntington During the American Revolution* (New York: Printed for Chas. Fred. Heartman, 1914).

Lamb, R., *Memoir of His Own Life, by R. Lamb, Serjeant in the Royal Welch Fuzileers* (Dublin: J. Jones, 1811).

Learned, M. D., ed., *Philipp Waldeck's Diary of the American Revolution* (Philadelphia: Americana Germanica Press, 1907).

Lee, C., *Anecdotes of the Late Charles Lee, Esq.*, Second Edition (London: Printed for J. S. Jordan, 1797).

Littell, J. S., ed., *Memoirs of His Own Time with Reminiscences of the Men and Events of the Revolution by Alexander Graydon* (Philadelphia: Lindsay and Blakiston, 1846).

Lloyd, Maj-Gen., "Major General Lloyd's Plan to Conquer America," *Political Magazine* (June, 1781), pp. 345–346.

Lomas, S. C., ed., *Report on the Manuscripts of Mrs Stopford-Sackville, Vols. I & II* (London: Mackie & Co. Ltd, 1904 & 1910).

Mauduit, I., *Strictures on the Philadelphia Mischianza or Triumph Upon Leaving America Unconquered* (London: Printed for J. Bew, Pater-Noster-Row, 1779).

Muenchhausen, F. von, *At General Howe's side, 1776–1778: the diary of General William Howe's aide de camp*, translated by Ernst Kipping and annotated by Samuel Smith (Monmouth Beach, N. J.: Philip Freneau Press, 1974).

Neeser, R. W., ed., *The Despatches of Molyneux Shuldham, January–July 1776* (New York: DeVinne Press, 1913).

Padelford, P., ed., *Colonial Panorama 1775: Dr. Robert Honyman's Journal for March and April* (Pasadena, California: San Pasqual Press, 1939).

Parliamentary Register; or History of the Proceedings and Debates of the House of Commons during the Fifth Session of the Fourteenth Parliament of Great Britain, Vol. X (London: Wilson and Co. 1802).

Parliamentary Register; or History of the Proceedings and Debates of the House of Commons during the Fifth Session of the Fourteenth Parliament of Great Britain, Vol. XII (London: J. Almon, 1779).

Parliamentary Register; or History of the Proceedings and Debates of the House of Commons during the Fifth Session of the Fourteenth Parliament of Great Britain, Vol. XII (London: Wilson and Co. 1802).

Putnam, I., *The Two Putnams: Israel and Rufus in the Havana Expedition 1762 and in the Mississippi River Exploration 1772–73, with some account of the Company of Military Adventurers* (Hartford: Connecticut Historical Society, 1931).

Raynor, D. and Skinner, A., eds., "Sir James Steuart: Nine Letters on the American Conflict, 1775–1778," *The William and Mary Quarterly*, 51 (4) (Oct. 1994), pp. 755–776.

Rhodehamel, J., ed., *Writings* (New York: The Library of America, 1987).

Ross, C., ed., *Correspondence of Charles, First Marquis Cornwallis, Vol. I & Vol. II* (London: John Murray, 1859).

Scheer, G. F., ed., *Private Yankee Doodle: A Narrative of some of the Adventures, Dangers and Sufferings of a Revolutionary Soldier* (Boston: Little, Brown and Company, 1962).

Scull, G. D., ed., *Memoirs and Letters of Captain W. Glanville Evelyn, of the 4th Regiment (King's Own) from North America, 1774–1776* (Oxford: James Parker and Co., 1879).

Scull, G. D., ed., *The Montresor Journals* (New York: New York Historical Society, 1882).

Seybolt, R. F., ed., "A Contemporary British Account of General Sir William Howe's Military Operations in 1777," *American Antiquarian Society* (April, 1930), pp. 74–76.

Simcoe, Lt. Col. J. G., *Simcoe's Military Journal: A History of the Operations of a Partisan Corps, Called the Queen's Rangers* (New York: Bartlett & Welford, 1844).

Sixth Report of the Royal Commission on Historical Manuscripts, Part I (London: George Edward Eyre and William Spottiswoode, 1877).

Sparks, J., ed., *The Writings of George Washington*, Vol. III (New York: Harper & Brothers, 1847).

Stevens, B. F., ed., *General Sir William Howe's Orderly Book, 1775–1776* (London: B. F. Stevens and Brown, 1890).

Stone, W. L., ed., *Letters of Brunswick and Hessian Officers During the American Revolution* (Albany, 1891).

Tallmadge, B., *Memoir of Colonel Benjamin Tallmadge* (New York: New York Times & Arno Press, 1968).

Tatum, E. H., ed., *The American Journal of Ambrose Serle*, Secretary to Lord Howe 1776–1778 (San Marino: The Huntingdon Library, 1940).

Thacher, J., *A Military Journal During the American Revolutionary War, from 1775 to 1783* (Boston: Richardson and Lord, 1823).

Tustin, J. P., ed., *Diary of the American War: A Hessian Journal, Captain Johann Ewald* (New Haven, Conn. and London: Yale University Press, 1979).

Uhlendorf, B. A., ed., *Revolution in America: Confidential Letters and Journals, 1776–1784, of Adjutant General Major Baurmeister of the Hessian Forces* (New York: Rutgers University Press, 1957).

Walker, P. K., ed., *Engineers of Independence: A Documentary History of the Army Engineers in the American Revolution, 1775–1783* (Washington, D. C.: U. S. Army Corps of Engineers, 1981).

Wheatley, H. B., ed., *The Historical and the Posthumous Memoirs of Sir Nathaniel William Wraxall*, Vol. I (London: Bickers & Son, 1884).

Willcox, W. B., ed., *The American Rebellion: Sir Henry Clinton's Narrative* (New Haven, Conn.: Yale University Press, 1954).

Wright, E., *The Fire of Liberty* (London: The Folio Society, 1983).

SECONDARY SOURCES
Books

Adams, R. G., *British Headquarters Maps and Sketches used by Sir Henry Clinton while in command of the British Forces operating in North America during the War for Independence, 1775–1782* (Ann Arbor: The William L. Clements Library, 1928).

Anderson, T. S., *The Command of the Howe Brothers During the American Revolution* (New York: Oxford University Press, 1936).

Bancroft, A., *Life of George Washington* (London: Printed for John Stockdale, 1808).

Bancroft, G., *History of the United States from the Discovery of the American Continent* (Boston: Little, Brown & Company, 1875).

Belcher, H., *The First American Civil War: First Period, 1775–1778* (London: Macmillan, 1911).

Bicheno, H., *Rebels and Redcoats* (London: HarperCollins, 2003).

Billias, G. A., ed., *George Washington's Generals and Opponents: Their Exploits and Leadership* (New York: Da Capo Press, 1994, originally 1964 and 1969).

Black, J., *Warfare in the Eighteenth Century* (London: Cassell, 1999).

Black, J., *War For America: The Fight for Independence, 1775–1783* (Stroud: Sutton Publishing Limited, 2001).

Botta, C., *History of the War of the Independence of the United States of America*, Vol. I (Newhaven: T. Brainard, 1840).

Brewer, J. and Hellmuth, E. (eds), *Rethinking Leviathan: The Eighteenth-Century State in Britain and Germany* (Oxford: Oxford University Press, 1999).

Brown, G. S., *The American Secretary: The Colonial Policy of Lord George Germain, 1775–1778* (Ann Arbor: University of Michigan Press, 1963).

Brown, W. A., *Empire or Independence: A Study of the Failure of Reconciliation, 1774–1783* (New York: Kennikat Press, 1966). First published 1941.

Burke, K., *Old World New World: The Story of Britain and America* (London: Little, Brown, 2007).

Burrows, E. G. and Wallace, M., *Gotham: A History of New York City to 1898* (New York: Oxford University Press, 1999).

Carrington, H. B., *Battles of the American Revolution* (New York: A. S. Barnes & Company, 1876).

Conway, S., *The War of American Independence 1775–1783* (London: Edward Arnold, 1995).

Cullum, G. W., "The Struggle for the Hudson", in Winsor, J. (ed.), *Narrative and Critical History of America, Vol. VI, Part I* (Boston and New York: Houghton, Mifflin and Company, 1886).

Curtis, E., *The Organization of the British Army in the American Revolution* (New Haven, Conn.: Yale University Press, 1926).

Cust, L., *A History of Eton College* (New York: Charles Scribner's Sons, 1899).

Cuthbertson, B., *A System for the Compleat Interior Management and Economy of a Battalion of Infantry* (Bristol: Rouths and Nelson, 1776).

Dixon, N., *On the Psychology of Military Incompetence* (London: Pimlico, 1994).

Doyle, J. A., in Ward, A. W., *et al.* (eds), *Cambridge Modern History*, vii (New York: Macmillan, 1909).

Ehwald, Colonel J. von, *A Treatise Upon the Duties of Light Troops* (London: C. Roworth, 1803).

Ferling, J., *Almost a Miracle: The American Victory in the War of Independence* (Oxford: Oxford University Press, 2007).

Field, T. W., *The Battle of Long Island, with Connected Preceding Events, and the Subsequent American Retreat* (Brooklyn: Long Island Historical Society, 1869).

Fischer, D. H., *Washington's Crossing* (New York: Oxford University Press, 2004).

Fisher, S. G., *The Struggle for American Independence* (Philadelphia and London: Lippincott, 1908).

Fortescue, J. W., *A History of the British Army, First Part to the Close of the Seven Years' War, Vol. II* (London: Macmillan and Co., Ltd, 1899).

Fortescue, J. W., *A History of the British Army, Second Part - From the Close of the Seven Years' War to the Second Peace of Paris, Vol. III* (London: Macmillan and Co., Ltd, 1911).

Fortescue, J. W., *The War of Independence: The British Army in North America, 1775–1783* (London: Greenhill Books, 2001).

French, D., *The British Way in Warfare 1688–2000* (London: Unwin Hyman, 1990).

Frothingham, R., *The Centennial: Battle of Bunker Hill* (Boston: Little, Brown and Company, 1875).

Fuller, J. F. C., *British Light Infantry in the Eighteenth Century* (London: Hutchinson and Co., 1925).

Gates, D., *The British Light Infantry Arm, c.1790–1815* (London: B. T. Batsford Ltd, 1987).

Goodale, G. L., *British and Colonial Army Surgeons on the 19th of April, 1775* (London: Middlesex South District Medical Society, 1899).

Gordon, W., *The History of the Rise, Progress and Establishment of the Independence of the United States of America* (New York: Printed for Samuel Campbell, 1801).

Greene, G. W., *The German Element in the War of American Independence* (New York: Hurd and Houghton, 1876).

Greene, J. P. and Pole, J. R., eds., *The Blackwell Encyclopedia of the American Revolution* (Oxford: Blackwell Publishers, 1991).

Greentree, D., *A Far-Flung Gamble, Havana 1762* (Oxford: Osprey Publishing, 2010).

Griffith, S. B., *The War for American Independence: from 1760 to the Surrender at Yorktown in 1781* (Chicago: University of Illinois Press, 2002).

Gruber, I. D., *Books and the British Army in the Age of the American Revolution* (Chapel Hill: University of North Carolina Press, 2010).

Gruber, I. D., *The Howe Brothers and the American Revolution* (New York: Atheneum, 1972).

Hatch, L. C., *The Administration of the American Revolutionary Army* (New York: Longmans, Green, and Co., 1904).

Johnston, H. P., *The Campaign of 1776 Around New York and Brooklyn* (New Jersey: Scholar's Bookshelf, 2005). First published 1878.

Keegan, J., *The Mask of Command* (London: Penguin, 1987).

Lodge, H. C., *The Story of the Revolution.* (New York: Charles Scribner's Sons, 1903).

Lossing, B. J., *Pictorial Field Book of the Revolution* (New York: Harper and Brothers, 1851).

Lowell, E. J., *The Hessians and the other German Auxiliaries of Great Britain in the Revolutionary War* (New York: Harper and Brothers, 1884).

Ludlow, J. M., *The War of American Independence* (London: Longmans, Green and Co., 1893).

Lyte, H. C. M., *A History of Eton College, 1440–1875* (London: Macmillan and Co., 1875).

Mackesy, P., *The War for America: 1775–1783* (London: University of Nebraska, 1993).

Nelson, P., et al., *The American Revolution in New York; Its Political, Social and Economic Significance* (Albany: University of the State of New York, 1926).

Neumann, G., *The History of the Weapons of the American Revolution* (New York: Harper and Row, 1967).

O'Shaughnessy, A., *The Men Who Lost America: British Command During the Revolutionary War and the Preservation of Empire* (London: Oneworld Publications, 2013).

Partridge, B., *Sir Billy Howe* (London: Longmans, Green and Co., 1932).

Pfister, A., *The Voyage of the First Hessian Army from Portsmouth to New York 1776* (New York: Printed for Chas. Fred. Heartman, 1815).

Sabine, H. W., *Murder, 1776 & Washington's Policy of Silence* (New York: Theo. Gaus' Sons, 1973).

Salmon, E., *General Wolfe* (Toronto: Cassell & Company, 1909).

Schecter, B., *The Battle for New York* (London: Jonathan Cape, 2003).

Shy, J., *A People Numerous and Armed: Reflections of the Military Struggle for American Independence* (Revised Edition) (Ann Arbor: University of Michigan Press, 1990).

Simms, B., *Three Victories and a Defeat: The Rise and Fall of the First British Empire, 1714–1783* (London: Penguin, 2007).

Smith, W., *An Historical Account of Bouquet's Expedition Against the Ohio Indians in 1764* (Cincinnati, Ohio: Robert Clarke & Co., 1868).

Spring, M. H., *With Zeal and with Bayonets Only: The British Army on Campaign in North America, 1775–1783* (Norman, Oklahoma: University of Oklahoma Press, 2010).

Stanhope, P. H., *History of England from the Peace of Utrecht to the Peace of Versailles, 1713–1783*, Vol. VI (London: John Murray, 1858).

Stedman, C., *The history of the Origin, Progress, and Termination of the American War*, vols. 1 & 2 (London: Published for the author, 1794).

Stephenson, M., *Patriot Battles: How the War of Independence was Fought* (New York: Harper Perennial, 2008).

Stiles, H. R., *A History of the City of Brooklyn*, Vol. I (Brooklyn: Published by Subscription, 1867).

Stoker, D., et al., eds., *Strategy in the American War of Independence: A Global Approach* (Abingdon: Routledge, 2010).

Strachan, H., *European Armies and the Conduct of War* (e-publication: Taylor & Francis e-Library, 2005).

Strachan, H., *The Politics of the British* Army (Oxford: Clarendon Press, 1997).

Trevelyan, G. O., *The American Revolution,* Vol. I (London: Longmans, Green & Co., 1905).

Underdal, S. J., ed., *Military History of the American Revolution* (Washington: Office of Air Force History, 1976).

Urban, M., *Fusiliers, How the British Army Lost America but Learned to Fight* (London: Faber and Faber, 2007).

Van Creveld, M., *Command in War* (Cambridge, Massachusetts: Harvard University Press, 1985).

Varnum, J. M., *A Sketch of the Life and Public Services of James Mitchell Varnum of Rhode Island* (Boston: David Clapp & Son, 1906).

Ward Jr, S., *The Battle of Long Island: A Lecture delivered before the New York Historical Society, February 7 1839* (New York: William Osborn, 1839).

Weintraub, S., *Iron Tears: Rebellion in America, 1775–1783* (London: Simon & Schuster, 2005).

Willcox, W. B., *Portrait of a General: Sir Henry Clinton in the War of Independence* (New York: Alfred A. Knopf, 1964).

Wright, R. K., *The Continental Army* (Washington, D. C.: Center of Military History, 1983).

Articles

Adams, C. F., "The Battle of Long Island," *The American Historical Review,* 1 (4) (Jul. 1896), pp. 650–670.

Bamford, W., "Bamford's Diary: The Revolutionary Diary of a British Officer," *Maryland Historical Magazine,* 27 (1932), pp. 240–259 and pp. 296–314; 28 (1932), pp. 9–26.

Bradford, S. S., ed., "A British Officer's Revolutionary War Journal, 1776-1778," *Maryland Historical Magazine,* 56 (1961), pp. 150–175.

Beers, H. P., "The Papers of the British Commanders in Chief in North America, 1754-1783," *Military Affairs,* 13 (2) (Summer, 1949), pp. 79–94.

Bereiter, G. D., "Campaigning in America: Captain Johann Ewald's Hessians in the American Revolution," *Constructing the Past:* Vol. 3, No. 1 (2002), pp. 6–34.

Black, J., "Britain as a Military Power, 1688–1815," *The Journal of Military History*, 64 (1) (Jan., 2000), pp. 159–177.

Black, J., "Eighteenth-Century Warfare Reconsidered," *War in History*, 1 (2) (1994), pp. 215–232.

Christie, I. R., "British Politics and the American Revolution," *Albion*, 9 (3) (Autumn, 1977), pp. 205–226.

Clark, J., "Responsibility for the Failure of the Burgoyne Campaign," *The American Historical Review*, 35 (3) (Apr. 1930), pp. 542–559.

Coffman, E. M., "The New American Military History," *Military Affairs*, 48 (1) (Jan. 1984), pp. 1–5.

Conway, S., "Britain and the Impact of the American War, 1775–1783," *War in History*, 2 (2) (1995), pp. 127–150.

Conway, S., "British Army Officers and the American War for Independence," *The William and Mary Quarterly*, 41 (2) (Apr. 1984), pp. 265–276.

Cuneo, J. R., "The Early Days of the Queen's Rangers August 1776–February 1777," *Military Affairs*, 22 (2) (Summer, 1958), pp. 65–74.

Diamond, S., "Bunker Hill, Tory Propaganda, and Adam Smith," *The New England Quarterly*, 25 (3) (Sep. 1952), pp. 363–374.

Fiore, J. D., "Carlo Botta: An Italian Historian of the American Revolution," *Italica*, 28 (3) (Sep. 1951), pp. 155–171.

Grossman, D., *On Killing: The Psychological Cost of Learning to Kill in War and Society* (Boston: Little, Brown, 1995).

Gruber, I. D., "Lord Howe and Lord George Germain: British Politics and the Winning of American Independence," *The William and Mary Quarterly*, 22 (2) (Apr. 1965), pp. 225–243.

Guttridge, G. H., "Lord George Germain in Office, 1775–1782," *The American Historical Review*, 33 (1) (Oct. 1927), pp. 23–43.

Higginbotham, D., "American Historians and the Military History of the American Revolution," *The American Historical Review*, 70 (1) (Oct. 1964), pp. 18–34.

Karsten, P., "The 'New' American Military History: A Map of the Territory, Explored and Unexplored," *American Quarterly*, 36 (3) (1984), pp. 389–418.

Kopperman, P. E., "'The Cheapest Pay': Alcohol Abuse in the Eighteenth-Century British Army," *The Journal of Military History*, 60 (3) (Jul. 1996), pp. 445–470.

Levy, J. S., "Theories of General War," *World Politics*, 37 (3) (Apr. 1985), pp. 344–374.

Linn, B. M., and Weigley, R. F., "The American Way of War revisited," *The Journal of Military History*, 66 (2) (Apr. 2002), pp. 501–533.

Mahan, A. T., "Admiral Lord Howe," *Atlantic Monthly*, 73 (1894), pp. 27–37.

Moomaw, W. H., "The Denouement of General Howe's Campaign of 1777," *The English Historical Review*, 79 (312) (Jul. 1964), pp. 498–512.

Morgan, E. S., "The American Revolution: Revisions in Need of Revising," *The William and Mary Quarterly*, 14 (1) (Jan. 1957), pp. 3–15.

Nelson, P. D., "British Conduct of the American Revolutionary War: A Review of Interpretations", *The Journal of American History*, 65 (3) (Dec. 1978), pp. 623–653.

Nelson, P. D., "Citizen Soldiers or Regulars: The Views of American General Officers on the Military Establishment, 1775–1781", Military Affairs, 43 (3) (Oct. 1979), pp. 126–132.

Newmyer, R. K., "Charles Stedman's History of the American War," The American Historical Review, 63 (4) (Jul. 1958), pp. 924–934.

Papadopoulos, R., "Broaching Military History to Wider Audiences," *Society for Military History Headquarters Gazette*, 19 (2) (Spring, 2006), pp. 3–5.

Peckham, H. H., "Military Papers in the Clements Library", *The Journal of the American Military History Foundation*, 2 (3) (Autumn, 1938), pp. 126–130.

Pohl, J. W., "The American Revolution and the Vietnamese War: Pertinent Military Analogies", *The History Teacher*, 7 (2) (Feb. 1974), pp. 255–265.

Powers, S. L., "Studying the Art of War: Military Books Known to American Officers and Their French Counterparts during the Second Half of the Eighteenth Century," *The Journal of Military History*, 70 (3) (Jul. 2006), pp. 781–814.

Rau, L., "Sergeant John Smith's Diary of 1776," *The Mississippi Valley Historical Review*, 20 (2) (Sep. 1933), pp. 247–270.

Robson, E., "The Expedition to the Southern Colonies, 1775–1776," *The English Historical Review*, 66 (261) (Oct. 1951), pp. 535–560.

Schlesinger, A. M., "The American Revolution Reconsidered," *Political Science Quarterly*, 34 (1) (Mar. 1919), pp. 61–78.

Seymour, W., "Turning Point at Saratoga," *Military History*, 16 (Dec. 1999), p. 46.

Siebert, W. H., "Loyalist Troops of New England," *The New England Quarterly*, 4 (1) (Jan. 1931), pp. 108–147.

Starkey, A., "Paoli to Stony Point: Military Ethics and Weaponry During the American Revolution," *The Journal of Military History*, 58 (1) (Jan. 1964), pp. 7–27.

Syrett, D., "The British Armed Forces in the American Revolutionary War: Publications, 1875–1998," *The Journal of Military History*, 63 (1) (Jan. 1999), pp. 147–164.

Tiedemann, J. S., "A Revolution Foiled: Queens County, New York, 1775–1776," *The Journal of American History*, 75 (2) (Sep. 1988), pp. 417–444.

Willcox, W. B., "British Strategy in America, 1778," *The Journal of Modern History*, 19 (2) (1947), pp. 97–121.

Willcox, W. B., "Too Many Cooks: British Planning Before Saratoga," *The Journal of British Studies*, 2 (1) (Nov. 1962), pp. 56–90.

Wyatt, F. and Willcox, W. B., "Henry Clinton: A Psychological Exploration in History," *The William and Mary Quarterly*, 16 (1) (Jan. 1959), pp. 3–26.

INDEX